MW01194310

A SELF-EVIDENT LIE

AMERICAN ABOLITIONISM AND ANTISLAVERY
John David Smith, series editor

The Imperfect Revolution: Anthony Burns and the Landscape
of Race in Antebellum America
GORDON S. BARKER

A Self-Evident Lie: Southern Slavery and the Threat to American Freedom
JEREMY J. TEWELL

A Self-Evident Lie

Southern Slavery and the Threat to American Freedom

JEREMY J. TEWELL

THE KENT STATE UNIVERSITY PRESS

Kent, Ohio

ALL RIGHTS RESERVED

ISBN 978-1-60635-145-1

Manufactured in the United States of America

Cataloging information for this title is available at the Library of Congress.

17 16 15 14 13   5 4 3 2 1

Contents

Acknowledgments   vii

Introduction: The Badge of Freedom?   1

1 The Myth of the Free-State Democrat   16

2 Inferiority   36

3 The Good of the Slave   50

4 The Good of Society   70

5 The Slaveocracy   87

6 Southerners and the Principle of Universal Liberty   100

7 Republicans, Northern Democrats, and the Principle
of Universal Liberty   120

Notes   140

Bibliography   156

Index   165

Acknowledgments

Nearly fourteen years have passed since the subject of this book began to develop in my mind. In that time, many gracious and thoughtful individuals have helped to improve the ideas contained in these pages. The encouragement I received at Pittsburg State University was more than a young historian could hope for. More recently, the outstanding doctoral program at Oklahoma State University provided me with the skills (not to mention the funding) necessary to complete this project.

I owe a particular debt of gratitude to James L. Huston for his inestimable assistance in the evolution and clarification of my central thesis. I would also like to thank John David Smith, editor of the American Abolitionism and Antislavery Series, and Joyce Harrison of Kent State University Press for their advice and support. Sarah E. Lookadoo (who is as good a friend as she is a writer) read the manuscript multiple times and bolstered my efforts with her considerable enthusiasm.

Special thanks are also due to my parents, John and Jean. They never failed to humor my love of history. Finally, I would be remiss if I did not express my gratitude to my feline friends—Ricky, Buddy, Peggy, and Rodney—for alleviating the occasional bouts of stress that accompany a life of historical research.

The Badge of Freedom?

Three months before his death, Benjamin Franklin stepped into the public spotlight for the final time. Although he had once published ads for slave sales, and had even owned a slave couple himself, beginning in the 1750s Franklin had gradually turned against the institution. As president of the Pennsylvania Society for Promoting the Abolition of Slavery, Franklin presented a formal petition to Congress in February 1790, denouncing both the slave trade and slavery itself. "Mankind are all formed by the same Almighty Being," it declared, "alike objects of his care, and equally designed for the enjoyment of happiness." Therefore, Congress had a solemn duty to grant liberty "to those unhappy men who alone in this land of freedom are degraded into perpetual bondage."[1]

Only fourteen years earlier, Americans had announced to the world that "all men are created equal." Franklin's reputation as an architect of that revolution was second only to George Washington's. Nevertheless, southern congressmen displayed unveiled contempt for Franklin and his petition. Senator Pierce Butler of South Carolina castigated the society's plan as a willful violation of the Constitution. In the House of Representatives, James Jackson of Georgia and William Loughton Smith of South Carolina suggested that the eighty-four-year-old Franklin was no longer in his right mind. Jackson was particularly vehement in his defense of slavery, insisting on the floor of the House that the institution was divinely sanctioned and economically vital to the southern economy.

As he had done in the past, Franklin decided to take his case to the public in the form of an anonymous parody. On March 23, 1790, a public letter appeared in the *Federal Gazette* under the signature "Historicus." In a disinterested tone, Franklin observed that Jackson's speech in Congress bore a striking resemblance to a speech delivered a hundred years earlier by Sidi Mehemet Ibrahim, a member of the Divan of Algiers, in response to a petition condemning the enslavement of European Christians. Assuming that Jackson had never read this speech, Franklin could not help but note "that men's interests and intellects operate and are operated on with surprising similarity in all countries and climates, whenever they are under similar circumstances."[2]

Indeed, "the African's" rationales for white slavery clearly presaged those invoked by Jackson and other Southerners in favor of black slavery:

> If we forbear to make slaves of their people, who in this hot climate are to cultivate our lands? And is there not more compassion and favor due to us as Mussulmen than to these Christian dogs? . . . Who is to indemnify the masters for their loss? . . . And if we set our slaves free, what is to be done with them? . . . Must we maintain them as beggars in our streets, or suffer our properties to be the prey of their pillage? For men accustomed to slavery will not work for a livelihood when not compelled. And what is there so pitiable in their present condition? Were they not slaves in their own countries? They have only exchanged one slavery for another and I may say a better; for here they are brought into a land where the sun of Islamism gives forth its light, and shines in full splendor, and they have an opportunity of making themselves acquainted with the true doctrine, and thereby saving their immortal souls. [They are] too ignorant to establish a good government. While serving us, we take care to provide them with everything, and they are treated with humanity. The laborers in their own country are, as I am well informed, worse fed, lodged, and clothed. . . . Here their lives are in safety.

As for those "religious mad bigots" with their "silly petitions," it was pure foolishness to argue that slavery was "disallowed by the Alcoran!" Were not the two precepts "Masters, treat your slaves with kindness; Slaves, serve your masters with cheerfulness and fidelity" ample evidence to the contrary? It was well known, explained the African, that God had given the world "to his faithful Mussulmen, who are to enjoy it of right as fast as they conquer it."[3]

The stability and happiness of the nation could not be sacrificed simply to appease the demands of a few fanatics. Such was the determination of the Divan of Algiers, which, according to Franklin, rejected the antislavery memorial. Following suit, Congress announced that it lacked the authority to act on Franklin's petition. Franklin did not live to see the cotton boom and the consequent entrenchment of slavery in southern life. Little did he know that Congressman Jackson's proslavery apology would become commonplace in the South during the first half of the nineteenth century. Nevertheless, Franklin's last public letter anticipated an important, and underappreciated, facet of the antislavery argument.

❖ ❖ ❖

The thesis of this book is that Northerners feared slavery, in part, because the rationales for black servitude were not inherently racial, and therefore posed a threat to the liberty of all Americans, irrespective of color. Southerners invoked five interrelated rationales in their defense of African slavery: race, moral and mental inferiority, the good of the slave, the good of society, and the lessons of history. Yet many of these rationales had been used in the past (as Franklin illustrated), and could be used in the future, to oppress people of any race. Northerners often expressed concern that proslavery arguments were subject to the mutable prejudices and economic motives of those who made them. Anyone could fall victim to the argument that they were "inferior," that they would be better off enslaved, that their enslavement served the interests of society, or that their subjugation was justified by history and religion. Preparing for his debates with Stephen A. Douglas in 1858, Abraham Lincoln wrote a neatly synthesized passage that highlighted the dangerous arbitrariness of proslavery justifications:

> If A can prove, however conclusively, that he may, of right, enslave B— why may not B snatch the same argument, and prove equally, that he may enslave A?
>
> You say A is white, and B is black. It is *color*, then; the lighter having the right to enslave the darker? Take care. By this rule, you are to be slave to the first man you meet, with a fairer skin than your own.
>
> You do not mean *color* exactly?—You mean the whites are intellectually the superiors of the blacks, and, therefore have the right to enslave them? Take care again. By this rule, you are to be slave to the first man you meet, with an intellect superior to your own.
>
> But, say you, it is a question of interest; and, if you can make it your *interest,* you have the right to enslave another. Very well. And if he can make it his interest, he has the right to enslave you.[4]

Because proslavery arguments were not strictly racial, some Northerners understood that the perpetuation of slavery, and its attendant rationales, made their own liberty, indeed everyone's liberty, contingent on circumstance—namely, the ability to defend oneself against those who would seek to subjugate. Freedom would depend on an individual's economic status, the prejudices of the majority, or the caprice of an aristocracy. They therefore held that the only effective safeguard of individual liberty was universal liberty, as expressed in the Declaration of Independence. As long as Americans believed that "all men" were endowed with inalienable rights to life, liberty, and the pursuit of happiness, everyone's liberty would be *self-evident,* regardless of circumstance. Each person's liberty would be respected simply by virtue of his or her status as a human being. Conversely, the justifications invoked to exclude a segment of society from the rights of man destroyed the self-evidence of those rights. Having rejected the Declaration's principle that all men are naturally free, Americans eliminated simple humanity as an unquestionable defense against oppression. This was dangerous because humanity was the only objective and unchanging evidence that an individual was entitled to freedom. Unless all men were assumed to be free because they were men, anyone, under the right circumstances, could be classified as weak or dangerous or inferior, and enslaved for those reasons. By failing to repudiate slavery, Americans necessarily broke the bond between humanity and liberty, thus making themselves vulnerable to proslavery rationales, especially when they happened to occupy a position of political, social, or economic weakness.

Furthermore, the capriciousness of these rationales, which was confirmed by historical evidence, proved that American slavery was simply another example of "might makes right." Like other forms of tyranny, it was determined by the desire and ability of the strong to oppress the weak. As a result, even through the lens of bigotry, white Northerners could look upon the slaves' condition and wonder if a similar fate could ever befall them. Black skin had been stigmatized as a badge of servitude, yet there was nothing to guarantee that white skin would always serve as an unimpeachable badge of freedom.

❖ ❖ ❖

It is incumbent upon anyone offering a new interpretation of the Civil War's causes to demonstrate that previous authors have missed an important component of the sectional conflict. It is obvious to most that slavery, as Lincoln stated, was "somehow" the cause of the war. From the southern perspective, it is not difficult to discern slavery's social and economic importance. However, northern hostility to the institution has proven much more challenging to explain. Historians have offered numerous interpretations in an effort to answer a seemingly straightforward question: What direct relevance did southern slavery have for Republicans (or Northerners in general)? The results have been fruitful, but not entirely satisfying.

These interpretive challenges may explain the recurring efforts to downplay slavery's significance. The ethnocultural interpretation is a clear example. Unlike slavery, foreign immigration was an immediate and understandably visceral experience for many Northerners. Given the massive influx of Catholic immigrants (and the consequent expansion of the Democratic Party), northern Whigs were primed for revolt even before the spring of 1854. While they highlight some of the fundamental causes of northern antislavery sentiment, ethnocultural historians, most notably William Gienapp, argue that slavery was not the initial catalyst for political realignment in the North. Rather, they emphasize the impact of nativism and the temperance movement. Similarly, political partisanship and overwrought emotionalism may have fostered the development of sectional animosity, but can hardly be said to have created it. The revisionists of the 1930s and 1940s, led by Avery Craven and James G. Randall, argued that better statesmanship might well have averted the war. By this logic, the conflict was not the result of fundamental or structural problems in American society. Yet as John Ashworth has recently noted, it makes at least as much sense to argue that the conflict over slavery produced a failure of statesmanship as it does to contend that a failure of statesmanship produced the conflict over slavery.[5]

Nor can moral fervor sufficiently account for the Republican Party's opposition to slavery's expansion. As Leon Litwack and Eugene Berwanger have pointed out, anti-black prejudice was nearly as prevalent in the North as in the South. Sympathy for the slaves and religious conviction may have been driving impetuses for some Northerners, but were not sufficient to sustain a popular political movement. One can reasonably assert that the devotion to white supremacy so often attributed to white Southerners was also common among northern whites. Nevertheless, the violent backlash triggered by abolitionist tactics in the 1830s encouraged Northerners to contrast the characteristics of slave society with their own, and in so doing generated a broader antislavery, or anti-southern, ideology. Riots, murders, and the House gag rule on abolitionist petitions fueled the suspicion that slaveholders and their allies held the liberties of white Northerners in contempt. Furthermore, this perception of southern despotism was closely related to northern antipathy for the southern work ethic (or lack thereof), which stood in sharp contrast to the values of hard work and upward mobility that many abolitionists exemplified.[6]

Indeed, economic opposition to southern bondage was undoubtedly a salient facet of the antislavery movement, considering the institution's threat to northern interests. Forty years after its publication, Eric Foner's *Free Soil, Free Labor, Free Men* remains one of the most influential volumes on antebellum politics, in part because its emphasis on slavery's threat to the North's economic and social values provides us with a structural explanation of Republican antislavery, not just an explanation of its timing. I stand quite convinced of the validity of Foner's argument that many Northerners opposed the spread of slavery because it inhibited upward social mobility by stigmatizing labor and, consequently, threatening their access to the West, which served as a safety valve for the growing population of white laborers. In addition, James L. Huston has argued that the emergence of a national market threatened to put northern workers and southern slaves into direct competition, thus depressing northern wages and further stultifying social progress. Yet it seems to me the primary weakness of the economic interpretation is that it fails to differentiate Republicans from northern Democrats. There is no reason to believe that the latter were any less devoted to the free-labor ideology. Many of those who supported the Kansas-Nebraska Act may have believed, as Douglas did, that climate would keep slavery out of the territories, and therefore that congressional prohibition was both meaningless and needlessly antagonistic to the South. But as David Potter suggested, the possible outcome of popular sovereignty was not the Republicans' only concern. Whereas northern Democrats failed to see any symbolic need for a national policy against slavery's expansion, Republicans believed such a policy was a vital statement of American values.[7]

Other historians have pointed to the specter of a Slave Power conspiracy against northern liberties. The Slave Power has been a prominent theme in Kansas studies, particularly Nicole Etcheson's recent book. This is hardly surprising, considering that northern settlers, facing hostile Missourians and an illegitimate legislature, described their condition as "white slavery." Bill Cecil-Fronsman's 1997 article, "Advocate the Freedom of White Men, as Well as that of Negroes," accurately describes the principal concern of many free-soil Kansans. Leonard Richards has also demonstrated that southern political power was a major concern to Northerners on a national level, primarily in respect to the Three-fifths Clause, southern parity in the Senate, and the complicity of northern "doughfaces." In addition, Gienapp and Michael Holt point to Republicans' insistence that the Slave Power undermined America's revolutionary heritage. Like their forebears, Republicans continued to imbibe such "republican" precepts as self-government, fear of conspiracy, and hostility to aristocratic privilege.[8]

Similarly, the political and symbolic importance of the Declaration of Independence has received attention from historians such as Michael Morrison, Garry Wills, Major Wilson, and Douglas Wilson. They have explained how Republicans, northern Democrats, and southern Democrats appealed to the legacy of the Revolution to legitimize their policies. For Southerners, the Revolution upheld property rights in slaves and served as a reminder of the dangers posed by centralized government. For northern Democrats, the Revolution upheld the principle of self-government (for whites alone) inherent in popular sovereignty. And for Republicans, the Revolution, and in particular, the Declaration of Independence, established the United States on the principle of universal human liberty. Of course, given the prejudice endemic in northern society, Lincoln and the Republicans could not advocate racial equality, but, according to Douglas Wilson, they recognized that "there was political advantage to be gained in preempting the most revered clause of the most revered statement of national purpose."[9]

In respect to my interpretation, however, the symbolic and political importance of the Declaration is tangential. It boils down to a somewhat amorphous conflict between democracy and aristocracy, or between liberty and the Slave Power. This is not meant as a criticism of the aforementioned historians. The majority of Republicans who invoked the Revolution did so without specifying precisely how Democrats' apparent repudiation of the Declaration threatened the liberty of white Americans.

The facet of the Republican position I will highlight is the more detailed argument that individual liberty, including the liberty of whites, depended on universal liberty (or at least the American people's continued devotion to that principle). Perhaps not surprisingly, given the prominence of this facet in Lincoln's speeches and letters, Lincoln scholars have come closest to elucidating the importance of universal freedom. According to Harry Jaffa, "there was no principle which justified enslaving Negroes which did not at the same time justify enslaving whites." He also points to Lincoln's insistence that Americans had to stand dedicated to the principle of universal freedom, lest they become victims of proslavery justifications. In the same vein, David Zarefsky has written that "slavery denied the rights of man and, in this very fundamental sense, threatened the entire edifice of natural rights." Therefore, the only protection for the liberties of whites "lay in recognizing that these liberties derived from their status as human beings and hence were shared by all other people, including blacks." Stephen Oates highlights Lincoln's belief that Democrats (both northern and southern) were attempting to overthrow the Declaration of Independence, thus transforming the United States into "a despotism based on class rule and human servitude." Likewise, Allen Guelzo observes that the Declaration became the rhetorical touchstone for Lincoln after the passage of the Kansas-Nebraska Act. The enslavement of blacks was a step away from the Declaration, he explains, and "a step toward the enslavement of everyone."[10]

It is fair to state that these authors have contributed significantly to the ideas in this book. However, their comments on the Declaration's importance to white liberty are somewhat scattered and, in my opinion, should be fleshed out as a complete interpretation. It is not my contention that this aspect of the antislavery argument in any way supplants the free-labor ideal or the more generalized resentment of a nefarious Slave Power. Yet I do believe that the idea that individual liberty depended on universal liberty should be added to the list of reasons for Northerners to have worried about slavery's impact on their own lives.

◆ ◆ ◆

Of the proslavery rationales mentioned here, the only one that has been specifically analyzed as a threat to whites is race. This is somewhat surprising, considering that white skin is generally assumed to have been the clearest badge of personal freedom. The stigmatization of black skin, going back to the 1550s, has been well described by Winthrop Jordan in his examination of the connotations Englishmen attached to black and white (which he attributes to their desire for negative reference groups). These assumptions would continue to define "blackness" as a mark of sin and inferiority, and a consequent qualifier for bondage, throughout the antebellum period.[11]

Nevertheless, a handful of historians, including Russel B. Nye, Carol Wilson, Calvin Wilson, Thomas D. Morris, and Lawrence R. Tenzer, have observed that, from a legal perspective, slavery was not entirely, or even primarily, based on race. Beginning with a Virginia statute of 1662,

Southerners determined slavery by the status of the mother. After several generations of white paternity, which was anything but uncommon, the result was a class of people who were white by all appearances, but legally held in bondage. Indeed, Northerners were quite aware that people who appeared fully white labored as slaves in the South. They called attention to countless advertisements in southern newspapers in which masters described their absconded property as having "blue eyes, light flaxen hair," and "skin disposed to freckle." One such slaveowner candidly admitted that his slave was "so nearly white that it is believed a stranger would suppose there was no African blood in him." With these descriptions in mind, a slightly waggish Northerner wrote to a Kansas newspaper expressing a desire to settle in the new territory, but then complained he was "almost afraid to come, for should I happen to tan a little under your hot sun I might be taken for a mulatto."[12]

Many abolitionists began to argue that the common sight of these light-skinned slaves would put poor whites at risk for abduction and enslavement. Carol Wilson and Calvin Wilson effectively examine the northern assertion that white children, in both the South and the North, were being kidnapped and sold as the offspring of white slaves. Harriet Beecher Stowe dramatically expressed this fear in her *Key to Uncle Tom's Cabin:* "When the mind once becomes familiarized with the process of slavery . . . and when blue eyes and golden hair are advertised as properties of *negroes*—what protection will there be for poor white people, especially as under the present fugitive slave law they can be carried away without a jury trial?"[13]

Other Northerners, both abolitionists and Republicans, concluded that the continuing effects of amalgamation were destroying race as the natural barrier between freemen and slaves, thus producing a willingness to impose bondage without so much as the pretext of an enslaved maternal line. Southern slavery embraced all complexions, noted a Wisconsin editor. He then warned that white skin was quickly supplanting black through the natural process of miscegenation, which would ultimately "obliterate all distinctions of color." William Lloyd Garrison went even further in personalizing the danger to northern whites, reminding them that Southerners actively sought light-skinned slaves, particularly women: "No person can say I am safe, my wife is safe, my mother or my child is safe; that complexion settles the question in America, that none but black people can be enslaved." In the fall of 1855 the *Liberator* took note of two slave children purchased in the nation's capital who, according to observers, possessed no visible trace of African blood. Garrison suggested that local photographers display their pictures in order to convince the public that Southerners were willing to enslave "any child in the land" if it would serve their financial interests. Congressman James Ashley of Ohio also warned his constituents that "the bleaching process" of amalgamation and the consequent appearance of white-skinned slaves could produce a willingness to impose bondage without any regard to color or birth.[14]

Yet as a rationale for bondage, race may be best described as a subjective manifestation of arbitrary characteristics. Even if each and every southern slave had been clearly black, slavery was still a threat to the liberty of others because these characteristics could be attributed to people with little or no reference to their racial background. Indeed, "the social construction of race" has been a key interpretation in the works of Eric Williams, Oscar and Mary Handlin, Kenneth Stampp, Edmund Morgan, William McKee Evans, and Barbara Fields. Williams argued that race had nothing to do with the choice of Africans as a labor force. They were simply the most vulnerable, and hence the most economical. Racism developed later as the justification for an existing practice. It was therefore apparent, as Stampp explained in his study of the peculiar institution, that race has no real meaning of its own; "its meanings accrue from ideas the powerful attach to it."[15]

❖ ❖ ❖

The belief that proslavery rationales were dangerously subjective was expressed by Northerners across the antislavery spectrum. Consequently, the evidence I present in this study comes from political as well as abolitionist sources. That being said, it is not always a simple task to draw a clear line between the abolitionist and Republican versions of antislavery. The traditional view of abolitionists is that they were a small group of evangelical Northerners who demanded "immediate" emancipation, denounced colonization and compensation for slaveowners, felt genuine sympathy for the plight of the slave, and were morally opposed to the racial prejudice endemic in American society. Republicans, on the other hand, looked to the gradual emancipation of slavery (through territorial restriction), and opposed the institution because of its deleterious socioeconomic impact. In reality, however, the dividing line was hazy at best. After antislavery developed into a political force in the 1840s and 1850s, the Republican Party could claim important leaders who, despite their support for gradual emancipation over immediatism, can be accurately designated as abolitionists, including Charles Sumner, Salmon Chase, and Owen Lovejoy.

Even if the typical abolitionist had a greater claim to morality than the typical Republican, morality was certainly not devoid of self-interest. As James Brewer Stewart has observed, immediate abolitionists "showed no less concern than other white Northerners about the fate of republican freedom" in a slaveholding country. The Golden Rule can easily be interpreted as a warning to individuals that the oppression of others opens the door to the possibility that they might be similarly oppressed. According to one evangelical paper published at the time of the Missouri crisis, if it were truly the duty of all men to do unto others as they would wish others to do unto them, slavery would come to an immediate end, "for no man is willing to become a slave himself," or to see his children enslaved. Consequently, Stowe, Garrison, James G. Birney, and other abolitionists were quick to warn white Americans that the slave's lot could potentially become their own. Like the Republicans, they feared that Americans no longer honored the ideals of the founding fathers. They warned that qualifying or rejecting universal liberty in order to justify black slavery would put people of all races at risk. Theodore Parker argued that the principles that allowed slavery in South Carolina would also establish it in New England. If Virginians could raise Africans for sale, he saw no reason why people could not raise Irishmen, Democrats, and Know-Nothings for sale in Massachusetts. "The bondage of a black man in Alexandria imperils every white woman's daughter in Boston," he explained. "You cannot escape the consequences of a first principle more than you can 'take the leap of Niagara and stop half way down.'" Abolitionists and Republicans also made a point of reminding Northerners that the slavery of antiquity—which Southerners were so fond of invoking—had been primarily white slavery.[16]

Because these arguments emphasized slavery's potential threat to whites, rather than the suffering of the slaves themselves, they easily fit the free-labor platform and political purposes of the Republican Party. It is not surprising that many historians have charged Republicans with hypocrisy, given the fact that they failed to offer civil equality as a corollary of their condemnation of slavery. In fact, many Republicans, particularly in the Midwest, vehemently denied any intention or desire to introduce social or political equality between the races. And many believed, or certainly claimed to believe, that blacks were morally and intellectually inferior to whites. Yet at the same time, they would not deny the black man's humanity. They would not embrace the fiction that slaves were simply another form of property, in the same category as pigs and cattle. In the final analysis, it was their common humanity that linked the black man's fate to the rights of white men. Republicans were thus forced to balance their own prejudice—and that of their constituents—with their insistence that whites and blacks were members of the same human family. As a result, they consistently attempted to segregate natural rights from social and political rights, maintaining that blacks were entitled to the former, but could be safely denied the latter. (Northern Democrats, on the other hand, insisted that the Republican platform would lead inexorably to political and social equality.) For Republicans, ultimate emancipation was as much a means to an end as an end in itself. In his second annual address to Congress in 1862, Lincoln argued that "in giving freedom to the slave, we assure freedom to the free—honorable alike in what we give and what we preserve." Yet given the prejudice of northern voters, most placed a greater emphasis on the second half of that equation. Lyman Trumbull, Illinois's first Republican senator, observed that Southerners had just as much right to enslave a white man in Kansas as they did to hold a black man in the same condition. White skin was no protection. He therefore maintained that "it is not so much in reference to the welfare of the negro that we are here." The Republicans' goal was to protect the rights and dignity of laboring whites.[17]

From a strictly political standpoint, Democrats spared no attempt to capitalize on northern prejudice by characterizing Republicans as racial egalitarians, while Republicans actively sought to portray Democrats as tools of the Slave Power and traitors to the nation's founding principles. The declension of American freedom, marked by a failure to respect the ideal of universal liberty, became a significant line of attack against both northern and southern Democrats. Republican editors and politicians made a point of connecting them to a defense of slavery in the abstract, characterizing southern papers that lauded slavery as the "special organs" of James Buchanan and, occasionally, Stephen A. Douglas. These editorials would often carry sensational titles—"The Buchanan Democracy Hate Freedom"—while the Democratic Party was frequently disparaged as "the bogus Democracy" or "the party calling itself democratic."[18]

Republicans also frequently included a special message for foreign-born Americans, warning them that they would be the most susceptible to enslavement and asking them to reconsider their devotion to the Democratic Party. This became an interesting facet of the Republicans' balancing act between nativism and an appeal to immigrants in 1856. "These Democratic rhapsodies over the peculiar institution are not confined to merely negro slavery," proclaimed the Springfield, Illinois, *Journal*. "The Douglas Democracy, it will be seen, say that 'the principle of slavery does not depend on difference of complexion,' but goes further and embraces within its folds likewise all the poor and laboring classes, no matter to what race or lineage they belong. They argue that the free-born sons of Ireland, of Germany, of Scotland, of America would be bettered and improved in their condition were they likewise brought into the bondage of the Southern slave. Was there ever a more monstrous doctrine promulgated? And yet it is to this that the present avowals of the Sham Democracy are rapidly tending."[19]

One might protest that Republicans were willing to accept the continuation of slavery in those states where it already existed, and were therefore complicit in the legitimization of proslavery rationales. Maintaining the ideal of universal liberty required the American people to repudiate slavery, but this did not require the immediate abolition of slavery in the South. Prohibiting the expansion of slavery, thus keeping it "on the course of ultimate extinction," would signify that the public considered it a necessary evil, to be tolerated temporarily as an aberration in a nation still dedicated to the proposition that all men possess equal rights to life, liberty, and the pursuit of happiness. "Let us, by our legislation, show that we really believe the declaration," announced the *New York Times*. Americans could not yet enforce the doctrine in every section of the country, but they could strive to "stay the plague," and affix the mark of national disapprobation on southern slavery.[20]

This was a major theme in Lincoln's campaign against Douglas and the application of popular sovereignty as the method for determining slavery's status in the territories. His greatest challenge was to convince northern audiences, including some of his fellow Republicans, that simple indifference to slavery was itself inimical to the liberty of whites. The question, as Lincoln saw it, was whether liberty would be universal (at least in theory) or whether the justifications for black slavery would survive to threaten the liberty of all—a danger he pointed to repeatedly, as when he criticized Douglas for convincing the public not to care about slavery and for qualifying the Declaration of Independence, which he viewed as the only sure defense against circumstance and the self-interest of the powerful. In order to fix my topic in the political context of the 1850s, I will begin with an examination of Lincoln's reaction to the Kansas-Nebraska Act and his subsequent debates with Senator Douglas.

Proceeding from Lincoln's argument, the next three chapters will examine each of the proslavery rationales I have identified (inferiority, the good of the slave, the good of society, and the lessons of history and Christianity) and demonstrate how northern whites could perceive each one to be a threat to their own freedom. Chapter five will highlight the northern argument that slaveholders constituted a burgeoning aristocracy. Chapter six will examine the antislavery response to Southerners' denials and qualifications of the Declaration of Independence, particularly in respect to the Dred Scott decision, while the final chapter will consider the debate between antislavery Northerners and northern Democrats after 1854 (including the historical accuracy of their respective claims) as well as the Republican Party's devotion to the ideal of universal liberty in the 1860 presidential campaign.

One of the primary challenges that confront students of antislavery is the need to extrapolate northern motivations from the sources at hand. Fortunately, antebellum Northerners left us an abundance of material with which to work, including newspapers, political tracts, published speeches, legislative petitions, and private correspondence. In the course of my research, I examined hundreds of newspapers and printed sources. Whether or not political speeches and newspaper editorials can reveal the actual depth of these antislavery arguments in the northern consciousness is certainly open to debate. But these are by far the most informative sources we have, and if the repetition of an argument by numerous individuals can be taken as evidence of its prominence, the antislavery positions examined in this study had a significant impact on the northern psyche. Consequently, the fear that black slavery posed a threat to white liberty cannot be dismissed as a mere conspiracy theory held by a paranoid minority. Furthermore, given the broadness of my topic, I saw no value in confining my research to a particular state or region—although a significant portion of my material emerged from the Old Northwest, which was the heart of the early Republican Party. Most of my sources will fall within the period of rapidly escalating tensions (1854–1860); however, some arguments will reach back into the nation's first half century, a period in which many aspects of the proslavery and antislavery arguments initially took shape.

Finally, it is important to clarify my use of the term "universal liberty." It is not meant to express a belief that American slaves (much less all human beings) would actually enjoy freedom at any point in the foreseeable future; rather it is a reference to Northerners' belief that liberty had to be maintained as a national ideal. Only by defining slavery as an aberrant and temporary evil could human bondage be delegitimized as a social arrangement and cordoned off from American society. If the principle of human liberty were not maintained (which it could not be if the American public sanctioned slavery's expansion and perpetuation), no one's liberty would be respected as "self-evident"—an inviolable aspect of the human condition—particularly if they were unable to defend themselves against the machinations of would-be aristocrats. So my use of the term is very much predicated on Lincoln's defense of the term "created equal." All men were endowed with inalienable rights, but Northerners' devotion to the concept was not tantamount to an argument that all human beings the world over should be immediately freed (certainly not for Republicans). It was an axiom adopted by the founding fathers to guide the nation in the future. And in this case, the territories were the future.

≒ 1 ≓

The Myth of the Free-State Democrat

"I am not in the habit of looking upon this struggle as a local one, and confined to Kansas," wrote the soon-to-be free-state governor, Charles Robinson, in 1855. "I regard it as one in which the whole nation is involved." In the age of Manifest Destiny, the West represented the nation's future, politically, economically, and symbolically. However, Manifest Destiny rarely served as a nationalizing force. Driven by separate sectional imperatives, westward expansion gave the conflict between North and South its "irrepressible" character. For more than forty years prior to the Civil War, Americans struggled to define slavery's status in areas where it did not yet exist or was not yet firmly established.[1]

Due to their increasing populations and their desire for additional political representation, Northerners and Southerners vied for control over the nation's territorial growth. Southerners felt the need to expand because of the depletion of the soil and the growing slave population. Many Americans, both Northerners and Southerners, agreed that if slavery could not expand it would eventually die. In the words of one proslavery editor in Kansas, limiting the institution to those states where it already existed would force Southerners "to choose between self-destruction and the agonies of a slow death." Likewise, northern society needed to expand in order to prevent a high population density that would increase competition for jobs and lower wages, thus undermining the free-labor ideology. Jefferson's hostility to urbanization had been predicated on this reasoning. According to the traditional republican view, land was the only source of personal independence, and personal independence was a prerequisite for those who expected to maintain their freedom in a participatory republic. Without an abundant supply of land, people would be forced to work for wages in an increasingly crowded market, which would make them dependent on their employers and, consequently, render them susceptible to blackmail and bribery. In this respect, Americans, with a sprawling continent at their doorstep, seemed particularly blessed. They envisioned the West as a safety valve through which people could make a fresh start when their fortunes declined.[2]

Yet many Northerners were convinced that their access to this land would be effectively blocked if they were forced to compete with slave labor. In the late 1850s, free laborers earned roughly a dollar a day, whereas the cost of a slave's daily labor was less than twenty-five cents. Competition with slaves could therefore be expected to severely depress wages. Psychologically, the effects were similar. Northerners argued that slavery undermined the work ethic of free laborers by stigmatizing hard work as servile. What could be more enervating, they asked, than having to compete with another man's slaves? Slavery therefore prevented upward social mobility, created a stagnant economy, and maintained a permanent class structure in which the bloated slaveholding aristocracy reigned supreme.[3]

❖ ❖ ❖

This conflict took a violent turn with the passage of the Kansas-Nebraska Act in the spring of 1854. Four years earlier, Congress had passed a series of measures that finally defused the crisis emanating from the Mexican War and the acquisition of California and New Mexico. Many Americans had hoped this would be a "final settlement" of the controversy over slavery's expansion. Yet with the acquisition of this territory, facilitating travel and communication between East and West became a salient issue. In fact, the war had not yet begun when Stephen A. Douglas of Illinois, then a thirty-two-year-old freshman congressman, began to advocate the construction of a railroad linking Chicago and San Francisco. In the fall of 1845, Douglas introduced a bill to organize the land west of Iowa as Nebraska Territory. The measure failed to pass, and while public support continued to grow, the possible location of a transcontinental road remained the subject of sectional and local rivalries almost a decade later.[4]

In February 1853, William A. Richardson, Douglas's ally and chairman of the House Committee on Territories, reported a new measure to provide Nebraska with a territorial government. The need for such legislation seemed obvious. "In the name of God, how is the railroad to be made if you will never let people live on the lands through which the road passes?" demanded the bill's author. Douglas, now chairman of the Senate Committee on Territories, concurred and favorably reported the measure. Yet despite widespread support for a transcontinental railroad, many Southerners opposed a move to organize the Louisiana Purchase territory north of 36° 30´. Slavery had been prohibited there under the terms of the Missouri Compromise in 1820, and any states carved from Nebraska would assuredly enter the Union as free states. Missourians were particularly wary. With the free state of Illinois to the east and Iowa to the north, they now faced the unwelcome prospect of a free territory on their western border, where much of their slave population was concentrated. It was therefore with considerable misgivings that Senator David Rice Atchison of Missouri agreed to support the bill. Nevertheless, Douglas was still unable to garner the votes he needed. With the support of every slave-state senator south of Missouri, the Senate voted to table the measure shortly before Congress adjourned.[5]

Douglas remained committed to Nebraska's organization, but as the new Congress assembled in December 1853, he found the terrain even more difficult than it had been during the previous session. Perhaps most notably, Atchison, who had spent the recess battling Thomas Hart Benton in the opening stage of the next senate campaign, now announced that he would see Nebraska "sink in hell" before voting to organize it as free territory. If Douglas could not pass the bill with Atchison's support, it was highly unlikely he would be able to do so without it. With this in mind, Douglas began to make a series of increasingly direct concessions to his southern colleagues. The new bill, reported out of his committee on January 4, made no reference to the Missouri Compromise, but repeated the language that had been employed in the New Mexico and Utah legislation of 1850: "when admitted as a State or States, the said territory, or any portion of the same, shall be received into the Union, with or without slavery, as their constitution may prescribe at the time of their admission." Southerners quickly made it clear to Douglas that this was insufficient, and within a week he added another section, which had supposedly been left out through "clerical error," explicitly stating the right of territorial residents to determine slavery's status within their borders. Southerners realized, however, that slavery would never have an opportunity to take root if the Missouri Compromise remained in effect. Two weeks after Douglas first introduced his bill, Senator Archibald Dixon of Kentucky pressed him to incorporate an outright repeal. Douglas agreed, fully aware that it would cause "a hell of a storm." He also decided to provide for two new territories, Nebraska, to the west of Iowa, and Kansas, to the west of Missouri. While it was not unreasonable to allow these regions the opportunity to develop separately from each other, many construed this measure as a means of reserving Kansas for slavery and Nebraska for freedom.[6]

Although Douglas may have hoped to placate Southerners while leaving the Missouri Compromise intact, his basic reasoning remained constant. Beginning with the bill's initial introduction, Douglas claimed that the principle of congressional exclusion had been superseded by "the leading feature of the compromise of 1850," which in his view was the "great principle of self-government." According to Douglas, Congress had repudiated the Missouri Compromise by refusing to extend it to the Pacific in 1848 (despite the support of the Polk administration) and in 1850 had determined "that the people of the territories, and of all the states, were to be allowed to do as they pleased upon the subject of slavery." The supersession argument was, however, clearly disingenuous on Douglas's part. He had publicly lauded the Missouri Compromise in 1849 as "a sacred thing, which no ruthless hand would ever be reckless enough to disturb." And as for the Compromise of 1850, many Northerners pointed out, quite correctly, that no one at the time believed that the New Mexico and Utah legislation had any bearing whatsoever on the Louisiana Purchase. Lincoln aptly noted the absurdity of the argument that those who favored the Wilmot Proviso in order to prohibit slavery in the Mexican Cession were actually fighting to allow slavery north of $36°\,30'$ by refusing to extend the line to the Pacific. The Missouri Compromise and the Compromise of 1850 were separate measures, he insisted, not general principles: "To argue that we thus repudiated the Missouri Compromise is no less absurd than it would be to argue that because we have so far forborne to acquire Cuba, we have thereby, in principle, repudiated our former acquisitions and determined to throw them out of the Union. No less absurd than it would be to say that because I may have refused to build an addition to my house, I thereby have decided to destroy the existing house! And if I catch you setting fire to my house, you will turn upon me and say I instructed you to do it!"[7]

To the extent to which it can be considered a principle, "congressional nonintervention" is perhaps a more accurate appellation than "popular sovereignty," considering that the actual sovereignty of territorial residents over the issue of slavery had been left intentionally ambiguous ever since Lewis Cass first championed the measure in his run for the White House in 1848.

The final version of the Kansas-Nebraska Act merely stated that territorial residents would be "perfectly free" to regulate their domestic institutions, "subject only to the Constitution." Northern Democrats, including Douglas, assumed that a territorial legislature could exclude slavery during the territorial stage. Southerners, on the other hand, assumed no such authority. In their minds, slave property should be as sacrosanct as any other form of property. Regulation could only occur as the territory entered the Union as a state. This ambiguity, while attractive as a means of garnering support in both sections, would later serve to divide the Democratic Party.

The Kansas-Nebraska Act easily passed the Senate on March 3. Only two Southerners voted against it, Sam Houston and John Bell, while party discipline kept all but four northern Democrats in line. President Pierce had agreed to make the bill a test of Democratic orthodoxy, but the House, whose members soon had to face their constituents, was less amenable to administration demands. Douglas exerted his influence, which, along with the legislative legerdemain of Alexander Stephens, secured the bill's passage on May 22 by a narrow vote of 113 to 100. More so than the Senate, the House vote revealed the sectional realignment of American politics. Half of the northern Democrats voted against the bill, as did every northern Whig, whereas two-thirds of southern Whigs joined the Democrats to support it.[8]

Douglas may have achieved an impressive legislative victory, but the Kansas-Nebraska Act was proved far from successful in its operation. Douglas had hoped that congressional nonintervention would define slavery as a state and territorial issue, thereby freeing Congress and the president to focus on greater issues. Instead, the dream of a transcontinental railroad was consumed by the sectional animosities engendered by the act, and the nation stood transfixed as Kansas descended into chaos and violence.[9]

Three years after the passage of Douglas's bill, Northerners could look back on a long series of outrages in Kansas. Proslavery Missourians had stolen elections for Kansas's delegate to Congress and for the territorial legislature. This legislature, fraudulent in spirit if not in fact, passed a draconian slave code, imposing a sentence of two years at hard labor for those who wrote or circulated antislavery material and threatening the imprisonment of anyone who simply denied the institution's legality. Those who aided escaped slaves or incited rebellion risked the death penalty. Southerners also threatened the life and expedited the departure of every governor who dared to oppose them. Cowed by their demands, President Pierce blamed the hostilities on New England emigrants (who, despite the propaganda, were relatively few in numbers), condemned the free-state Topeka Constitution as "revolutionary," and authorized the use of federal troops to disperse the free-state government. Then, in February 1857, the proslavery legislature attempted to solidify its gains by calling for the election of a constitutional convention.[10]

Not surprisingly, free-soil opponents often lamented their "enslavement" by a proslavery minority. Broadsides advertising mass meetings were emblazoned with the words "No White Slavery!" Sara Robinson, wife of the free-state governor, observed that Kansans "feel the iron heel of the oppressor, making us truly white slaves." (The imprisonment of Gov. Robinson at Lecompton during the summer of 1856 illustrates her point.) Somewhat ironically, considering the northern reaction to the Kansas-Nebraska Act, free-soil Kansans expressed acceptance of popular sovereignty as a democratic principle, but decried Southerners' violation of that principle. In an anguished remonstrance, free-state leaders told Congress that the Kansas-Nebraska Act had granted popular sovereignty to proslavery Missourians, but had imposed "serfdom" on the territory's actual residents.

> The doctrine of self-government is to be trampled under foot here, of all other places in the world, on the very spot which had been hallowed and consecrated. . . . The compact is to be basely broken, and the ballot of the freeman torn from our hands, almost before the ink of the covenant is dry. . . . The question of *negro* slavery is to sink into insignificance, and the greater portentous issue is to rise up in its stead, whether or not *we* shall be slaves, and fanatics who disgrace the honorable and chivalric men of the south shall be our masters to rule us at their pleasure.[11]

❖ ❖ ❖

Republicans condemned the violence and fraud that resulted from the Kansas-Nebraska Act. Yet in Lincoln's view, this was not the most troubling aspect of Douglas's measure. The status of freedom and slavery in the public mind was his primary concern.

Lincoln believed slavery's status in the West would determine the character of the entire nation. He therefore argued that Kansas-Nebraska was a dangerous watershed in American history. By relinquishing control over slavery's expansion to territorial settlers, popular sovereignty both fostered and reflected national indifference to the future of human servitude. In other words, it presented freedom and slavery as equally acceptable options for local majorities in their dealings with vulnerable minorities. And this indifference implied national approval of slavery. The endorsement or toleration of slavery's expansion (and indefinite continuation), under the terms of popular sovereignty, or any other policy, would signify that the American people approved of slavery *in principle*. Beginning with his Peoria speech in October 1854, Lincoln denounced "this declared indifference" to the spread of slavery because "it assumes that there can be moral right in the enslaving of one man by another." It was "a dangerous dalliance for a free people"—evidence that "liberty, as a principle, we have ceased to revere."[12]

This would develop into a major theme in his debates with Douglas four years later. Tolerating slavery's expansion connoted an assumption that slavery was "not a wrong." No man, Lincoln reasoned, could logically express indifference toward something he considered immoral. But it made perfect sense if the issue at hand was trivial or morally acceptable. The real difference between Douglas and his followers on the one hand and the Republicans on the other was that Douglas "is not in favor of making any difference between slavery and liberty—that he is in favor of eradicating, of pressing out of view, the questions of preference in this country for free or slave institutions; and consequently every sentiment he utters discards the idea that there is any wrong in slavery."[13]

Because popular sovereignty implied that slavery was not wrong, its supporters, like the proslavery apologists, were naturally compelled to qualify or otherwise reject the Declaration of Independence. How could Americans continue to proclaim that "all men" possessed inalienable rights to life, liberty, and the pursuit of happiness when they countenanced the expansion and perpetuation of human servitude? Popular sovereignty debauched public opinion—which, in Lincoln's view, was "everything" in a republic—by rejecting the universal rights of man: "Near eighty years ago we began by declaring that all men are created equal; but now from that beginning we have run down to the other declaration, that for some men to enslave others is a 'sacred right of self-government.'" These principles were clearly incompatible; therefore, "whoever holds to the one must despise the other." By fostering northern apathy, popular sovereignty had the same corrosive effect as the proslavery ideology. Acceptance of the institution's expansion, or indifference to it, necessarily destroyed the principle of universal freedom. For this reason, Lincoln believed that Douglas and the northern Democrats posed as much of a threat to American liberty as did southern slaveholders.[14]

Qualifying the Declaration's assertion of universal liberty in order to allow for black slavery was dangerous because it would leave the door open for additional qualifications. "I should like to know," Lincoln asked, "taking this old Declaration of Independence, which declares that all men are equal upon principle, and making exceptions to it—where will it stop? If one man says it does not mean a Negro, why not another say it does not mean some other man?" Without liberty for all (or at least a recognition of that principle), the rationales that were used to exclude one class of people could be used to exclude any other class. No one's liberty would be self-evident. Everyone's liberty would be contingent on circumstance. And it was for this reason that Lincoln explicitly accused Democrats of attempting to replace universal liberty with "the opposite idea that slavery is right in the abstract, the workings of which as a central idea may be the perpetuity of human slavery and its extension to all countries and colors."[15]

The Declaration of Independence was therefore the ultimate American palladium—a guarantee that white Americans could never fall victim to arguments favoring their subjugation. Regardless of circumstance or misfortune, the freedom of each individual would be respected simply by virtue of his or her humanity. And it was to protect the Declaration's principle of universal freedom that Lincoln opposed popular sovereignty. "Is there no danger to liberty itself in discarding the earliest practice and first precept of our ancient faith?" he asked at Peoria. "In our greedy chase to make profit of the Negro, let us beware lest we 'cancel and tear in pieces' even the white man's charter of freedom."[16]

Not surprisingly, Senator John Pettit of Indiana became a harbinger of national declension in the eyes of Lincoln and many Republicans. In a three-hour speech delivered before the Senate on February 20, 1854, Pettit, a northern Democrat, argued vociferously that Congress possessed the constitutional authority to prohibit slavery in the territories. Yet he supported the Kansas-Nebraska Act, insisting that there was "a great difference between power and the exercise of power." In his view, popular sovereignty would "put at rest forever this exciting question of slavery, and banish it from these halls." It would settle the debate over slavery's expansion upon just and equitable principles, allowing North and South equal access to the territories. Pettit also denounced the "ultra extreme abolitionism" of those who castigated Stephen Douglas. In particular, he condemned the antislavery defense of human equality: "It is alleged that all men are created equal, and the Declaration of Independence is referred to, to sustain that position. However unpopular, or however displeasing it may be to the mass of my fellow-citizens, I am constrained to dissent from any such position or dogma. It is not true in fact; it is not true in law; it is not true physically, mentally, or morally that all men are created equal. . . . I hold it to be a self-evident lie."

> Sir, tell me that the imbecile, the deformed, the weak, the blurred intellect in man, is my equal, physically, mentally, or morally, and you tell me a lie. Tell me, sir, that the slave in the South, who is born a slave, and with but little over one half the volume of brain that attaches to the northern European race, is my equal, and you tell me what is physically a falsehood. Sir, you tell me that the native African, upon his burning sands, and in his native wilderness, is my equal, and I hesitate not to hoot at the idea. . . . Sir, it is not true that even all persons of the same race are created equal. . . . Are you the equal of the man who daily and nightly wallows in the gutter, and vomits upon all, and nauseates all who come into his presence? Are you his equal? If you are, you are not mine.[17]

Although some antislavery Northerners (who would soon coalesce into the Republican Party) doubtlessly concurred with Pettit's racial assumptions, they were scandalized by his direct assault on the Declaration of Independence. The phrase "self-evident lie," as a description of that document, quickly became a catchphrase for the political retrogression of the Democratic Party and the deleterious spirit of the Kansas-Nebraska Act. "When Pettit, in connection with his support of the Nebraska Bill, called the Declaration of Independence a 'self-evident lie,'" Lincoln explained, "he only did what consistency and candor require all other Nebraska men to do."

> Of the forty-odd Nebraska senators who sat present and heard him, no one rebuked him. Nor am I apprised that any Nebraska newspaper, or any Nebraska orator, in the whole nation has ever yet rebuked him. If this had been said among Marion's men, Southerners though they were, what would have become of the man who said it? If this had been said to the men who captured Andre, the man who said it would probably have been hung sooner than Andre was. If it had been said in old Independence Hall seventy-eight years ago, the very doorkeeper would have throttled the man and thrust him into the street. Let no one be deceived. The spirit

of seventy-six and the spirit of Nebraska are utter antagonisms; and the
former is being rapidly displaced by the latter.

Pettit's fellow Indianan, Congressman Samuel Parker, denounced the senator for impugning the founders' intentions. "He insists most vehemently
that that old fogy, Thomas Jefferson, when he promulgated the 'self-evident
truth' that 'all men are created equal' did not clearly understand what he
was talking about." Indeed, Pettit's aggressive (one might say self-righteous)
manner did nothing to endear him to his colleagues, regardless of their
political affiliation. Lewis Cass suggested he was unbalanced. Thomas Hart
Benton dubbed him "dirty dog Pettit"—a sobriquet that would continue to
dog the senator through the remainder of his political career.[18]

Douglas was far more reverential to the Declaration than Pettit, yet his
officially stated indifference to the spread of slavery forced him to limit its
meaning. He repeatedly proclaimed his belief that the signers of the Declaration "referred to the white race alone, and not to the African, when they
declared all men to have been created equal." In fact, Douglas was certain
that the signers meant to exclude all "inferior races," such as Native Americans, the Chinese, and the Japanese. "They were speaking," he insisted, "of
British subjects on this continent being equal to British subjects born and
residing in Great Britain."[19]

Lincoln echoed the feelings of many Republicans when he accused Douglas of making a "mangled ruin" of the Declaration of Independence. As a
mere statement of equality between British subjects in America and those
across the pond, it was stripped of all relevance and meaning to succeeding
generations of Americans, many of whom, he noted, were not descendants
of British colonists. Indeed, he was quick to remind his foreign-born listeners, Germans in particular, that, in Douglas's construction, not only *could*
they be excluded from the Declaration, *they already were excluded.* With
the exception of white Americans, Britons, Irishmen, and Scots, the white
people of the world "are all gone to pot along with the judge's inferior races!"[20]

In response to Douglas's argument, which Roger B. Taney also made
in the Dred Scott decision, that the founders could not have included
blacks due to the fact that they had accepted slavery (and in many cases
had owned slaves themselves), Lincoln insisted that the Declaration was
never intended as an edict of emancipation or a description of reality, but
rather as a statement of principle that set forth the ultimate goal of universal
liberty. "They meant to set up a standard maxim for free society, which

should be familiar to all, and revered by all," he announced. And while this maxim would never be perfectly attained, it should be constantly looked to as the critical objective of a free society. At the very least, inequality and subjugation should not be allowed to expand.[21]

The greatest difficulty Republicans faced was the need to counter Douglas's explicit appeal to white supremacy. Although there were certainly gradations, particularly in Illinois, white racism was as much a fact of life in the North as in the South. And while Douglas promised the audience at the first joint debate at Ottawa to address himself to their judgment, "and not to your passions or your enthusiasm," he was quite eager to affix the odium of abolition and racial equality on his opponents. Willfully obfuscating the difference between abolitionists, who advocated social and political equalitarianism, and the vast majority of Republicans, who did not, he insisted that opposition to the spread of slavery was tantamount to support for racial equality, especially when Republicans invoked the Declaration of Independence. "I believe this government was made by our fathers on the white basis . . . made by white men for the benefit of white men and their posterity forever," he intoned. "I do not question Mr. Lincoln's conscientious belief that the negro was made his equal, and hence his brother; but for my own part, I do not regard the negro as my equal, and positively deny that he is my brother or any kin to me whatever." In this same vein, Douglas accused Lincoln of conspiring to create an abolition party in 1854, accused "Black Republicans" of making war on the Supreme Court and favoring black citizenship, characterized "Fred Douglass, the negro" as a close Lincoln advisor, and continued to insist that the founding fathers did not include blacks, "nor any other barbarous race," when they declared all men to be created equal.[22]

In order to circumvent Douglas's racist appeals, Lincoln insisted that the signers of the Declaration posited a universal equality of natural rights, not social or political rights. "I think the authors of that notable instrument intended to include all men," he explained, "but they did not intend to declare all men equal in all respects." They had not meant to declare all men equal in color, intellect, morality, or social capacity (as Pettit suggested). However, they did define all men to be equal in their rights to life, liberty, and the pursuit of happiness. Lincoln was politically obliged to disclaim any tendency toward racial equalitarianism and to announce his own support for white supremacy, which included reserving the territories for free white laborers. Yet he also argued that the American public had to accept the Declaration as a statement of the universality of *natural rights.* "The judge will have it that if we do not confess that there is a sort of inequality between the white and black races which justifies us in making them slaves, we must, then, insist that there is a degree of equality that requires us to make them our wives." This, however, was counterfeit logic. A black man may not have been his equal "in many respects," Lincoln averred, "but in his right to eat the bread, without the leave of anybody else, which his own hand earns, he is my equal and the equal of Judge Douglas, and the equal of every living man."[23]

Lincoln also maintained that these assaults on the Declaration of Independence were a new phenomenon. The Kansas-Nebraska Act had turned Democrats away from their traditional devotion to the principle of universal freedom and threatened to debauch the public mind with a dangerous indifference to the liberty of others. Prior to the introduction of the Kansas-Nebraska Act, no one, he argued, including Douglas, had ever alleged that blacks were not included in the Declaration—that is not until "the necessities of the present policy of the Democratic party, in regard to slavery, had to invent that affirmation." He therefore insisted that Americans should redeem their devotion to universal liberty by rejecting the "spirit of Nebraska" and readopting the spirit of seventy-six, which accepted slavery only as a necessary evil that would eventually end. This would be accomplished when they arrested the spread of slavery, and once again placed it "where the public mind shall rest in the belief that it is in the course of ultimate extinction."[24]

Given the indifference undergirding popular sovereignty—and the tacit acceptance of proslavery rationales it implied—Lincoln dismissed the very notion of a "free-state Democrat" in the struggle for Kansas. As far as Lincoln and his fellow Republicans were concerned, the Democratic Party, with its pliant northern wing, had become little more than a vehicle for the southern Slave Power. It was apparent to them that all true advocates of free soil would flock to the Republican banner, an assumption that Lincoln expressed before a Springfield audience shortly after the election of delegates to the Lecompton convention. Musing on the role of Democrats in the election, Lincoln found it difficult to believe that any honest advocate of free soil could remain with the party of Jackson: "Allow me to barely whisper my suspicion that there were no such things in Kansas as 'free-state Democrats'—that they were altogether mythical, good only to figure in newspapers and speeches in the free states. If there should prove

to be one real living free-state Democrat in Kansas, I suggest that it might
be well to catch him, and stuff and preserve his skin as an interesting speci-
men of that soon-to-be extinct variety of the genus Democrat."[25]

◆ ◆ ◆

Nevertheless, Lincoln realized that Douglas exercised enormous influence
over public opinion. He accused the Little Giant of using that influence to
prepare the public mind for the nationalization of slavery. Unfortunately,
Douglas's influence had increased dramatically among Northerners after
his break with President Buchanan over the Lecompton Constitution.

Upon taking office in March 1857, Buchanan chose Robert J. Walker
to serve as governor of Kansas. Pierce's three appointees to the position,
Andrew Reeder, Wilson Shannon, and John Geary, had all found the territory to be an intractable hornet's nest. Although a native of Pennsylvania,
Walker had moved to Mississippi, which appointed him as a U.S. senator
in 1835; later, he served with Buchanan in Polk's cabinet as secretary of the
treasury. As the new governor, Walker also had Douglas's support. Indeed,
Douglas had begged Walker to accept the position, telling him "the whole
success of the Kansas-Nebraska Act in that territory is to a great extent
dependent on your consenting to go."[26]

Walker agreed, with the understanding that the legitimate residents of
Kansas would be permitted to choose their own institutions. In his inaugural address, he boldly notified the proslavery legislature that Congress
would not accept Kansas statehood unless a majority of its residents had
approved the constitution in a direct vote, "excluding all fraud and violence."
Buchanan concurred, assuring Walker that "on the question of submit-
ting the constitution to the bona fide residences of Kansas, I am willing to
stand or fall." Southerners, however, began to push back against Walker's
agenda, which ultimately eroded the president's resolve. Democratic state
conventions in Georgia and Mississippi denounced the governor's med-
dling, as did the Alabama state senate and many southern newspapers.
The territory's proslavery leaders also became increasingly uneasy as more
and more settlers arrived, giving Kansas a clear free-state majority. In the
territorial election that October, Northerners finally won control of the
legislature, thanks in no small part to Walker's determination to discard
fraudulent returns.[27]

When the Lecompton convention met shortly thereafter, the proslavery delegates decided to offer the form of a referendum without the
substance. Kansans could choose between the "Constitution with slavery"

or the "Constitution without slavery." However, the latter option provided that the slave property already in Kansas would not be interfered with. Republicans denounced this subterfuge as the "Lecompton swindle." Not only did it deny Kansans a right to reject the entire document, the provision protecting existing slave property would effectively establish Kansas as a slave state, considering that the prohibition on importation would be almost impossible to enforce.

Douglas agreed: "Is that the mode in which I am called upon to carry out the principle of self-government and popular sovereignty—to force a constitution on the people against their will?" Buchanan, meanwhile, submitted the constitution to Congress, and urged legislators to approve it. Because the Lecompton document had been thoroughly stigmatized as a proslavery usurpation, Buchanan was (and still is) denounced as a supplicating doughface, while Douglas found himself hailed as the champion of free soil. As such, he gained notable Republican support—much to Lincoln's chagrin. Horace Greeley, whose *New York Tribune* reached a large national audience, counseled Illinois Republicans to support Douglas for reelection to the Senate. "His course has not been merely right," Greeley proclaimed, "it has been conspicuously, courageously, eminently so." Opposing the Little Giant under these circumstances would be to court the charge of radicalism and abolitionism. Douglas also won support from Republican leaders such as former Speaker of the House Nathaniel Banks and Senator Benjamin Wade of Ohio. Senator Henry Wilson of Massachusetts expressed hope that Douglas would become a Republican, where he would be "of more weight to our cause than any other ten men in the country." Even William H. Seward, who had championed the free-state Topeka Constitution and had castigated Douglas for postulating a moral equality between freedom and slavery, came to agree with Douglas that popular sovereignty, and not congressional prohibition, was the best means of securing the territories for free labor.[28]

According to this rationale, climate had already prohibited slavery in the West, thus making northern Democrats free soilers by default. As with later revisionist historians, Douglas argued that slavery had reached its natural limits. Although the repeal of the Missouri Compromise had been intended to placate Southerners, Douglas had never been shy about stating his assumptions. Within a week of declaring the compromise line "inoperative," he insisted that Kansas was destined to become a free state: "In that climate, with its production, it is worse than folly to think of its being a slave-holding country." (The admission of California as a free state four years earlier had already vindicated this assumption in Douglas's mind.) Nor was Douglas the first to express this belief. David Potter credits President Polk with being the first to develop the idea, later popularized by Daniel Webster in his Seventh of March address, that physical conditions in the territories would necessarily preclude slavery.[29]

The climate argument even casts a slight antislavery glow on the Buchanan administration and its northern supporters. The dispute between Buchanan and Douglas was about the procedure of the Lecompton convention rather than its ultimate outcome. Given the nebulous quality of popular sovereignty, which was reflected in the wording of the Kansas-Nebraska Act, it is difficult to see a dramatic difference between the two men on the general operation of popular sovereignty. In his first message to Congress in December 1857, the president explicitly defended the convention's actions as a fulfillment of the principles of the Kansas-Nebraska Act—which, he noted, only required submission of the slavery question to the people. It did not require submission of a state constitution in its entirety. However, this was not Buchanan's primary concern. Just as Douglas accused the Republicans of fostering an unnecessary sectional division for political gain, Buchanan's position implied much the same thing about Douglas himself. In the end, not unlike Douglas, he had little doubt that Kansas would be a free state. That being the case, there was no need for Republicans to antagonize the South with sanctimonious harping on the evils of slavery *or* for the Douglas Democrats to constantly moralize about the right of a majority to exclude the institution. Governor Walker had made the point a bit too bluntly for southern sensibilities when he declared in his inaugural address that Kansas lay north of an "isothermal line" beyond which slavery could not exist. And although he would soon condemn Buchanan for failing to back his promise for a full referendum on the Lecompton Constitution, the president maintained his belief in the inevitability of majority rule on the slavery question.

Indeed, Buchanan believed that the best way to give the free-state majority control over the issue (and to deprive the Republican Party of its chief source of propaganda) was to admit Kansas to statehood under the Lecompton document. "Should [Kansas] be admitted into the Union with a constitution either maintaining or abolishing slavery against the sentiment of the people," he explained, "this could have no other effect than to continue and to exasperate the existing agitation during the brief period required to make the constitution conform to the irresistible will of the majority." If the constitution's provisions on the subject of slavery were unacceptable to the majority of the population, he insisted that "no human power can prevent them from changing it within a brief period." On the eve of the final vote on Lecompton (under the provisions of the English Bill), the editor of the *Fort Scott* (Kans.) *Democrat* argued in favor of the organic act in the belief that Kansas would be a free state regardless of what the document might say. As a state, Kansas would be able to regulate her own affairs. "This, we believe and understand, has been the chief design of President Buchanan in advising the adoption of the Constitution framed at Lecompton." By opposing the measure, Republicans were simply looking to "manufacture political thunder for 1860." The president seemed to concur, announcing that the peace and quiet of the nation as a whole was far more important than "the mere temporary triumph of either of the political parties in Kansas."[30]

Some free-state leaders saw the logic in Buchanan's thinking. After all, in the election for officers under the Lecompton Constitution held on January 4, 1858, the Republicans had won control of the state legislature. The administration even convinced Governor Robinson to support Lecompton. In an open letter, Robinson suggested that "Kansas would be the gainer by being admitted under any conceivable Constitution, if the agitation could thus be ended" than to remain as a territory. Once admitted to statehood, Kansans could rid themselves of the Lecompton Constitution "in thirty minutes time and by the dash of a pen." Conversely, as the practical results of statehood became clear, including the likely election of Robinson and James Lane as United States senators, Kansas's proslavery leaders began to oppose admission under Lecompton. Furthermore, later that year, some Southerners would defy the administration and come out in favor of Douglas's reelection, including Henry Wise, Alexander Stephens, and (much to Buchanan's irritation) Vice President John C. Breckinridge.[31]

❖ ❖ ❖

On a strictly personal level, Douglas opposed slavery. He privately called it "a curse beyond computation" and "a dangerous tumor." Yet he did not consider it morally or politically exigent. On the contrary, sectional agitation stultified the nation's Manifest Destiny, and perhaps threatened its very existence. As James L. Huston explains, Douglas refused to discuss slavery as an institution, all but ignoring the various facets of the antislavery argument. Because of his belief that slavery had reached its natural limits, Douglas seems to have assumed that slavery posed no threat to northern interests. It would exist only where climate allowed and where the people wanted it. Not even the Supreme Court's decision in the Dred Scott case had the potential to thwart the popular will. (Douglas dismissed out of hand the idea that the Court would pass a similar decision protecting slavery in the free states.) If the people of a territory wanted slavery, he explained, they would pass laws to protect it; if they were opposed to slavery, the institution would be "as dead as if it was prohibited by a constitutional prohibition." Given this reality, sectional agitators were nothing more than self-interested fanatics. In Douglas's view, there was absolutely no reason why the nation could not continue half slave and half free.[32]

As a result of Douglas's stance on Lecompton—and the power of the climate argument in general—Lincoln was at pains to explain to his audiences, and to some Republicans, the differences between the Republican platform and Douglas's position (notwithstanding Lincoln's dismissal of "free-state Democrats" the previous year). Lincoln watched with considerable anxiety as eastern Republicans seemed to fall over themselves in their rush to praise Douglas for his opposition to Lecompton. The stance taken by Greeley, whose *New York Tribune* had between five and ten thousand subscribers in Illinois, was especially troubling. "What does the New-York Tribune mean by its constant eulogizing, and admiring, and magnifying [of] Douglas?" Lincoln angrily asked Lyman Trumbull. "Does it, in this, speak the sentiments of the republicans at Washington? Have they concluded that the republican cause, generally, can be best promoted by sacrificing us here in Illinois?"[33]

The Douglas of 1858 held precisely the same position he had held in 1854, Lincoln insisted. Douglas's policy was still predicated on national indifference to the expansion of slavery. It was still debauching public opinion by excluding blacks from the Declaration of Independence, thus denying the universality of human liberty and destroying simple humanity as an unimpeachable defense against tyranny. In the very same speech in which he had initially defied the Buchanan administration by denouncing Lecompton, Douglas made it quite clear that his only concern was the fairness of the democratic process, not the fate of slavery: "It is none of my business which way the Slavery clause is decided," he announced. "I care not whether it is voted down or up."[34]

Again and again, Lincoln would point to Douglas's "care not" comment (which he deemed "the accepted maxim" of the Democratic Party) as irrefutable evidence that the Little Giant was no Republican. He was not a

Republican, Lincoln explained, because he did not demand congressional prohibition of slavery in the territories, a policy Lincoln considered vital to the integrity of American liberty. Unlike popular sovereignty, this policy—the cornerstone of the Republican Party—treated slavery as a wrong. Slavery would carry the mark of moral condemnation, and the principle of the Declaration would be sustained, only as long as Americans prohibited slavery's expansion, with the expectation that the institution would eventually end—in other words, by treating it as a necessary evil, as the founders had done.

Popular sovereignty simply would not do. In Lincoln's view, the practical outcomes of a policy should not obscure the danger of its philosophical underpinnings. Although he considered the climate barrier to be nothing more than a "lullaby," he nonetheless insisted that "if Kansas should sink today, and leave a great vacant space in the earth's surface, this vexed question would still be among us." Popular sovereignty tacitly legitimized slavery by defining it as an innocuous issue (analogous, as Douglas argued, to any local law or regulation), and in so doing, it undermined the ideal of universal liberty, which was the only guarantee that everyone's natural rights would always be respected. Douglas's "care not" policy destroyed the nation's moral compass, "penetrating the human soul and eradicating the light of reason and the love of liberty in this American people." The only way to safeguard the liberty of all was to stigmatize slavery as an aberrant institution and accept the Declaration's principle that all men are equal in their rights to life, liberty, and the pursuit of happiness.[35]

What would be the result if Douglas succeeded? The American people, by failing to repudiate slavery and sustain the Declaration of Independence, would destroy the self-evidence of their own liberty, exposing themselves to proslavery rationales whenever they happened to be economically or politically vulnerable. If white Americans consigned the black man to perpetual bondage, Lincoln warned, there was no guarantee "that the demon you have roused will not turn and rend you." For the future president, America's strength was a result not of its military might, but rather of the people's devotion to the nation's founding principles:

> What constitutes the bulwark of our own liberty and independence? It is not our frowning battlements, our bristling sea coasts, our army and our navy. These are not our reliance against tyranny. All of those may be turned against us without making us weaker for the struggle. Our reliance is in the love of liberty which God has planted in us. Our defense is in the

spirit which prized liberty as the heritage of all men, in all lands everywhere. Destroy this spirit and you have planted the seeds of despotism at
your own doors. Familiarize yourselves with the chains of bondage and
you prepare your own limbs to wear them. Accustomed to trample on the
rights of others, you have lost the genius of your own independence and
become the fit subjects of the first cunning tyrant who rises among you.[36]

The belief that other, non-African, groups could be excluded from
the Declaration was rational because the rationales for slavery were not
inherently racial. From 1854 to 1859, Lincoln repeatedly highlighted the
capriciousness of slavery by drawing an analogy between black servitude
and divine-right monarchy. In an 1859 letter to a Boston meeting celebrating Thomas Jefferson's birthday, Lincoln observed that "it is now no child's
play to save the principles of Jefferson from total overthrow in this nation."
The arguments used to justify slavery—calling the Declaration of Independence a "self-evident lie" or insisting that it applied only to "superior
races"—were identical in their effect: "supplanting the principles of free
government, and restoring those of classification, caste, and legitimacy."
These arguments "would delight a convocation of crowned heads plot-
ting against the people. They are the vanguard, the miners and sappers
of returning despotism. . . . We must repulse them, or they will subjugate
us." This sentiment was at the heart of what was perhaps Lincoln's most
unified explanation of his opposition to popular sovereignty:

> Now, sirs, for the purpose of squaring things with this idea of "don't care if
> slavery is voted up or voted down," for sustaining the Dred Scott decision,
> for holding that the Declaration of Independence did not mean anything at
> all, we have Judge Douglas giving his exposition of what the Declaration of
> Independence means, and we have him saying that the people of America
> are equal to the people of England. According to this construction, you
> Germans are not connected with it. Now I ask you, in all soberness, if these
> things, if indulged in, if ratified, if confirmed and indorsed, if taught to our
> children, and repeated to them, do not tend to rub out the sentiment of
> liberty in the country, and to transform this government into a government
> of some other form? Those arguments that are made, that the inferior race
> are to be treated with as much allowance as they are capable of enjoying;
> that as much is to be done for them as their condition will allow—what are
> these arguments? They are the arguments that kings have made for enslav-

ing the people in all ages of the world. You will find that all the arguments in favor of kingcraft were of this class; they always bestrode the necks of the people—not that they wanted to do it, but because the people were better off for being ridden. That is their argument, and this argument of the judge is the same old serpent that says: "you work and I eat, you toil and I will enjoy the fruits of it." Turn in whatever way you will—whether it come from the mouth of a king, an excuse for enslaving the people of his country, or from the mouth of men of one race as a reason for enslaving the men of another race, it is all the same old serpent, and I hold if that course of argumentation that is made for the purpose of convincing the public mind that we should not care about this should be granted, it does not stop with the Negro.

Lincoln then conceded that Americans had no choice but to accept slavery where it already existed, just as the founding fathers had done. This, he explained, was a matter of necessity. But yielding to necessity did not destroy the principle of universal liberty so long as Americans continued to look to that principle as their ideal and ultimate goal.[37]

⊰ 2 ⊱

Inferiority

The primary rationalization for slavery was the alleged inferiority of those enslaved. Yet despite the inveterate racism of white Americans and the determination of antislavery leaders to maintain white supremacy, some did recognize that inferiority, as a justification for slavery, was a nebulous standard, and ultimately a subjective one. In 1849 Henry Clay wrote a letter—later quoted by Lincoln—expressing this concern:

> I know there are those who draw an argument in favor of slavery from the alleged intellectual inferiority of the black race. Whether this argument is founded in fact or not, I will not now stop to inquire, but merely say that if it proves anything at all, it proves too much. It proves that among the white races of the world any one might properly be enslaved by any other which had made greater advances in civilization. And, if this rule applies to nations there is no reason why it should not apply to individuals; and it might easily be proved that the wisest man in the world could rightfully reduce all other men and women to bondage.[1]

Indeed, this danger seems to have weighed on Lincoln's mind. Jotting down notes in preparation for the debates with Douglas, he once again invoked Pettit's dismissal of the Declaration of Independence as a "self-evident lie," and observed that his opponent "regularly argues against the doctrine of the equality of all men." And while Douglas did not "draw the conclusion that the superiors ought to enslave the inferiors, he evidently wishes his hearers to draw that conclusion." But the difficulty remained:

Who might be regarded as inferior? Was inferiority restricted to blacks alone? Lincoln thought not. The "common object" for both Pettit and Douglas "is to subvert in the public mind, and in practical administration, our old and only standard of free government, that 'all men are created equal,' and to substitute for it some different standard." What that substitute would be was not difficult to discern, Lincoln insisted. "It is to deny the equality of men, and to assert the natural, moral, and religious right of one *class* to enslave another." In Springfield Lincoln summarized this danger with a simple question: "Who shall say, 'I am the superior, and you are the inferior?'" And in Chicago he beseeched his audience to "discard all this quibbling about this man and the other man, this race and that race and the other race being inferior, and therefore they must be placed in an inferior position. Let us discard all these things, and unite as one people throughout this land, until we shall once more stand up declaring that all men are created equal."[2]

For those with a clearer abolitionist cast than Lincoln and the majority of the Republican Party, this warning assumed a prominent position. Russel B. Nye has noted that abolitionists were anxious to demonstrate that if "slavery were the best system for inferior races, it was also the best for inferior classes, regardless of race." In 1850, the Reverend Charles Elliott, a leading Methodist clergyman, published *The Sinfulness of American Slavery*, which refuted the argument that "the negroes are by nature inferior to the whites, and may therefore be justly held as slaves." If this meant that God made some men with capacities inferior to others, and that the latter could rightfully enslave the former, Elliott explained, "this argument will prove that some citizens of every country have a right to enslave other citizens of the same country; nay, that some have a right to enslave their own brothers and sisters." In an 1860 congressional speech that was widely reprinted in northern newspapers, Owen Lovejoy of Illinois (whose brother, the abolitionist editor Elijah Lovejoy, had been murdered by an angry mob in 1837) conceded that blacks were inferior, but asked whether it was right to enslave people for that reason. "This, to me, is a most abhorrent doctrine," he explained. Because "inferiority" was an amorphous concept, people could be enslaved for any condition that left them in a position of vulnerability—poverty, isolation, physical weakness, or low intelligence. Such a doctrine "would place the weak everywhere at the mercy of the strong," Lovejoy insisted. "It would place the poor at the mercy of the rich; it would place those that are deficient in intellect at the mercy of those that are gifted in mental endowment." Two months later, Charles Sumner made a similar point in his famous speech, "The Barbarism of Slavery." Justifying the enslavement of blacks by their inferiority not only consigned an entire race to bondage, regardless of the capacities of individuals, but also "leaves it uncertain whether the same principle may not be applied to other races," including, he added, "persons of obvious inferiority in the white race." The danger is apparent when one attempts to ascertain precisely which whites Sumner considered obviously inferior. Similarly, the *National Era* castigated Andrew Johnson, recently elected senator from Tennessee, for justifying slavery on the basis of physical and mental inferiority. "This Senatorial philosopher"—who "was once a poor man and an industrious mechanic"—failed to understand the implications of his own argument. If one man had twice the physical strength of his neighbor, "is that a reason why he should seize him, send him to his field, and make him cut rails for nothing? If so, you might have to change places with some of your slaves."[3]

❖ ❖ ❖

There was no objective reason why the allegation of inferiority could not be extended to other races and ethnicities. As noted in the previous chapter, Senator Douglas had already interpreted the Declaration of Independence so as to exclude such "inferior" groups as Native Americans, the Chinese, and the Japanese. These people exhibited nothing but "ignorance, superstition and despotism," Douglas maintained, and were therefore "utterly incapable of governing themselves." So while Douglas did not believe that enslavement was necessarily the appropriate option, the rights of these "inferior races" were properly subject to civil law—in other words, to the will of the majority. And as can be seen in the history of American settlement, characterizations of inferiority—and a subsequent deprivation of rights—had never been strictly confined to Africans.[4]

If it had been possible, white Americans would have enslaved Native Americans in large numbers. Indians had proven more difficult to hold in bondage, however, because of the proximity of their compatriots. Indian slaves could easily abscond and native tribes could mount murderous reprisals against white settlements. (Once again, strength was a salient factor in the bondsman's condition.) Consequently, most Indians enslaved by whites during the colonial period were shipped to the West Indies and exchanged for Africans. Yet, if large-scale bondage was impracticable, coercion was still common fare for those defined as intellectually or racially inferior.[5]

Native Americans were by no means the only victims of white expansion. Mexicans also stood in the way. Manifest Destiny reflected both the growing pride that characterized American nationalism and the idealistic vision of social perfection that fueled the manifold reform movements of the period. However, it was highly ethnocentric. Running throughout the arguments for expansion was an explicitly racial justification. Throughout the 1840s, many Americans defended the idea of westward expansion by citing the superiority of the "American race"—by which they meant white people of northern European origins. As had been the case with American Indians, white Americans did not believe that Mexicans had an inherent right to the land they possessed. As an "inferior people," they lacked the capacity to develop a truly republican form of government.

Not unlike Northerners in the 1850s, Mexican officials and newspaper editors thirty years earlier had expressed the concern that characterizations of inferiority could be expanded. Gene Brack has argued that the Mexican public adamantly opposed ceding territory to the United States in large part because of their awareness of Americans' treatment of people they considered "inferior." In the early 1820s, Mexican newspapers reprinted a letter written by John C. Calhoun in which the secretary of war recommended the forced relocation of Native Americans. Mexican officials assigned to Washington, D.C., were alarmed by American prejudice against Indians and blacks and expressed the belief that Mexicans, due to their culture and appearance, would soon fall under the same rubric. On the eve of the Mexican War, a Mexican diplomat quoted a New Orleans newspaper that characterized his countrymen as "semi-Indian" and "semi-Negro." He then noted that in the United States blacks and Indians were not considered "part of the human race." This, of course, could only facilitate the self-justifying belief that Mexicans would benefit from American hegemony.[6]

Foreign-born Americans, most notably the Irish, also faced pejorative characterizations. Between 1845 and 1854, nearly three million immigrants arrived in the United States, of whom 1,200,000 were Irish. Economic competition, mixed with cultural and religious differences, led to widespread friction between the newcomers and native-born Americans. By the early 1850s, many nativists couched their opposition to Irish Americans in racial terms. The character of "Paddy"—dirty, ragged, violent, even simian—was considered immutable, rather than a consequence of his surroundings. As Dale Knobel explains, "once it became a habit to speak of the Irish as different and thus to think of them as different, it was not a great leap to treat them as different by nature rather than nurture." A contributor to *Harper's Monthly* in the 1850s, describing two "bogtrotters," wrote that "the Celtic physiognomy was distinctly marked—the small and somewhat upturned nose, the black tint of the skin; the eyes now looking gray, now black; the freckled cheek, and sandy hair. Beard and whiskers covered half the face, and the short, square shouldered bodies were bent forward with eager impatience." The Irish were also repeatedly portrayed in political cartoons as vicious and apelike. Hence a group of white Europeans could be defined as an inferior race. Given this prejudice against them, what security would the Irish and Germans have that they and their children would not be "reduced to slavery in this land of their adoption?" asked the *Anti-Slavery Bugle*. "Is color any protection? No indeed."[7]

Their Catholicism contributed to making foreign-born Americans objects of condemnation. Many historians have pointed out that nativism and antislavery were in some respects political cousins, outgrowths of the Second Great Awakening. Northern Protestants hated slavery and Catholicism for the same reasons. They felt that both were autocratic, repressive, and economically stultifying. "These two malign powers have a natural affinity for each other," noted an antislavery paper.[8] Foreigners, particularly Irish Catholics, were characterized as lazy, drunken, and subservient—a threat to the upward mobility that defined free labor.

Yet many Republicans viewed nativism as a distraction at best or another form of bigotry at worst. And they actively appealed to foreign-born voters. Northern newspapers repeatedly quoted an editorial in John Van Evrie's New York *Day Book,* which in their view favored the enslavement of poor Americans, including Germans and the Irish. Van Evrie was rabidly proslavery and a staunch supporter of James Buchanan in 1856. He argued that impoverished children and their parents would be better off enslaved: "Let our legislature pass a law that whoever will take these parents and take care of them and their offspring, in sickness and in health—clothe them, feed them, and house them—shall be legally entitled to their service; and let the same Legislature decree that whoever receives these parents and their children, and obtains their services, shall take care of them as long as they live." According to an Ohio newspaper, "this is what the Democratic party propose to do with the poor *Americans, Irish and Germans and their Children."* These papers also quoted Robert Wickliffe, the largest slaveholder in Kentucky and a delegate to the 1856 Democratic convention in Cincinnati, who intemperately announced that "if there are not niggers enough to supply the demand for slave labor, he was in favor of making slaves of the damned Dutch and Irish." Indeed, Wickliffe voiced his preference for these "white negroes." A Wisconsin editor warned his readers that this was simply an honest expression of the true sentiments of the Democratic Party: "Let them go on; give them their way and the time is not remote when slavery will not be confined to the African race."[9]

Republicans also pointed to the use of "inferiority" arguments against the Chinese and the Japanese. In 1859, they highlighted an editorial that appeared in the Washington *Union,* President Buchanan's official organ, which appeared to suggest that Chinese slaves would be an economical option for California's labor needs: "for one-fourth of the annual interest of an African slave, the Californian may have a laborer who will answer all the purpose of the negro." The *National Era* expressed outrage that a party "which claims to have been founded by Jefferson," no longer content with the enslavement of Africans, "should now propose to enslave the oldest civilized people in the world. The Chinese have no African blood in them, and their enslavement would at once destroy the peculiarity of slavery in this country, of being confined to the African race." In his speculations on "inferior races," Sumner alluded to "the polished Japanese," an official delegation of whom were then in Washington. The federal government had recently spent $50,000 entertaining the Japanese embassy, observed one editor, while New York City had expended $100,000 for the same purpose. "Yet if any of these inferior people should become residents of the state of Illinois, the theory of Douglas would place them at the mercy of the State, and their *status* would depend solely on legislation."[10]

If non-African races and ethnic groups could be enslaved due to their perceived inferiority, some Northerners feared that anyone could be enslaved for the same reason. Congressman James Ashley of Ohio concluded that the ultimate purpose of southern slaveholders could be "fairly adduced from the fact that they do not hesitate to-day at enslaving Indians, Mexicans, Chinamen," and, he noted, "even whites of American birth and unmixed blood." Ashley's fellow Ohio Republican Benjamin Stanton also sought to clarify the danger: "It will be remembered, if mere superiority gives the title, then it is not simply that a white man may enslave the Negro because he is inferior, but that he may enslave another white man who is his inferior. It is the inferiority of the slave and the superiority of the master upon which the right rests. It is not, therefore, a question of race or complexion."[11]

❖ ❖ ❖

Even if one were to concede that a particular group of people was "inferior," it did not follow that these people should therefore be enslaved. The vast majority of Northerners, including abolitionists and Republicans, maintained that blacks were inferior to whites. Indeed, Eric Foner has noted that there was "a strong overtone of racism" in the antislavery movement. So while antislavery leaders condemned the unjust denial of natural rights to the slave, there were still widespread legal proscriptions against African Americans in the North. C. Vann Woodward has argued that Jim Crow was born in northern cities, not in the antebellum South. According to Leon Litwack, "the northern Negro remained largely disfranchised, segregated, and economically depressed." Among abolitionists, even Harriet Beecher Stowe contrasted the "rudely indulged" passions of Africans with "the colder and more correct white race." The Unitarian clergyman Theodore Parker suggested that "the Caucasian has hitherto shown the most instinct of progress." Yet he went on to reproach the nation for robbing "the feeble Indian" and "the feebler Mexican," and for playing the tyrant over the African, "her weakest child."[12]

Indeed, some argued that the enslavement of inferior people was decidedly unchristian. Senator Henry Wilson of Massachusetts (later vice president under Ulysses S. Grant) disclaimed any intention of interfering with slavery as a local institution in the southern states. However, he was adamant that it should never become a national institution (sanctioned by Congress in the territories). In his view, the United States should not give its imprimatur to an immoral practice, thus implicating all of its citizens. "I believe, and the people of Massachusetts believe," he explained, "that slavery is a violation of the holy commands to love our neighbor, and to do unto others as we would that others should do unto us." After listening to one of Senator Pettit's lengthy disquisitions on inferior races, and the foolishness of recognizing them as equals, Wilson beseeched the Senate to adopt a more Christian, not to mention democratic, approach.

> The Senator from Indiana [Mr. Pettit] has made a long argument tonight to prove the inferiority of the African race. Well, sir, I have no contest with the Senator upon that question. I do not claim for that race intellectual equality; but I say to the Senator from Indiana that I know men of that race who are quite equal in mental power to either the Senator from Indiana or myself—men who are scarcely inferior in that respect, to any Senators upon this floor. But, sir, suppose the Senator from Indiana succeeds in

establishing the inferiority of that despised race, is mental inferiority a valid reason for the perpetual oppression of a race? Is the mental, moral, or physical inferiority of man a just cause of oppression in republican and Christian America? Sir, is this Democracy? Is it Christianity?

The phrase "all men are created equal" was not a "self-evident lie" as Pettit claimed, but rather a source of protection to the weakest members of society, a guarantee that one's humanity would always carry the assumption of freedom, regardless of personal circumstances. A truly republican and Christian nation, Wilson argued, should seek to educate and elevate those who were inferior, not oppress them. Lincoln agreed: "In pointing out that more has been given you, you cannot be justified in taking away the little which has been given him. . . . If God gave him but little, that little let him enjoy."[13]

According to Lovejoy, the principle of enslaving human beings due to their inferiority was the antithesis of the golden rule: "If a man is a cripple, trip him up"; if he is old and feeble, "strike him, for he cannot strike back"; if he is unintelligent, "take advantage of him, and if a child deceive him." This, he concluded, was the doctrine of devils and Democrats, "and there is no place in the universe outside the five points of hell and the Democratic party where such doctrines would not be a disgrace." As Lovejoy spoke, he approached the Democratic benches to address southern members directly. Enraged by this show of impudence, Roger Pryor of Virginia shook his fist and demanded that Lovejoy take his seat, precipitating a row that garnered considerable attention in the northern press. Thirty or forty congressmen surrounded the two men, shouting and gesticulating wildly. The speaker eventually restored some semblance of order, but the recriminations continued to fly. "You shed the blood of my brother on the banks of the Mississippi twenty years ago," Lovejoy cried. "I am here today, thank God, to vindicate the principles baptized in his blood." William Barksdale of Mississippi then exclaimed that Lovejoy was "a perjured negro thief" and told him "the meanest slave in the South is your superior."[14]

Others argued that inferiority was actually a consequence of slavery, rather than a justification for it. Considering the enervating effects of oppression along with southern laws that prohibited the education of slaves, an Ohio newspaper acknowledged that blacks were inferior, but told Southerners that this inferiority was "in consequence of the degraded condition you wish to keep them in, for their good!" In the debate over the Kansas-Nebraska Act, Senator Archibald Dixon of Kentucky invoked the Declaration of Independence and asked Ohio's Benjamin Wade if he believed whites and blacks were equal. Wade unhesitatingly answered in the affirmative. It was true that blacks were generally poor, despised, and without influence, but these considerations did not pertain to their equality of rights. "I say, in the language of the Declaration of Independence, that they were 'created equal.'" Yet they seemed inferior, according to Wade, because Southerners had "trampled them under foot, and made them apparently unequal by your own wrong." In the summer of 1855, the *Illinois State Register,* a supporter of Senator Douglas, offered a justification of slavery on the basis of black inferiority. In response, the *Alton Weekly Courier* encouraged its readers to consider the effects that centuries of bondage would produce. If whites rather than blacks had been placed in that position, "would the white race not be an inferior race?"[15]

❖ ❖ ❖

The arbitrariness of the inferiority rationale made it apparent, as Owen Lovejoy argued, that enslavement was determined solely by the desire and ability of the strong to oppress the weak. This made everyone's liberty contingent on the vicissitudes of circumstance—namely the transience of strength. Faced with an increasingly strident proslavery defense, some Northerners came to this conclusion. They repeatedly suggested that American slavery was analogous to other examples of human tyranny. Daniel Webster presaged this argument in his famous Seventh of March address. Although he was advocating sectional rapprochement and compromise—and would suffer the opprobrium of his fellow New Englanders for so doing—he could not help but observe "the wide difference of opinion" between the North and South in respect to slavery's general nature and character. For Southerners, the institution was economically vital, morally superior, and biblically sanctioned. From the northern perspective, slavery was morally iniquitous. According to Webster, Northerners believed that slavery "is founded merely in the right of the strongest; that it is oppression." In the end, slavery was like "all unjust wars; like all those conflicts by which mighty nations subject weaker nations to their will."[16]

Slavery and subjugation were not peculiar products of the African American experience. Because of the subjectivity of proslavery rationales, anyone who found themselves vulnerable or unpopular could be oppressed or, if practicable, reduced to bondage. As illustrated by the Know-Nothings' popularity between 1854 and 1856, there was no shortage of hostility directed toward foreigners, Catholics in particular. In this vein, a Kansas newspaper, the *Herald of Freedom,* argued that the South was "changing front on the subject of slavery," and warned that slaveholders' historical rationales would put its Irish and German readers at risk. As previously noted, Native Americans, Mexicans, the Chinese, and the Japanese were also characterized and treated as "inferior races." In response to the *Washington Union*'s suggestion that the Chinese could serve as an economical labor force in the absence of black slaves, the *Columbus Republican Journal* expressed doubt that "the slave power would always remain satisfied with reducing negroes alone to servitude." Other races of men, regardless of color or ethnicity, "must be brought under the yoke, when the power becomes sufficiently strong to subjugate." Slavery in the Roman period was not limited by race or color, it noted, and there was no reason to assume that the modern slaveocracy would not be "equally indiscriminate, when it gets the strength to execute its purpose."[17]

In 1858, William Seward suggested that the freedom of northern laborers would not last indefinitely given the current proslavery outlook. The only reason they were not already enslaved, he told a New York audience, was because they could not "as yet, be reduced to bondage." As a longtime opponent of nativism, he also warned them that it ultimately would not matter if they were native or foreign born. And at the very beginning of the speech in which he posited an "irrepressible conflict" between North and South, he observed that the confinement of slavery to blacks was "only accidental." Slavery's main principle was not racial, he explained. It was the weak and debased condition of the laborer.[18]

Other Northerners employed the same logic. According to Russel Nye, the northern laborer was often warned that he would be the first to be enslaved, "since his was the weakest political and economic position in society." In response to a *Richmond Enquirer* article noting that "the strong in mind or body were born to command," and conversely that nature had made slaves of the weak, the editor of a Michigan newspaper warned that "according to this doctrine, my brother shopman, if you, by reason of sickness or misfortune are enervated in body and mind, why you are a SLAVE!" This could only be expected, said the editor, because the difference in color between slaves and free whites was becoming so slight, particularly in Virginia, that it was almost impossible to differentiate between the two. Further highlighting the danger of "weakness," William Goodell argued that "If slaveholding be a natural right, then all men have a right to be slaveholders, and to make slaves of all whom they can overpower and control."[19]

The noted Scottish journalist William Chambers also gave voice to this concern. Along with his brother, Chambers was coeditor of *Chambers' Journal of Popular Literature.* In 1853, he undertook a tour of the United States and Canada that led to the publication of two books, *Things as They Are in America,* and *American Slavery and Colour.* While visiting Richmond, Chambers attended a slave auction, a spectacle he deemed "the most curious I ever witnessed." He spoke with slaveowners, would-be buyers, and with the slaves themselves, and discovered a surprising degree of cheerfulness among all parties, although the slaves facing separation from family members willingly expressed their sorrow. Summing up the experience, he expressed doubt as to the fairness of selling a man, even if that man was inferior. After all, it was only from "a variety of fortunate circumstances" that his new owner could claim superiority. In any event, Chambers's American tour gave him a firm understanding of the southern position—or at least the northern interpretation of it. On the first page of *American Slavery,* he presented the southern argument and noted the dangers it posed to the weakest members of society:

> "Race! Do not speak to us of race—we care nothing for breed or colour. What we contend for is, that slavery, whether of black or white, is a normal, a proper institution in society." So proclaim southern writers in the United States. The principle of enslaving only coloured persons, descendants of imported Africans, is now antiquated, and a scheme which embraces slavery of every race and variety of complexion is at length put forward as a natural and desirable arrangement for all parties. . . . Any one could have foreseen that it must come to this. The prodigious and irregular amalgamation of races in the south . . . led to a pretty nearly pure, nay, absolutely pure breed of white slaves. A new style of reasoning is consequently required. If slavery is to be at all vindicated, it must not now be on the narrow basis of colour, but on the broad grounds, that there is an inherent right in the stronger and more wealthy classes to reduce the poorer, and, it may be, more ignorant orders to a state of perpetual bondage.

Even the most cursory glance at the southern press would, in his view, disabuse anyone who doubted the accuracy of this description.[20]

In the end, it was up to the American people to repudiate the notion that slavery was normal and proper, for a supposedly beneficent institution could not be logically confined to any particular race. In terms similar to Lincoln's oft-expressed concern for the status of slavery in the public mind, a Pennsylvania newspaper stated that the "soundness of the popular heart" depended on the nation's perception of the institution's morality or immorality. This was important, said the editor, because the assumption that slaveholding is right and benevolent "confounds all our notions of right and wrong." If the American people acquiesced in the southern position, class, color, race, and ethnicity would prove no barrier to an individual's enslavement. "A universal degeneracy" would seize the country. Thousands would join the Democratic Party in denouncing the Declaration of Independence and insisting that men should own their servants. Then it would only be "by sleepless vigilance" that the poor and friendless could "avoid becoming mere chattels and things."[21]

The *New York Tribune's* political editor, William Henry Fry, also penned an 1860 campaign tract that emphasized southern intentions. Once the South succeeded in enslaving the white laborers of the North, the United States would degenerate into a nineteenth-century reproduction of Roman despotism. Why would it be any different? According to Fry, history provided indisputable proof that the "cause of slavery was the same everywhere . . . and so must be its highest development." It was born of warfare and human rapacity. "Cities and villages are given to flames and pillage, and the inhabitants not killed to the conqueror's yoke. Slavery never can be other than its origin made it. It is simply the triumph of brute force."[22]

❖ ❖ ❖

The causal relationship between inferiority and slavery raises what was perhaps the most important question: Was "inferiority" a necessary prerequisite for enslavement? Some Southerners subscribed to the "American school" of anthropologists, which advanced the notion of polygenesis—the separate creation of different human races. John C. Calhoun, Jefferson Davis, and James Henry Hammond all invoked polygenist arguments (usually consisting of the supposed disparity in cranial measurements between whites and blacks).

However, many Southerners rejected the theory. While on the surface polygenism may have strengthened the claim that Africans were inferior, and hence proper candidates for enslavement, the verbose defender of slavery George Fitzhugh opposed such a claim, not only because it was contrary to scripture, but also because it encouraged brutal masters to treat their slaves "not as weak, ignorant and dependent brethren, but as wicked beasts, without the pale of humanity." By this reasoning, slavery was as much a consequence of weakness and vulnerability as it was of racial inferiority. In fact, Fitzhugh suspected that "inferiority of race is quite as good an argument against slavery as in its favor." In a recent article, Christopher Luse has observed that abolitionists and southern Christians used the same religious arguments to denounce the inhumane treatment of southern slaves. Both argued that blacks and whites shared a common humanity, and that all people were moral beings with the capability for improvement. One southern missionary who studied African cultures admitted that "the charge of African inferiority . . . comes with an ill grace from Americans." After all, one only had to look back a few centuries to see that Anglo-Saxons had once been "stupid idolators." Of course, the difference between southern Christians and abolitionists was that Southerners viewed abolitionism as "false benevolence." Black slaves may have been human beings with immortal souls, but that did not mean their enslavement was contrary to humanity or Christian doctrine.[23]

Furthermore, while Southerners may have justified slavery on the basis of African inferiority, in reality they did not always seek inferior people as slaves. Slave dealers, noted a Milwaukee paper, never dwelt upon the "inferiority" or the dark color of their property as selling points, "but on the contrary are glad to be able to exhibit them as of light complexion and to recommend them as sprightly and intelligent." In fact, the very attributes that Southerners advanced as justifications for slavery "are the very things which most depreciate the value of slaves and are carefully ignored in offering them for sale."[24]

Considering that slaves were occasionally employed as skilled laborers—mechanics, potters, blacksmiths—there was no apparent reason why slave labor could not be extended on a larger scale to employments other than agriculture. Fry's campaign tract argued that Southerners had rejected the inferiority argument in favor of class-based servitude and sought to replicate the slavery of antiquity, in which members of every profession—from shopkeepers and mechanics to teachers and doctors—were enslaved. The enslavement of doctors and other professionals may strain credulity, but when one considers the enormous value of slave property, it is reasonable to assume that slaveowners, if they had ever faced a significant reduction in the profitability of cotton, would have attempted to maintain the value of their investment by applying it to other vocations.[25]

Many Northerners expressed alarm when white Southerners confounded inferiority with labor. In his infamous "Mudsill" speech, Senator

James Hammond of South Carolina noted that northern laborers were physically and intellectually equal to their employers, yet insisted that, due to their poverty and lack of personal security, slavery would be as much an "elevation" for them as it was for Africans. According to one Republican paper, Chief Justice Taney's invocation of inferiority in the Dred Scott case was "a miserable dodge." Instead, the decision was a blatant proscription of labor: "If those who read Taney's decision will, where it declares that 'colored' men have no rights which 'white men' are bound to respect, substitute 'laboring' for colored—and 'idlers' for white men, the real merit and intention of the decision will be arrived at."[26]

Given the widespread belief that slavery stigmatized labor and undermined personal work habits, Northerners could easily posit the degradation of all laborers, white and black. Along with the poor and the weak, they could be defined as "inferior," regardless of their race. And having accepted the perceived inferiority of blacks as a reason for excluding them from the rights of man, white laborers could no longer appeal to their own natural human rights. In words very similar to Lincoln's 1858 campaign speeches, one Wisconsin editor warned his readers of the dangers of complacency:

> We ask those laboring men who do not believe that negro slavery is right, but are influenced by arguments such as these [that slavery is confined to the African race], to consider carefully whether in their selfish indifference to the rights of an inferior class, they are not bringing contempt upon their own freedom. . . . Poor, degraded, despised by [slaveholders] . . . there is no justification of slavery, based upon the inferiority of the negro race, which does not apply with equal force and pertinency to him. . . . With the fact so palpably before us that wherever slavery exists, the laboring man nominally free is as subject and wretched as the slave himself, it is folly to suppose that the slave holder will continue always to rest his justification upon the assertion that the black men are inferior to the white, or upon any other assumption, than *that all men who labor* are incapacitated to be free.

And once the Slave Power succeeded in spreading the institution across the whole country, "it will be too late for the poor men of the North who are now recreant to the cause of justice and their own highest interests, to prevent the imposition upon their own necks of a yoke which they considered a trivial thing when borne by the necks of others."[27]

⊰ 3 ⊱

The Good of the Slave

"It is of no use to write on this subject," Thomas R. Bayne replied to a query from the Kansas State Historical Society in 1895. "The Northern people don't now understand what slavery was and never will." Bayne had been one of the slaveholding settlers of Kansas Territory. Like many Southerners, he felt frustrated by the determination of abolitionists and antislavery politicians to paint slavery as a moral abomination and slaveholders themselves as inveterate sinners. It was occasionally true that the institution was paternal in nature and not wholly devoid of affection. Marcus Freeman, one of Mr. Bayne's former slaves, fondly recalled the relationship. His master "was kind to his slaves," Freeman insisted, and he "thought a great deal of me." Freeman had been given as a "gift" to Bayne when they were both infants. With a slight hint of pride, the ex-slave noted that at one point someone had offered to purchase him for $1,800, but Bayne would not hear of it. The experiences of childhood had precluded any such notions. Bayne and Freeman had grown up together, according to the latter, just as if they "had been two little puppies."[1]

Ironically, Freeman was giving voice to a proslavery argument that southern whites had adopted at least thirty years prior to the Civil War. One of the first and most influential examples can be found in Thomas R. Dew's *Review of the Debate in the Virginia Legislature of 1831 and 1832.* Dew, a thirty-year-old professor of political economy at the College of William and Mary, was alarmed by the support some Virginians had recently expressed for the abolition of slavery in the commonwealth. Expressing dismay that Thomas Jefferson had provided the "sanction of his great name" to the antislavery cause, Dew insisted that Southerners had no reason to regret or apologize for the institution of slavery. In his view, the southern way of life was well within the mainstream of Western history, analogous to Greek democracy and other slaveholding societies of antiquity. Southerners could also claim a superior morality, in which the master's economic self-interest protected African bondsmen from the specter of want and extermination that would otherwise haunt such an inferior race. To emancipate a slave, explained Dew, was to throw him "into the hands of those who have no scruples of conscience—those who will not perhaps treat him so kindly." Indeed, the master-slave relationship was similar in paternalistic affection to the relationship between parents and children and husbands and wives. No one even insinuated, he observed, "that slaves in Virginia were not treated kindly. And all, too, agree that they were most abundantly fed; and we have no doubt but that they form the happiest portion of our society." In short, "a merrier being does not exist on the face of the globe than the Negro slave of the United States."[2]

As Dew and other Virginians debated slavery's future, the South was beginning to alter its stance on human servitude. Just beneath the surface, a proslavery ideology had already taken shape. Although the Revolution may have weakened the slaveholder's position, Southerners had demanded the institution's continuation as a social and economic necessity. They openly recognized that it was incompatible with the ideals of 1776 and apologized for it as a "necessary evil," but they also manifested an intense defensiveness when challenged, as evidenced by Congressman Jackson's response to Franklin's abolitionist petition. And as time went on, slavery only became more profitable and more entrenched in the southern landscape. The early 1830s proved to be the tipping point. In 1832, Virginia was still reeling from Nat Turner's rebellion. The previous August, Turner and fifty followers had exterminated about sixty whites—men, women, and children—in Southampton County. Rather than blame themselves, white Southerners denounced the baneful influence of the burgeoning abolitionist movement, which had been symbolically inaugurated by the introduction of William Lloyd Garrison's *Liberator* in January 1831. Dew was not alone when he contended that slaves were almost invariably content until "the wily philanthropist" agitated their minds with notions of equality. As the decade wore on, Southerners became increasingly defensive and paranoid, developing a siege mentality that refused to tolerate outside criticism.[3]

Slavery then ceased to be a "necessary evil" and became "a positive good," sanctioned by history and biblical teachings. Not only was it a blessing to southern whites, it was a blessing to the slaves themselves. Slaves enjoyed cradle-to-grave protection. They were not cast aside when they fell sick, got too old to work, or were unneeded. They also had the comfort of knowing that their family would always be taken care of. By the 1850s, Senator James Hammond could confidently proclaim that it would be difficult to find a single Southerner "who feels the system to be the slightest burthen on his conscience."[4]

❖ ❖ ❖

If slavery was the beneficent and paternalistic institution that Southerners claimed, could it not be applied with equal morality to whites as well as blacks? This question became a prominent aspect of the Republican argument in 1856 and would continue to serve as a lightning rod for northern indignation. In fact proslavery paternalism was a significant factor in the Republican Party's opposition to the expansion of slavery. Northerners had occasionally voiced their concern prior to this time, as in 1839, when the *Anti-Slavery Lecturer* quoted Professor Dew's proslavery defense and then warned that the day would eventually come when all American laborers would be slaves of the rich. The same paper also quoted South Carolina governor George McDuffie's prediction that northern laborers would soon be reduced to bondage.[5]

But the true smoking gun—the apparent evidence of southern designs— was an anonymous editorial that appeared in the *Richmond Enquirer* on December 15, 1855. It offered a trenchant and wide-ranging vindication of slavery in the abstract. "Until recently, the defense of slavery has labored under great difficulties," the author explained, "because its apologists took half-way ground." By confining themselves to a defense of *black* slavery, Southerners gave up "the slavery principle" and involved themselves in hopeless inconsistencies. Their appeals to religion, history, and humanity transcended race—the Bible "ordained, authorized and enforced white slavery"—therefore a defense of "mere negro slavery," and the admission that slavery in the abstract was wrong, yielded these arguments (and also denied biblical truth). Furthermore, it failed to recognize the fading of racial lines caused by amalgamation. Indeed, the author was quick to point out that "the laws of all the Southern States justified the holding of white men in slavery," provided that they were descended from a slave through the maternal line.

The South, however, had changed its line of defense, the author was proud to note, and now the North was "completely cornered, and dumb as an oyster." Southerners could compare their moral, physical, and religious condition with the North, or any other society, and take pride in their institutions:

> They will see that Slavery is a positive good, and not a necessary evil. . . . Let them read history, and balance the evils that have grown out of the little short-lived experiment of free society against those of slavery, and they will find the evils of the former a hundred to one compared to those of the latter. Crime, famine, ignorance, anarchy, infidelity and revolution stare the reader in the face on every page of the history of universal liberty. A single season of want in Ireland and Scotland will exhibit more human suffering than Mrs. Stowe could glean from the annals of slavery through all time and all countries. Slave society is co-extensive with man in time and space.

This was simply the immutable law of God, he argued, and Northerners would eventually recognize the futility of universal freedom. As for race, the author fully conceded that it was "far more obvious that negroes should be slaves than whites," because the former were unfit for anything beyond simple labor. "Yet the principle of slavery is itself right," he insisted, "and does not depend on difference of complexion."[6]

Republicans reprinted portions of this editorial in scores of newspapers. They quoted it again and again on the campaign trail, in state legislatures, and in the halls of Congress. In their hands the statement "slavery does not depend on difference of complexion" joined "a self-evident lie" as a mantra not only for the South, but for the Democratic Party as a whole. It assumed a prominent place in the circular issued by the first Republican National Committee in March 1856. As William Gienapp notes, Republican leaders wanted an appeal that would command support along a wide spectrum of antislavery sentiment. Consequently, the circular, written largely by Francis P. Blair, focused on slavery's threat to "the freedom of white laborers" and called for the arrest of slavery's expansion. The Republican Party would transform the territories into "a constellation of free, bright republics, constituted of the white race alone; untarnished by a slave of any color." Yet if slaveowners successfully infected the West with black servitude, they would inevitably reduce the white population to the same hopeless poverty that characterized nonslaveholders in the South. And according to the committee, this dichotomy between wealthy planters and poor whites "explains the recent article in the Richmond *Enquirer,* the oracle of

Southern interests, which elaborately argues the right of subjecting whites, as well as blacks, to slavery." The doctrine promulgated in the *Enquirer* "is a positive sanction to the bondage of the white race."[7]

Republicans repeated this argument throughout the 1856 campaign. Mason W. Tappan of New Hampshire delivered a typical Republican speech to the House of Representatives in July 1856 entitled "Modern 'Democracy,' the Ally of Slavery." Expressing fear that the "hateful badge" of servitude would no longer be confined to the black race, he quoted the "complexion" editorial as evidence of Democratic designs. Israel Washburn Jr. of Maine quoted the same editorial and informed the House that "the *Richmond Enquirer,* the leading southern journals, and intelligent Pro-Slavery men generally, admit that there is no foundation in reason for limiting slavery to the negro, and maintain that the whites who are ignorant and dependent upon the labor of their hands for subsistence ought to be held in Slavery, and that it would be better for them to be slaves than freemen." Likewise, Ohio's Timothy C. Day highlighted the "Democratic" principle "that it is better for labor to be owned than to be employed." At a public meeting in Philadelphia, John M. Read also quoted from the "complexion" editorial and denounced Democrats for attempting to convince Pennsylvanians that they should "prefer being 'owned' instead of being hired." About the same time, the *Decatur State Chronicle* hung the article like an albatross around northern Democrats' necks:

> Mr. Douglas says the democracy are the same every where—that they are identical all over the world. This paper [the *Enquirer*] contends, that the democracy has just started a *new* doctrine, but a few weeks old, which is the most popular political idea that the world has ever seen. The doctrine is, that the slave owner, the slave breeder—the black democracy, may carry slavery wherever a rat may burrow; or the American flag may flutter in the breeze. . . . This is the democracy, which the people in Illinois—of Macon county are to respect and worship, and call glorious democracy. That sheet, confessedly democratic, maintains, that slavery is correct in principle; that it is the national, normal, logical condition of the race of man, and that that principle is as applicable to the *white* man as well as to the black.

Taking their cue from the *Enquirer,* Republicans repeatedly presented the enslavement of labor, irrespective of race, as the "crown jewel" of the Democratic platform.[8]

Indeed, the complexion editorial's apparent relevance as a statement of Democratic principles was enhanced by the *Enquirer*'s undoubted status as a respected party organ. The paper was founded at Jefferson's behest in 1804, and in the succeeding decades it continued to endorse the states' rights principle of the Virginia and Kentucky resolutions. By the 1840s, the *Enquirer* was widely read in both the South and the North. In his study of the southern press, Carl Osthaus argues that the paper could be found in "every respectable reading room in the United States." Lincoln's law partner, William H. Herndon, subscribed to the *Enquirer*, and Lincoln was well acquainted with its arguments. "I have noticed in Southern newspapers, particularly the Richmond *Enquirer*, the Southern view of the free states," Lincoln told a Michigan audience in August 1856. They defend slavery on principle, he noted, and "insist that their slaves are far better off than Northern freemen." Later that year he referred to the *Enquirer* as "an avowed advocate of slavery, regardless of color" and denounced the "mistaken view" that northern laborers constituted a permanent underclass.[9]

But as Lincoln suggested, the *Enquirer* was not the only advocate of class-based slavery. The Richmond *Examiner* printed an editorial that echoed many of the *Enquirer* editorial's sentiments and phrases, including the statement that slavery was "right, natural, and necessary, and does not depend on difference of complexion." During the 1856 campaign, Republican editors offered a long list of Democratic quotations lauding slavery as a superior form of labor. Under such titles as "Slavery Not to be Confined to the Negro Race," "Northern Freemen Read This!," and "Northern Laborers But Slaves," this list circulated from one newspaper to another—with only minor changes—as an indictment of the Democratic Party. On several occasions, they simply labeled it "The New 'Democratic' Doctrine."[10]

Along with the *Richmond Enquirer* and Richmond *Examiner*, it included the following quotation from the *Charleston Standard:* "Slavery is the natural and normal condition of the *laboring* man, whether WHITE or *black. . . .* Master and slave is a relation in society as necessary as that of parent and child; and the Northern States will yet have to introduce it. Their theory of free government is a delusion." This was often followed by the *Muscogee Herald,* an Alabama newspaper: "Free society! We sicken at the name. What is it but a conglomeration of GREASY MECHANICS, FILTHY OPERATIVES, SMALL-FISTED FARMERS, and moon-struck THEORISTS." A quotation from the *Southside Democrat* (Virginia) then announced its hatred for everything "free"—"FREE farms, FREE labor,

FREE society, FREE will, FREE thinking, FREE children and FREE schools."
Finally, in addition to the previously mentioned statements of John Van
Evrie, regarding impoverished families in New York City, and Robert
Wickliffe, in favor of making slaves of the "Dutch and Irish," the list also
highlighted Louisiana senator Solomon W. Downs's views on the moral
superiority of slave labor:

> I call upon the opponents of slavery to prove that the WHITE LABORERS
> of the North are as happy, as contented, or as comfortable as the slaves
> of the South. In the South the slaves do not suffer one-tenth of the evils
> endured by the white laborers of the North. Poverty is unknown to the
> Southern slave, for as soon as the master of slaves becomes too poor to
> provide for them, he SELLS them to others who can take care of them. This,
> sir, is one of the excellencies of the system of slavery, and this the superior
> condition of the Southern slave over the Northern WHITE laborer.

As the campaign entered its final weeks, Republicans added new statements from the pages of the *Enquirer.*

> Make the laboring man the slave of one man instead of the slave of society
> and he would be far better off. Two hundred years of Liberty have made
> white laborers a pauper banditti. Free society has failed, and that which
> is not free must be substituted. Free society is a monstrous abortion, and
> slavery the healthy, beautiful and natural being which they are trying
> unconsciously to adopt. The slaves are governed far better than the free
> laborers at the North are governed. Our negroes are not only better off as
> to physical comfort than free laborers, but their moral condition is better.

The list of proslavery quotations would conclude with a warning that
this was "the doctrine which 'Democracy' so called, would introduce in
Iowa"—or Wisconsin, or whatever state the list appeared in. And lest there
be any doubt about the significance of the upcoming election, it reminded
voters that "JAMES BUCHANAN, the presidential candidate of the men
and of the party who hold these odious views," would surely prove a fit
instrument for those "who would make WHITE MEN slaves."[11]

◆ ◆ ◆

One might ask whether Northerners' fear of class-based slavery was irra-
tional, or perhaps disingenuous. Was there truly a possibility that southern

leaders would attempt to enslave white laborers? Or were Republicans simply cherry-picking the most outrageous statements in an effort to discredit the Democratic Party? To properly consider these questions, one must look to the source of this proslavery outlook.

The preceding editorials and arguments are in large part attributable to one man, George Fitzhugh of Port Royal, Virginia. On the surface, Fitzhugh was not a particularly notable character. One of many descendants of Virginia's distinguished Fitzhughs, he settled into a languid and less-than-remunerative legal career. In 1829, he married Mary Metcalf Brockenbrough and moved into her family's decaying mansion on the banks of the Rappahannock. With bats flapping in the crevices of his writing chamber, Fitzhugh researched local history and his own ancestry. He took particular pride in his first Virginia forebear, William Fitzhugh, who had strong ties to the British court and exemplified the noblesse oblige of the planter-aristocracy. A lifelong insomniac, Fitzhugh spent many a night reading antislavery papers, including the *Liberator* and the *New York Tribune,* as well as conservative English journals like *Blackwood's Magazine,* the *North British Review,* and the *Edinburgh Review.* He was a devotee of Thomas Carlyle, the British philosopher who argued that emancipation within the empire had been a "shortsighted philanthropy" and denounced democracy as the inarticulate "voice of chaos." Although he was well acquainted with Virginia's political leadership and took an active role in local Democratic politics, Fitzhugh never pursued elective office and served only briefly as a law clerk in the attorney general's office during the Buchanan administration. As a whole, Fitzhugh had the reputation of being slightly absentminded yet altogether genial toward friends and opponents alike.[12]

He was also a bold advocate of southern society, and by 1849 he had embraced his new vocation as the author of proslavery polemics. His first work, *Slavery Justified, by a Southerner,* was an unsigned twelve-page pamphlet intended strictly for local consumption. However, it introduced the themes he would soon bring to a national audience. "Liberty and Equality are new things under the sun," he explained. Furthermore, they had not only failed to ameliorate human misery, but had proven to be highly injurious to the people's happiness and well-being.[13]

Northerners argued that slavery was simply another manifestation of "might makes right," but Fitzhugh effectively turned this argument on its head. As he suggested in the titles of his two books, *Sociology for the South, or the Failure of Free Society* and *Cannibals All! or Slaves Without Masters,* universal liberty was an oxymoronic concept. By ushering in free competition, universal liberty begot a "war of wits" between the strong and the weak and fostered a destructive attitude of every man for himself. Free society was thus reminiscent of Hobbes's state of nature, a "dog-eat-dog" situation in which the most vulnerable members of society inevitably suffered. Northerners posited a harmonious relationship between employer and employee, arguing that even the most humble laborer could reap the rewards of his diligence and work his way up the social ladder. But to Fitzhugh, this free-labor ideal was purely fallacious. Self-interest made employers and laborers enemies. The former were determined to keep wages as low as possible in order to maximize profits, while the latter teetered on the edge of starvation. The pursuit of profit encouraged employers to cast their employees aside when they were no longer essential to the bottom line, thus depriving families of security when the breadwinner was sick, injured, elderly, or unneeded. In short, free society gave the employer as much control over labor as any slaveholder, but allowed him to abdicate his paternal responsibilities. As a result, northern laborers were, in Fitzhugh's words, slaves, but were denied "the rights of slaves." They were "slaves without a master!"[14]

As noted in chapter two, some Northerners characterized slavery as unchristian because it exploited the weakest members of society. Fitzhugh suggested that this was actually true of freedom, not slavery. Christian morality, he observed, had little place in free-market capitalism: "'To do unto others as we would they should do unto us' would be acts of suicidal self-sacrifice."[15]

In Fitzhugh's view, the iniquities of the modern world were the result of a historical process that had run amok. With their emphasis on individualism, the Reformation and the Enlightenment had gone too far, depriving men of the religious and political institutions they needed for survival. An isolated man was unnatural, he insisted, and would prove to be "as helpless and ridiculous as a bee setting up for himself." With the end of feudalism and the decline of the Catholic Church, "might makes right" and "every man for himself" came into full play, and as a natural consequence, the strong were able to subjugate the weak much faster than they had ever done before. Beggary began after the abolition of serfdom, which, according to Fitzhugh, had prevented class struggle by uniting the interests of tenants and landholders. By this logic, the Glorious Revolution was a tragic development because it had stripped the prerogatives of the crown, the nobility, and the Church, "the natural friends, allies, and guardians of the laboring class," in favor of the moneyed interests represented in the House of Commons. (It was no accident that the Bank of England was chartered shortly thereafter.) More to Fitzhugh's liking was the subject of John Locke's criticism in *Two Treatises of Government,* Sir Robert Filmer, whose book *Patriarchia* presented government as an extension of the family, an institution that brought together people of different needs and abilities for the sake of their mutual support.[16]

Nor did his iconoclasm spare the Lockean acolytes of 1776. While Locke was "a presumptuous charlatan," Jefferson was "the architect of ruin" and "the inaugurator of anarchy," who had enshrined laissez faire as America's seminal philosophy. Jefferson had engineered the disestablishment of the Anglican Church in Virginia, which was yet another blow to paternalistic institutions. In short, whereas the Sage of Monticello had believed "that government is best which governs least," Fitzhugh subscribed to Carlyle's dictum that "the world is too little governed."[17]

Fitzhugh's remedy was to "identify the interests of the weak and the strong," which slavery did better than any other institution. Slaveholders provided their workers with all the necessities of life, in sickness and in health, in infancy and in old age, "not according to his labor, but according to his wants." In this respect, slavery was the best form of socialism. If the master fell on hard times and was no longer able to take care of his slaves, they were "transferred" and would then "participate in the profits" of another master. A slave could take comfort in the knowledge that his family would be taken care of, with or without him. Unlike free laborers, there was no competition among slaves for work. Nor was there a war between master and slave. Unlike the northern capitalist, whose self-interest impelled him to pay his employee as little as possible, the master's self-interest prevented any reduction in the slave's allowance, lest he harm or lose the slave in the process. Furthermore, because slaves were part of the family, his affection for the bondsman would also keep the master from casting him aside in old age. A master loved a dependent slave for the same reason that he loved his dog, not because he was always useful, but because he was the master's personal responsibility. Consequently, Fitzhugh explained, southern slaves had "no dread of the future—no fear of want." They could sleep peacefully and luxuriate in mental repose. In fact, they were "the happiest, and, in some sense, the freest people in the world."[18]

The free laborer, by contrast, was beset with soul-crushing worries. The threat of unemployment made the specter of homelessness and hunger a constant companion. If his wife or child fell ill, he could not look over their bedside. If he could no longer work, he and his family would starve. Given this life of uncertainty, Fitzhugh expressed doubt that free laborers ever slept at all. "They are fools to do so," he suggested, "for, whilst they sleep, the wily and watchful capitalist is devising means to ensnare and exploit them." According to this reasoning, free laborers did not have a fraction of the liberties of southern slaves. Northerners, moreover, were fully aware of the failures of their own society, even as they denounced servitude in the South. Why else, Fitzhugh asked, would northern society be infested with so many utopians, transcendentalists, reformists, and other assorted "isms"?[19]

Republicans often invoked Fitzhugh's books, along with the aforementioned list of newspaper quotations, as evidence of southern intentions. Lincoln never referred to Fitzhugh by name, but Herndon, who purchased a copy of *Sociology* for his and his partner's edification, recalled that this work "aroused the ire of Lincoln more than most pro-slavery books." It appears to have aroused Herndon's ire as well. In a public letter to the editors of the *Illinois Journal,* he observed that Fitzhugh described himself as a Democrat. "This I do not doubt," he quipped, caustically noting that *Sociology* was "a good Democratic book." The failure of liberty and the desirability of slavery for members of all races were "fixed ideas of the southern despots." There was no escaping a principle, Herndon explained. "Slavery is right or it is wrong. If it is justice and right toward one race, so it must be to all. The South enslaves one race, so she must necessarily, if adopted as a principle, contend for the enslavement of some of the white race." Israel Washburn of Maine was among several politicians who cited *Sociology* in the House and noted that it had been "extravagantly commended" in the slave states. Among the abolitionists, William Lloyd Garrison often castigated the Virginian as "the Don Quixote of Slavedom." Fitzhugh had attempted, without success, to initiate a cordial correspondence with Garrison, as he had with other abolitionists. In respect to Fitzhugh's contentions in *Cannibals All!,* Garrison observed, "Such idiocy may pass current as wit and wisdom among the cradle-plunderers and slave-drivers at the South, but the rest of the world will rate it at its true value."[20]

Northerners were unaware, however, that Fitzhugh was also the author of the infamous "difference of complexion" editorial, as well as many others. Shortly before the release of *Sociology for the South* in 1854, he had accepted a contributing editorship with the Richmond *Examiner,* which claimed the largest circulation of any southern newspaper at that time. More than a dozen of his articles appeared in the *Examiner* that spring and summer, many of which presaged his arguments in *Sociology*. He denounced laissez faire, free trade, and free labor; and he appealed to southern educators to teach proslavery arguments to the next generation. The following year Fitzhugh won an editorial position with the *Richmond Enquirer*, which, as previously mentioned, enjoyed tremendous authority as a Democratic organ in both the South and the North. Furthermore, Fitzhugh's biographer, Harvey Wish, contends that the other editorials and statements quoted by Republicans in 1856 were clearly influenced by Fitzhugh's positions. Consequently, despite his relatively low profile, the lawyer from Port Royal exercised considerable influence on the national debate.[21]

But to what extent did Fitzhugh actually represent the mainstream of southern opinion? By invoking his words time and time again, many Republicans implied they were descriptive of the Slave Power's nefarious agenda. Eugene Genovese, who expresses admiration for Fitzhugh from a Marxist standpoint, has stated that Fitzhugh's ideas were "neither typical nor representative," but did represent the logical outcome of the slaveholders' philosophy. Many historians, however, have maintained that his views were nothing but aberrant musings, albeit highly quotable ones. Albert Beveridge expressed doubt that his position on servitude "was held by any large number in the South." Going a step further, Robert Loewenberg has argued that Fitzhugh's proposal to enslave white laborers was an outright embarrassment to the southern position. In respect to the northern reaction, David Donald contends that Lincoln and other Republicans mistook the "idiosyncratic" Fitzhugh as a representative thinker and erroneously claimed that the Democratic Party stood in support of white slavery. Robert Johannsen has likewise argued that Lincoln "should have known (if he was the reader recent writers have claimed him to be) that Southerners themselves rejected Fitzhugh's extreme arguments."[22]

Yet it is not entirely clear that they did in fact reject his views. It is probably true, as both Wish and Genovese state, that any "anti-Yankee, proslavery tract" would have won southern approval in the hysterical years following the passage of the Kansas-Nebraska Act. Still, one cannot dismiss the fact that his works were disseminated in the most respected southern journals—the *Examiner*, the *Enquirer*, and *De Bow's Review*—or that they were widely read and received fulsome praise from the most prominent southern reviewers. In January 1860, James Doolittle of Wisconsin told the Senate that Southerners had adopted the doctrine that slavery was the natural and normal condition of the laboring man. James Chestnut promptly denied the charge. It was the African laborer, he insisted, not the white, for whom slavery was a natural and beneficial condition. Doolittle then proceeded to quote Fitzhugh's editorials, as well as his books, which, Doolittle argued, had been "commended very generally by the leading Democratic press to the people of the South." In a conciliatory tone, he claimed not to question Chestnut's rejection of class-based slavery, but nonetheless insisted that the South was tending in that direction:

> I do not say that all the leading men and presses of the South today take the ground that the laboring man is a slave, whether white or black, but I do maintain that some of their leading presses and some of their leading men do take that position, and do justify slavery upon the ground that the true way to reconcile this troublesome question of capital and labor is simply this: that capital should own its labor, and not hire it.

As Lawrence Tenzer points out, Fitzhugh's anonymous editorials were never challenged by printed rebuttals, which in his view implies "a virtually total acceptance on the part of Southern readers"—although this is undoubtedly an overstatement. Nor can one deny that Fitzhugh had a clear impact on southern leaders. According to Genovese, "Miller, Hammond, Holmes, Thornwell, Harper, Simms, Memminger, Hughes, Edmund Ruffin, and a host of others moved step by step toward the defense of slavery in the abstract." Wish notes Fitzhugh's influence on such southern luminaries as R. M. T. Hunter and James Mason. It therefore seems safe to contend that antislavery Northerners were not being overly disingenuous when they held up "Fitzhughian" comments as evidence of southern designs.[23]

It would also appear that the notion of the "wage slave" made inroads into southern culture. In 1855, the South Carolina lawyer and poet William J. Grayson lamented the treatment of northern laborers in his fifty-page poem *The Hireling and the Slave.* Like Fitzhugh, Grayson stressed the beneficence of servitude and the free laborer's desperate need for a paternalistic master. For the hireling:

> Free but in name—the slaves of endless toil . . .
> In squalid hut—a kennel for the poor,
> Or noisome cellar, stretched upon the floor,
> His clothing rags, of filthy straw his bed,

With offal from the gutter daily fed. . . .
These are the miseries, such the wants, the cares,
The bliss that freedom for the serf prepares. . . .
The black slave, by contrast:
Taught by the master's efforts, by his care
Fed, clothed, protected many a patient year,
From trivial numbers now to millions grown,
With all the white man's useful arts their own. . . .
Guarded from want, from beggary secure,
He never feels what hireling crowds endure,
Nor knows, like them, in hopeless want to crave,
For wife and child, the comforts of the slave

The same theme can also be seen in the multitude of novels Southern-ers penned in response to *Uncle Tom's Cabin.* One pithily expressed its intended moral in the title: *Uncle Robin in His Cabin in Virginia and Tom without One in Boston.*[24]

On the other hand, it is not safe to assert that Fitzhugh was actually advocating the enslavement of white laborers in the United States, although it is not surprising that Republicans viewed his statements in that light. C. Vann Woodward has suggested that Republicans took Fitzhugh's more troubling statements out of context in order to discredit northern and southern Democrats. But capturing the larger context of Fitzhugh's argu-ments can be quite challenging, considering that his various writings are not exactly monuments to clarity. His style "suffered seriously from a lack of organization and tiresome repetition," which, according to Wish, often led him to "abbreviate his ideas in a dangerous fashion." John Ashworth also takes note of Fitzhugh's "linguistic inconsistencies" and "penchant for the startling overstatement." Indeed, the latter was especially prominent. "How can we contend that white slavery is wrong," Fitzhugh asked in *Cannibals All!,* "whilst all the great body of free laborers are starving; and slaves, black or white, throughout the world, are enjoying comfort?"[25]

The "slavery principle"—or the "patriarchal principle"—transcended race, and could not be surrendered if Southerners intended to justify and maintain domestic servitude. Yet despite Fitzhugh's vociferous condemna-tion of free society, Wish makes the point that he was primarily interested not in reforming the North, but rather in demonstrating the normality and moral integrity of the South. In May 1856, he wrote an editorial for the *Enquirer* disclaiming any desire to enslave white laborers: "We do not hope, nor wish, to see slavery like ours introduced at the North. There is no room for black slaves, and we never wish to see white men made slaves."[26]

As for the question of whether blacks and whites were equally suited for servitude, Fitzhugh believed that dependence was racially inherent for blacks but a matter of circumstance for whites. "Almost all negroes require masters," he opined, but among whites only "the children, the women, the very weak, poor, and ignorant" needed the benefits of paternalism. (Of course, ignorance and weakness are subjective terms.) Blacks, in other words, were inherently incapable of competing in the "war of wits," while many whites *could* successfully compete. So even though he may have rejected polygenesis at first—by 1861 he declared himself a convert to the racialist views of Nott and Van Evrie—Fitzhugh never expressed doubt that blacks were inherently inferior. He fully subscribed to the herrenvolk ideal of confining blacks to menial labor, thus allowing the southern white man to become "a noble and a privileged character" like the Roman citizen of antiquity. Black slavery elevated whites, "for it makes them not the bottom of society." All whites were therefore equal in respectability, he noted, if not in terms of wealth. Yet, in the hopes of ameliorating economic disparities, Fitzhugh became a vocal advocate of active state governments that would sponsor education and internal improvements for the betterment of their citizens.[27]

Still, in the end he hoped that Americans would adopt the principle "that men should be *governed,* not 'Let Alone,'" and that each person should be governed "according to his wants, and moral and intellectual capacity." Precisely what this meant is open to debate. Ashworth writes that Fitzhugh did not address the question of whether his desired form of slavery would allow for temporary or limited bondage; but in fact he did. After the success of *Sociology,* he began a correspondence with the New York abolitionist A. Hogeboom, which was published by the *Liberator,* the *Examiner,* the *Enquirer,* and *De Bow's Review.* In his letters to Hogeboom, Fitzhugh seems to have envisioned a form of voluntary indentured servitude. In a statement redolent of Van Evrie's proposal in the New York *Day Book,* he explained that he would allow destitute women to sell themselves and their children "for life, or for a term of years." He also expressed support for those agricultural laborers who might want to sell themselves "for a year at a time." During this period of servitude, moreover, they would be treated much differently than African slaves. Indeed, this is implied in the oft-quoted "difference of complexion" editorials, in which he stated that it was "far more obvious that negroes should be slaves than whites—for they are only fit to labor, and not to direct." To Hogeboom he noted that it would be unwise and "unscientific" to govern white men in the same manner as African slaves due to the former's superior capacities. Although the New Yorker disagreed with Fitzhugh's ideas, he cordially acknowledged the subtleties of the Virginian's position.[28]

Fitzhugh's more vehement criticisms of free society were also mitigated by his acceptance of the Jeffersonian conception of land as a safety valve for wage laborers. Although Fitzhugh deemed "free society" in general to be a failure, he drew most of his evidence from industrialized European nations where land was scarce and labor abundant. Ireland, for example, would not have experienced mass starvation in the late 1840s if the people there had not been "freed" from the beneficent protection of feudal lords. For the foreseeable future at least, American laborers had the ability to escape the clutches of the greedy capitalist. For this reason, Fitzhugh claimed that there was not a "sane man in America" who advocated the literal enslavement of white men. It would be unwise, impracticable, and inexpedient. "We all agree," he explained in the *Enquirer,* "that so long as the poor may become independent freemen and land-holders, by emigrating to the west . . . it is better that they should become independent freemen, than sink down into the apathetic, lethargic, but secure and comfortable position of slaves."[29]

Fitzhugh was a bit inconsistent on this point, however. In response to a critic of *Cannibals All!,* he once again disclaimed any desire to promote the enslavement of white Northerners. Despite all his musings on the failure of free society, he conceded that the "social forms of the North and South are each excellent, and should not be changed or tampered with." Southern society was normal and natural, while that of the North was exceptional, but the latter could endure until the continent was densely populated, which might not happen for a very long time. Indeed, Fitzhugh kept postponing the loss of this safety valve. In *Sociology for the South* he suggested that the West would "soon" fill up with settlers; later he suspected that "several centuries may elapse," then "thousands of years," and finally, he conceded that it "may never occur." And until such time, this exceptional form of society would continue to answer well for northern workers. But on other occasions, he seemed to posit an "irrepressible conflict" between the two sections. *Sociology* contained a prediction that slavery would be everywhere abolished or everywhere reinstituted. In one of his 1856 *Enquirer* editorials, he argued that the "evils of free society" should not be extended to new lands and future generations. Free society and slave society were incompatible and could not coexist among civilized men. "The one must give way and cease to exist," he contended, while the other became universal. Wish notes the similarity of this view to those expressed by Lincoln and Seward. In 1858, Douglas lambasted Lincoln for suggesting that the nation could not continue half slave and half free, and for predicting a sectional "crisis" in his "House Divided" speech. Lincoln later noted that neither he nor Seward deserved the "enviable or unenviable distinction of having first expressed that idea." Unaware of Fitzhugh's authorship, he claimed that the *Richmond Enquirer* had broached the notion of an irrepressible conflict "two years before it was expressed by the first of us." In any event, it is worth noting that neither Lincoln nor Fitzhugh believed or hoped that the issue would be decided on the battlefield.[30]

❖ ❖ ❖

Unfortunately, the subtleties of Fitzhugh's position were all too easily lost in his generalized endorsements of slavery in the abstract and his condemnation of free society. Not surprisingly, Republicans continued to invoke them in the years following Buchanan's election. In an effort to highlight a longer-term conspiracy than Fitzhugh's writings alone could provide, they also cited an 1836 speech in which Congressman Francis Pickens of South Carolina had opined that American society would eventually divide between capitalists and laborers rather than along strictly racial lines. "Let not gentlemen from the North start at this truth," Pickens intoned. "We are yet a people in our infancy. Society has not yet been pressed down to its classifications. Let us live through an era, and we shall discover this great truth. All society settles down into a classification of capitalists and laborers. The former will own the latter."[31]

New ammunition also presented itself. The Panic of 1857 exacerbated sectional hostilities by contrasting the northern and southern economies and, at least in Southerners' minds, vindicating the paternalistic principle intrinsic in slavery. They now had undeniable proof that free society was inherently unstable and insecure. The floundering of the nation's banking system triggered widespread unemployment, particularly in eastern cities. Men demonstrated in the streets, attended "hunger meetings," and voiced their demand for government assistance. Republicans responded by stepping up their support for a higher tariff to shield American workers from foreign competition and a homestead law to provide distressed Northerners with greater access to western lands. Congress passed a law lowering the price of public land to twenty-five cents an acre, but President Buchanan vetoed it, insisting that laboring men had no desire for the government's "charity." Southerners, on the other hand, boasted that their economy had been left relatively untouched. "The wealth of the South is permanent and real," crowed *De Bow's Review,* "that of the North fugitive and fictitious. Events now transpiring are exposing the fiction as humbug after humbug explodes."[32]

The chief spokesman for this newly enhanced hubris was Senator James Henry Hammond of South Carolina. A passionate advocate of nullification and states' rights, Hammond had edited the *Southern Times* and had served in the House of Representatives and as governor of South Carolina, although his political career had been cut short by poor health and family scandal. He was elected by the state legislature to succeed Andrew Butler in 1857 and soon enraged the North with a swaggering exposition on slavery's morality and freedom's failure. On March 4, 1858, he proclaimed to the Senate that Southerners were "unquestionably the most prosperous people in the world." Southern cotton constituted the bulk of the nation's exports and had single-handedly saved the North from economic ruin. "You dare not make war on cotton," he cried. "No power on earth dares make war upon it. Cotton is king."[33]

In response to Senator Seward's condemnation of slave labor, Hammond clearly echoed Fitzhugh's defense of the paternalistic principle. Seward may have been correct that much of the world had abolished slavery in name, but Hammond insisted that it would always exist in reality. Slavery would only be abolished, he explained, when God repealed the inescapable fact of poverty. The northern worker who lived by his daily toil, "and scarcely lives at that," was all too often crushed by the vagaries of the marketplace and the avarice of his employer. The liberty of the northern laborer "was no more than a choice of whether to beg or steal, to starve or go to prison." Consequently, Hammond informed his northern colleagues, their "whole class of manual laborers and operatives, as you call them, are slaves." The only real difference between these northern slaves and southern blacks was that southern slaves enjoyed job security and were well compensated. "There is no starvation, no begging, no want of employment among our people," he argued. Nor were southern slaves forced to compete with each other for jobs or resources. Northern slaves, on the other hand, "are hired by the day, not cared for, and slightly compensated," a fact that could be easily proven by the deplorable conditions in northern cities. "Why, sir, you meet more beggars in one day, in a single street of the City of New York," Hammond declared, "than you would meet in a lifetime in the whole South."[34]

Republicans responded to Hammond as they had to the barrage of proslavery editorials two years earlier. Although northern Democrats shied away from Hammond's remarks, Republicans presented them as further evidence of "the new Democratic doctrine." A Kansas newspaper captured the sentiments of many when it expressed outrage that those who earned their bread by the sweat of their brow and "adorned and beautified the earth" with railroads and steamers and palaces, and who converted a sterile soil into a blossoming garden, would ever be characterized as slaves. Surely those who gave their votes to President Buchanan "must feel themselves highly flattered," it remarked, in being ranked with the chattel laborers of the South. Similarly, Congressman Philemon Bliss of Ohio inveighed against Southerners who had claimed that "the northern free laborer was far worse off than the bought and sold chattel of the slave plantation" and highlighted the potential danger that northern laborers might be enslaved by quoting from both Hammond's speech and the *Enquirer's* "complexion" editorial. According to Seward, the fundamental assumption of slavery was "that labor in every society, by whomsoever performed, is necessarily unintellectual, groveling and base; and that the laborer, equally for his own good and for the welfare of the state, ought to be enslaved."[35]

This defense of slavery in the abstract continued to serve as a major bone of contention in the 1860 campaign. In the Senate, Southerners voiced their approval of Hammond's paternalistic sentiments. According to Jefferson Davis, slavery was but a "form of civil government for those who by their nature are not fit to govern themselves." Senator Hunter, in his defense of the "social system of the South," exalted slavery as "the normal condition of human society," and "best for the happiness of both races." His colleague James Mason similarly proclaimed that slavery was "ennobling to both races, the white and the black." In response, Sumner announced his dismay that senators "insensible to the true character of slavery" would presume to laud it as a form of high civilization. Fitzhugh, on the other hand, expressed delight that the southern leadership in Congress had adopted his doctrine. They had finally realized that it was safe to proclaim it, he observed, "because it is popular with the people." With no small degree of pride, he mused, "Yes! It has been solemnly announced in Congress that Southern society is *normal*, Northern society *exceptional* and *experimental*."[36]

Douglas's choice of Georgia senator Herschel V. Johnson as his running mate allowed Republicans to tie northern Democrats even more closely to the southern position. In terms similar to those quoted endlessly by Republicans in 1856, Johnson had announced that "capital should own its labor." And as before, Northerners did not hesitate to express their incredulity. How could a man who uttered such a vile calumny come before the northern public and ask for the second-highest office in the land? "Are you willing to stand tamely by and hear this Southern slave-driver taunt *you* with the name of *slaves?*" inquired the *Cedar Falls Gazette.* Just as Lincoln had condemned Douglas's position for failing to recognize anything wrong with slavery, others noted that Douglas never rebuked or found fault with any of his southern colleagues when they denounced northern working-men as "mudsills" or "white slaves."[37]

In short, antislavery Northerners had more than enough evidence to convince themselves that the paternalistic aspect of the proslavery argument was a potential threat to white laborers. As Fitzhugh explicitly maintained, there was nothing inherently racial in the assertion that slaves were better off enslaved. And as with the charge of inferiority, the public's devotion to the principle of universal human liberty was the only sure defense poor and working-class whites had against slavery's supposed blessings. In reality, however, paternalism was not the most prominent facet of the proslavery argument. Southern slavery was simultaneously an example of slavery in the abstract *and* a form of specifically racial servitude. Notwithstanding the popularity of Fitzhugh's views, or the politicians who occasionally echoed them, Southerners generally defended black slavery as a means of enhancing and sustaining white liberty.

⊰ 4 ⊱

The Good of Society

The belief that individual liberty depended on universal liberty can be seen as a counterpoint to the southern argument that black slavery provided a safeguard for the freedom of white Americans. For many Northerners, the rationales for African bondage were not strictly racial, and could therefore be applied to anyone, regardless of race. In addition to the South's insistence on slaves' inferiority and the celebration of slavery's benefits, its societal defense of slavery could be applicable to whites as well as blacks. According to Southerners' own logic, individuals did not threaten social stability because they were a particular color—they threatened society because they were poor.

First, it is important to understand the southern position. Despite the "bleaching" effects of amalgamation, and the racially unspecific appeal to slavery's benign paternalism, most Southerners viewed white skin as an unimpeachable badge of personal liberty. Rather than reject the Declaration of Independence entirely, they sought to defend the ideal of equality for whites alone. As Eugene Genovese points out, most Southerners still wanted to believe, despite the incongruity, that they could have Locke, Jefferson, and slavery, too. They may not have rejected the paternalist argument (at least not for blacks), but it seems clear their ideal society was divided by race, not economic class. In this respect, the good of the slave took a backseat to the interests of society as a whole.[1]

❖ ❖ ❖

On the eve of the Civil War, the fifteen slave states were home to about 385,000 slaveholders. Out of a million and a half free families in the South, only one-fourth had slaves at their direct disposal. And of those 385,000 individuals, only a small fraction can be classified as large planters—those who owned twenty slaves or more. The vast majority owned fewer than ten slaves; 50 percent owned fewer than five. Considering the relatively small number of large slaveholders and the sizeable majority of nonslaveholders, some may find it difficult to explain why the South was so obdurately wedded to its peculiar institution.[2]

For those who personally owned slaves, their bondsmen represented a $3 billion investment. For other white Southerners, the economic benefits of slavery were less straightforward, but not insignificant. Some resented slavery and the influence of their wealthier neighbors, but many lived in the orbit of the plantation system. Small farmers depended on local plantations for access to cotton gins and for financial assistance in times of need. There were also extensive kinship networks. Wealthy planters were not aristocrats in the European mold, however much they may have attempted to style themselves as such. In most cases they were new money without a long family history of influence and privilege. Consequently, the poorest resident of a county might easily be a cousin of the wealthiest planter. These economic and familial ties undoubtedly helped to mute class tensions.

In addition to its economic importance, slavery was a powerful social institution. Because the African presence in certain parts of the slave states was considerable—and nearly overwhelming in states like Mississippi and South Carolina—slavery became an important form of race control. Southern whites considered the legal servitude of blacks to be absolutely necessary for the maintenance of white supremacy. Despite their insistence that slavery was a blessing to those held in bondage, Southerners could not deny their sense of unease, a feeling that was betrayed by the ubiquity of slave patrols and the hysterical reaction that followed Nat Turner's insurrection and John Brown's raid on Harpers Ferry.[3]

There was far more to nonslaveholders' support of slavery than simple fear, however. As George M. Fredrickson has explained, slavery created "a psychologically satisfying sense of racial superiority" for all southern whites. Most Southerners advocated what the sociologist Pierre L. van den Berghe has called "herrenvolk democracy." According to van den Berghe's explanation, these are regimes like South Africa and the United States, societies that are "democratic for the master race but tyrannical for the subordinate groups." Indeed, democracy in the Old South was "no sham," as Fredrickson points out. Universal white manhood suffrage existed in most states, which made nonslaveholders a significant political force. James Oakes contends that Southerners actually took the lead in the democratization of state constitutions in the 1820s and 1830s—although reform was somewhat slow to reach the eastern states, South Carolina in particular. In any case, given the need to mollify the nonslaveholding majority, the planter elite actively appealed to their constituents' sense of racial pride. Herrenvolk egalitarianism was the only ideology that could guarantee a white consensus.[4]

In short, black slavery made southern whites feel better about themselves by obfuscating class divisions. Prejudice may be accurately defined as a desire to create the comparative illusion of superiority for oneself by denigrating people one views as different. Slavery defined all whites as fundamentally superior. In so doing, it fostered an assumption that all whites were fundamentally equal, regardless of class. A white man could be as poor as dirt and as dumb as a fence post and still wear his skin as a badge of superiority—a sign of his membership in the "natural aristocracy." This was particularly significant for those southern whites who would otherwise have had little reason to feel superior. It is therefore disingenuous to contend that nonslaveholders (later the common soldiers of the Confederacy) had no stake in slavery simply because they owned no slaves. Certainly all the perpetrators of racial violence in the years after the war were not former slaveholders angry over the loss of their labor force. Nothing was more humiliating to nonslaveholders than the idea of being placed on any sort of equality with blacks, of having to compete with them for jobs or for a place in the social hierarchy. By dividing society along racial lines, slavery raised all classes of whites to the master class. On the eve of the war, Georgia governor Joseph E. Brown reminded his constituents that slavery "is the poor man's best Government." The poor southern white man did not belong to a menial class, he claimed: "The Negro is in no sense his equal. He belongs to the only true aristocracy, the race of white men."[5]

Indeed, just as northern Democrats fostered anti-black prejudice in order to court immigrant workers (those who had to vie with blacks for the second-lowest rung on the social ladder), southern politicians were not at all hesitant to remind nonslaveholders of their social stake in the institution. "With us," argued Calhoun in 1848, "the two great divisions of society are not the rich and the poor, but white and black; and all the former, the poor as well as the rich, belong to the upper class, and are respected and treated as equals ... and hence have a position and pride of character which neither poverty nor misfortune can deprive them." Virginia governor Henry A. Wise (to whom Fitzhugh had dedicated *Cannibals All!*) contended that black servitude constituted the very foundation of white liberty. "Break down slavery," he argued, "and you would with the same blow destroy the great democratic principle of equality among men."[6]

The same ad hominem appeals to white supremacy also found their way into proslavery newspapers. Despite its publication of Fitzhugh's much-maligned endorsements of class-based slavery, the *Richmond Enquirer* perfectly expressed the herrenvolk idea: "The presence of the Negro population, occupying an inferior social position, and excluded from political privileges, imparts to the white laborer a peculiar sense of personal pride and independence." The southern laborer stood on the same legal and social level as the rich and the powerful, and hence "exhibits a dignity of character and an elevation of feeling found among the same class in no other social system." Bill Cecil-Fronsman notes that Kansas's proslavery papers couched their arguments in these terms because most of the migrant Missourians were small farmers rather than large planters. "Color, not money marks the class," announced the *Atchison Squatter Sovereign.* "Black is the badge of slavery; white the color of the freeman, and the white man, however poor [and] whatever his occupation feels himself a sovereign."[7]

Historians seem to have reached a consensus on the importance of the herrenvolk ideology to the southern mind. William Barney argues that nonslaveholding whites opposed emancipation because their self-respect would no longer be "reinforced by a color line separating free from slave." J. Mills Thornton III concurs in his study of antebellum Alabama. African slavery, he argues, dispensed with classes among whites, and he makes it quite clear that this was the reason the nonslaveholding majority defended the institution, even to the point of secession and war. Thornton also highlights the argument promulgated by southern politicians that poor whites would be hurt the most by emancipation. Unlike the wealthy landowners, who had the means to maintain their status, it was the working whites who would be thrown into a degrading competition for employment and social standing with former slaves. But with bondage recognized as the natural and legal status for blacks, every white man could rest secure in the belief that he was no one's inferior.[8]

Although the paternalist and the herrenvolk ideologies were not totally incompatible, there was certainly tension between the two. Ultimately, the paternalists, with their appeal to slavery's beneficence (regardless of race), gave way to a vociferous appeal to white supremacy. As we have seen, Fitzhugh, the arch paternalist, fully conceded black inferiority, and defended an exalted position for whites. Given the size and political influence of the nonslaveholding population, slavery's "benefits" would be reserved for blacks alone. In fact, some defenders of slavery denounced any form of hierarchy within white society. While the paternalists had pointed to historical examples of white slavery as instructive, others rejected them as unnatural. In a pamphlet endorsed by Jefferson Davis and J. D. B. De Bow, the ethnologist and New York *Day Book* editor John Van Evrie denounced any type of white subordination as unjust and "artificial." All whites, he insisted, were endowed by God with the capacity and right to govern themselves. In the spring of 1861, the new Confederate vice president, Alexander H. Stephens, forcefully announced that white equality and black subordination were the only natural basis for society and would therefore serve as the "cornerstone" of the new southern nation. "Many governments," he noted, "have been founded on the principles of subordination and serfdom of certain classes of the same race; *such were, and are in violation of the laws of nature.* Our system commits no such violation of nature's laws. With us, all the white race, however high or low, rich or poor, are equal in the eyes of the law." The cornerstone of the Confederate States of America would rest upon "the great truth that the Negro is not equal to the white man, that slavery—subordination to the superior race—is his natural or normal condition."[9]

At first blush, it might seem that Northerners, being equally racist, would have posed no threat to African slavery. But a quick examination of the 1860 census returns provides convincing evidence that Northerners and Southerners would have had vastly different conceptions of race control. In many areas of the South, blacks constituted a majority or a sizeable minority of the population. Over 57 percent of South Carolinians were African slaves. Slightly more than 45 percent of Alabamians were held in bondage. Even in Tennessee and Arkansas, roughly one in every four people was a black slave. In Illinois, on the other hand, it was rather unlikely that 7,628 blacks would overwhelm the remaining population of 1,704,323. Likewise, the 326,073 residents of New Hampshire were unlikely to be dominated by 494 free blacks. Even the 56,949 free blacks of Pennsylvania had little chance of overpowering 2,849,266 of their fellow Pennsylvanians. It is therefore not difficult to understand that Southerners would have considered bondage to be the only reliable means of maintaining "proper" race relations, while Northerners would not.[10]

Because blacks were not property in the North, and because their numbers were not sufficient to threaten white supremacy, Northerners were in a far better position to perceive the threat slavery posed to their own freedom. Their white skin and racial prejudice notwithstanding, they understood that accepting black slavery could allow themselves and their posterity to be encompassed by the institution's subjective criteria. Having accepted the rationales for African bondage, there was no guarantee that they themselves would never be defined as inferior or dangerously dependent.

◆ ◆ ◆

White supremacy was an important component in what many white Americans—South and North—viewed as a stable and secure society. But there was another component that had long been stressed in American history—the need for a virtuous citizenry. A virtuous citizen was both educated and independent. And according to republican theory, for a participatory republic to function, those entrusted with the franchise had to possess adequate knowledge of pertinent issues. Jefferson famously proclaimed that "those who expect to be ignorant and free expect what never was and never will be," a sentiment many Americans fully endorsed. Yet citizens also required personal independence, which would protect them from coercion and enable them to pursue the common good, rather than their own purely selfish interests. The greatest impediment to personal independence was poverty, or simply the absence of economic autonomy. People without productive property—which in the eighteenth and nineteenth centuries meant land—were necessarily dependent on others for their livelihood. They could therefore be bought, bribed, intimidated, or swayed by a demagogue into attacking the property of those who *could* maintain the independence requisite for genuine liberty. Said Jefferson in his *Notes on the State of Virginia,* "Dependence begets subservience and venality, suffocates the germ of virtue, and prepares fit tools for the designs of ambition."[11]

The prevailing fear among landed elites was the possibility of an agrarian redistribution of property. This was the paradox of republicanism: property trumped liberty because private property, in the Lockean sense, was the physical manifestation of self-ownership. As Locke explained in his *Second Treatise,* because each individual owns his own person, he also owns his labor, and therefore he owns the fruits of his labor. Whatever individuals mixed their labor with—picking an apple off a tree, building a house, or working for a salary—they owned the end product. Consequently, private property became the essence of personal freedom. It was the product of one's liberty, and, by this reasoning, it could not be taken away without consent. To do so would be an attack on liberty itself—hence Americans' insistence on "no taxation without representation" in the 1760s and 1770s. However, if a person did not own sufficient property to maintain economic independence, he became a threat to the property of others. This is why a property requirement for voting was universal during the colonial period and remained widespread in the United States prior to the 1820s. A typical assumption had been voiced by Gouverneur Morris during the Constitutional Convention when he expressed certainty that mechanics and manufacturers, "who receive their bread from employers," would sell their votes to would-be aristocrats.[12]

In fact, there was a long tradition of justifying not only disfranchisement, but also varying degrees of servitude, as a necessary element of a stable society. According to Edmund Morgan, the eighteenth-century commonwealthmen, along with their Virginia counterparts, considered poverty to be as great a threat as tyranny. Not unlike Virginia's blacks, England's poor were social pariahs—unclean, shiftless, vicious, and decidedly unworthy to be trusted with political influence that could endanger the property rights of the elite.[13]

None of the British proposals for the enslavement of the poor came to fruition, but, in Morgan's view, the fact that they were even entertained suggests "that the English poor of this time seemed to many of their betters to be fit for slavery." One of the most notable proposals can be found in Andrew Fletcher's *Two Discourses Concerning the Affairs of Scotland*. Fletcher, a member of the Scottish parliament and supporter of William III, denounced the Christian Church for coddling his impoverished countrymen. By establishing almshouses and hospitals, it had enabled them to live without the need for gainful employment. The result was 200,000 "idle rogues" wandering the countryside and destabilizing Scottish society. The most effective solution, he argued, would be to enslave them and put them at the service of men of property. In response to those who worried about the possibility of ill treatment, Fletcher noted that economic self-interest would prevent even "the most brutal man" from mistreating "his beast." As Morgan points out, these words "might have come a century and a half later from a George Fitzhugh."[14]

Virginians, on the other hand, lived under a different, and in their minds, felicitous, dynamic. After the tumult of Bacon's Rebellion, in which former indentured servants joined Nathaniel Bacon's campaign against western Indians and eastern elites, Virginia's political establishment began to see racism as an effective means of improving the material and psychological condition of poor whites and, in so doing, to soothe class animosities. Virginians were therefore able, in Morgan's analysis, to assume the mantle of republicanism. They did not have to fear a dangerous mob because their rabble had already been enslaved and effectively detached from society.

In fact, Fitzhugh presaged Morgan's argument in *Cannibals All!*. As a corollary to his defense of herrenvolk democracy, he contended that black slavery allowed the franchise to be safely extended to non-propertied whites because of their devotion to white supremacy. More so than Northerners, southern whites without property felt a strong sense of racial unity with property owners. This made the South safer for democracy and, as a consequence, the leader in democratic reforms. Along these lines, Fitzhugh proudly noted that "the slaveholding South is the only country on the globe that can safely tolerate" freedom of speech, freedom of the press, and universal white manhood suffrage. (This surely would have come as a surprise to anyone in the South who attempted to express antislavery sentiments.) The South was "the friend of popular government" because "the interests and feelings of many non-property holders are identified with those of a comparatively few property holders." It was not necessary to the security of property that the majority of voters should possess it, he explained. "But where the pauper majority becomes so large as to disconnect the mass of them in feeling and interest from the property holding class, revolution and agrarianism are inevitable." Fitzhugh declined to assert that northern society was tending in that direction, but he nevertheless felt compelled to observe that property was becoming more concentrated in the North and that pauperism was increasing.[15]

Indeed, since the argument had already been made to enslave impoverished and disorderly Europeans, it was unclear why American whites should necessarily be immune to the possibility of enslavement if they happened to become an "unstable element." Senator Douglas insisted that the American government had been "made by the white man for the benefit of the white man." As for the rights of others, he believed they should be respected as long as their exercise was "consistent with the safety of society." Yet, if blacks could be enslaved because of their dependence, what would prevent the enslavement of whites if they should have the misfortune to fall into pauperism and thereby endanger social stability?[16]

In light of the South's critique of northern society, the republican paradox had apparently not been resolved because Southerners were still confounding blackness and poverty. Northerners were quick to note that Southerners condemned their "servile class of mechanics and laborers" as being "unfit for self-government." Along these same lines, Governor George McDuffie of South Carolina insisted that it was dangerous to endow the poor with freedom and power, which could then be directed against the property of their social betters: "Hence the alarming tendency to violate the rights of property by agrarian legislation." If slaves, "bleached or unbleached," were allowed equal political privileges, McDuffie reasoned that no rational man would consent to live in such a society if he could possibly help it. With these assertions in mind, Benjamin Stanton, the Republican candidate for the eighth congressional district of Ohio in 1858 (and future chairman of the House Committee on Military Affairs), wrote a public letter in which he summarized the southern position:

> It will be seen at once that the real issue between the Republican and Democratic parties is whether the productive labor of the country, the rugged toil which is required to develop its resources, and augment its wealth, population, and power, shall be performed by freemen or slaves. It is now the well settled doctrine of the Democratic party of the South . . . that the laboring masses of every country, must of necessity be a degraded, ignorant, and servile class, who have not intelligence enough to govern the country, and that the tendency of free labor society is constantly anarchy and agrarianism, and that therefore they should not be entrusted with power, but should be placed under the absolute dominion and control of that more intelligent class who wield the capital of the country.
>
> How easy and natural the conclusion is that laboring men, women and children are property, as much the legitimate subjects of commerce as horses and cattle.

Stanton's political hyperbole notwithstanding, it seems clear that some slaveholders were eschewing universal liberty in favor of republicanism. The latter was fundamentally incompatible with the former because the right to private property eclipsed the personal freedom of anyone who threatened property rights.[17]

Within the many southern speeches and editorials Northerners cited as evidence of the Slave Power's designs, the political threat posed by laborers was a common refrain. In one of his *Enquirer* editorials, Fitzhugh declared that free society was insufferable because it was "everywhere starving, demoralized, and insurrectionary." The *Washington Union*—"the national organ of Buchanan"—referred to the northern settlers in Kansas as "a miserable blear-eyed rabble who have been transferred like so many cattle to that country." Senator Andrew Butler of South Carolina, whom northern editors referred to as the uncle of "assassin" Preston Brooks, was quoted as saying that a man had no right to vote in South Carolina unless he owned ten slaves or real estate valued at $10,000. And included with Herschel Johnson's widely denounced pronouncement that "capital should own its labor" was his observation that the "slaves" in northern workshops were vulnerable to political intimidation by their employers: "They are driven to the polls at the beck of their masters under penalty of being discharged." But by far the most infamous and clearly stated condemnation of northern laborers' political power was Hammond's "Mudsill" speech. "Your slaves are white," he instructed the North, and "are your equals in natural endowment," which engendered a feeling of galling degradation among a potentially unstable social element. Southerners denied their slaves political rights for a reason, and he suggested that Northerners would be wise to consider the possible implications of universal white manhood suffrage. Being in the majority, northern slaves "are the depositories of all your political power," and could therefore use that power for their own purposes: "If they knew the tremendous secret, that the ballot-box is stronger than any army, with bayonets, and could combine, where would you be? Your society would be reconstructed, your government reconstructed, [and] your property divided." Hammond then issued a warning that Southerners, angered by northern insults and interference with their slaves, could easily send forth lecturers and agitators to instruct these degraded northern laborers on the potentialities of the ballot box.[18]

❖ ❖ ❖

Disfranchisement due to a lack of property was one thing; enslavement as a result of poverty was quite another. Yet the latter possibility was not without a foundation in reality. Beginning in 1618, the British government swept up thousands of poor children and sent them to America to serve as apprentices, with or without their family's approval. However, many were sold to southern planters and, not unlike other new arrivals in the tobacco colonies, were dead within a year. Prior to 1776, the authorities in London also forcibly transported between 50,000 and 70,000 convicts to the American colonies, as well as thousands of other "undesirables," including beggars, prostitutes, Quakers, Cavaliers, Irishmen, and Scottish Jacobins. Yet these numbers, while not insignificant, were dwarfed by the 300,000 indentured servants who took their chances in the British colonies. Although they willingly agreed to temporarily exchange their labor for the hope of a better life down the road, upon arriving in America they often found that they were de facto chattels, and could be bought, sold, and abused with impunity. As Gary B. Nash has written, "most depictions of early America as a garden of opportunity airbrush indentured servants out of the picture while focusing on the minority who arrived free." Their indentures may have been temporary (for those who survived), but the anguish of servitude was no less real.[19]

Indentured servitude was not the only form of economic bondage that haunted American society. After 1848, Congress was forced to consider the future of peonage in the Mexican Cession. Under Mexican law, a creditor could force a debtor to remain in his employ until the debt was paid—a condition that could also bind the debtor's heirs. Southerners tended to look favorably upon the continuation of peonage, viewing it as an issue of personal property analogous to slavery. Jefferson Davis, for example, defended peonage, asserting that it was a species of property, and denying that Congress had any right to interfere with it. In response, Stephen Douglas denounced "this revolting system by which white men, our own kindred, may be reduced to a system of slavery." Referring to this exchange, James Huston notes that Douglas's conception of morality would not allow the liberty of whites to be determined by majority rule, even though popular sovereignty consigned blacks to the caprice of the majority. Douglas may indeed have felt that way, but it is difficult to see an objective principle that could have prevented the subjugation of whites if a majority had been so inclined.[20]

Nor did Republicans ignore the specter of peonage as a threat to white liberty. The circular issued by the first Republican National Committee in April 1856 raised the issue: "What will result from the creation of a cordon of slave states across the continent?" The answer, they suggested, could be found in the condition of the nominally free population of Mexico, where slavery was abolished in name yet still existed in practice. Once the slave-ocracy came to power in the new territories, they would inevitably charge their workers more for supplies than they paid them in wages, "and the result is, that the laborer is constantly falling more and more in debt, and the law subjects him to his creditors until he works out his indebtedness." The ultimate effect of this system would be "to compel a man to sell himself and his family." The circular then took note of the pervasive poverty found in southern society, and, as evidence of the Slave Power's pernicious designs, once again quoted Fitzhugh's statement that slavery "does not depend on difference of complexion." It concluded that under this doctrine there would be an even more direct enslavement of the white race than that which currently pertained under debtor vassalage in Mexico.[21]

A related issue arose shortly before the election of 1860. In August, the *Portland Weekly Oregonian* related a disturbing development out of New Mexico and an equally disturbing reaction from Democrats in Congress. A few proslavery men had settled in New Mexico, and finding it unprofitable or impractical to bring their black slaves, they had "made slaves of poor white people." In the same manner as Mexican landowners, these proslavery men advanced clothing and supplies, but paid the lowest possible wages, thus imprisoning their workers through indebtedness. But unlike Mexican landowners, these Southerners refused to abide by the laws and customs that had protected peons from abuse by their masters. "They wanted the privilege of WHIPPING these WHITE MEN, WOMEN, AND CHILDREN," explained the editor, and the territorial legislature accordingly passed a law denying the courts jurisdiction over any case involving the "correction that masters may give their servants for neglect of their duties." Here was the principle of slavery in the abstract carried out. Congress, however, had the authority to nullify territorial statutes under the terms of New Mexico's organic law. Accordingly, Senator Henry Wilson of Massachusetts introduced an amendment to abrogate the offensive provision, but Republicans could not overcome Democratic opposition. Among those voting against the amendment were Jefferson Davis, Albert Gallatin Brown, James Chestnut, Andrew Johnson, R. M. T. Hunter, Robert Toombs, John Slidell, and Louis Wigfall. Douglas was not present, but given his earlier opposition to peonage, one suspects he would have supported the measure. The *Portland Weekly Oregonian* was also dismayed by the fact that one of Oregon's own senators, Joseph Lane, had voted with the southern bloc: "What do you think of this white men of Oregon? How would you like your employers to cudgel and WHIP you, and when you seek redress, find the courts shut against you?" It was therefore a sad commentary on the current state of the Democratic Party that some had sought to make Lane Senator Douglas's running mate. (Not coincidently, Lane did become the vice presidential nominee under John C. Breckinridge. One of his sons also fought for the Confederacy.)[22]

Such were the principles of "the new democratic doctrine." Not only were laborers better off in bondage, the stability of American society depended on it. Herrenvolk democracy may have created an illusion of superiority for southern whites, but the vagaries of economic fortune could expose anyone to the fate of the peon or the rationalizations of property holders. As history proved time and again, slavery was simply another example of "might makes right."

◆ ◆ ◆

Southerners often invoked historical precedent in an attempt to validate their belief that slavery was a vital component of a good society. They were particularly eager to prove that the institution carried the approbation of Christian experience. Proslavery newspapers offered lengthy disquisitions on scripture's recognition of human bondage. The title of a pamphlet written by a southern clergyman in 1850 was fairly typical of the southern thesis: *A Defense of the South Against the Reproaches and Encroachments of the North: In Which Slavery Is Shown to Be an Institution of God Intended to Form the Basis of the Best Social State and the Only Safeguard to the Permanence of a Republican Government.*[23]

Once again, Professor Dew's apologia provided a model for later pro-slavery writers. "There is no rule of conscience or revealed law of God that can condemn us," he assured his fellow slaveholders. There was nothing whatsoever in the Old or New Testaments to even suggest that the southern master committed an offense. As proof, he pointed to biblical patriarchs who were also slaveowners. "Abraham had more than 300; Isaac had a 'great store' of them." Even Job had "a very great household." Nor did Christ presume to "meddle" with the established institutions of mankind. Jesus had accepted all, Dew insisted, including "the monarch and the subject, the rich and the poor, the master and the slave." And with a thinly veiled reference to Nat Turner's recent revolt, he angrily condemned the supposed philanthropy of northern abolitionists: "What a rebuke does the practice of the Redeemer of mankind imply upon the conduct of some of his nominal disciples, who seek to destroy the contentment of the slaves, to rouse their most deadly passions, and to lead them on to a night of darkness and confusion!" He then suggested that Northerners misunderstood the Golden Rule. It may properly govern personal conduct, but it did not mean that men should be wrested from their "calling," even if their calling was to be a slave. The southern historian and novelist William Gilmore Simms also took pains to highlight biblical passages that seemed to legitimize the southern position. He noted that the angel of the Lord had explicitly enjoined a runaway slave owned by Sarah (Abraham's wife) to "return unto thy mistress, and submit thyself under her hands." The apostle Paul had likewise urged slaves to submit to their masters and advised a runaway to return to his owner.[24]

Apart from biblical sanctions, the very fact that slavery and serfdom had been an integral part of so many great societies encouraged Southerners to draw comparisons. Ancient Egypt, Greece, Rome, Carolingian France, and Norman England had all rested on some form of paternalistic servitude. These were the societies that had produced the greatest art, the greatest literature, and the greatest architectural monuments to human ingenuity. These were the societies that Americans consciously sought to emulate. "There is not a respectable system of civilization known to history," crowed Virginia's R. M. T. Hunter, "whose foundations were not laid in the institution of domestic slavery."[25]

Although many Southerners may have been unwilling to admit the logical implications of their religious and historical appeals, Northerners were quick to note that biblical slavery had been *white* slavery. Of course this was also Fitzhugh's purpose in rejecting race as the *sine qua non* of servitude. In an editorial for *De Bow's Review* he accurately observed that black slavery was "of very recent origin." And then, in one of his more controversial statements, he argued that anyone who suggested "the white race is not the true and best slave race" contradicted all history. In fact the very image of "Liberty" in the United States (which appeared on almost every American coin and banknote) was a white woman holding or wearing a Phrygian cap, the symbol of emancipation in ancient Rome.[26]

This is precisely why Northerners viewed slavery as yet another manifestation of "might makes right." In response to L. Q. C. Lamar's effort to show that the Bible sanctioned slavery, Congressman Sidney Edgerton of Ohio noted that "if it did, it was white slavery." Indeed, the Mississippian did not even attempt to sustain slavery on the basis of race or color, but "upon the more startling assumption that the stronger class has a right to enslave the weaker." While addressing a Cincinnati audience in 1859, Lincoln noted that his fellow Kentuckians attempted to establish the rightfulness of slavery by reference to the Bible. This defense was problematic, he explained, because "whenever you establish that slavery was right by the Bible, it will occur that that slavery was the slavery of the white man—of men without reference to color." The *National Era* also expressed alarm over the capriciousness of historical servitude. The slavery of antiquity had been white slavery, it declared in 1854, and "had its origin in just such cause as black Slavery in our day has grown out of." Six years later, it was still reminding its readers that the slaves of Moses's time were white men, as were those held in the Roman Empire: "They were either the unfortunate poor sold into slavery for debt, or else they were captives taken in war" who were then sold into slavery instead of being executed. (Fitzhugh had taken the latter fact and suggested that slavery was more "durable" if those held in bondage were of a different nationality than their masters. But Republicans often took this statement and styled it as a threat to Irish and German Americans.)[27]

The most widely employed piece of biblical "evidence" for the divine origins of slavery was the Curse of Ham. The original story in Genesis 9:18–27 was that Ham, the son of Noah, had looked upon his father's nakedness as Noah lay drunk in his tent after the flood. Precisely what "looked upon" meant has long been the subject of debate. For some it implies castration, for others merely a lack of reverence. In either case, Noah's other two sons, Shem and Japheth, carefully covered their father without looking upon him. When Noah awoke and discovered what Ham had done, he cursed Canaan, Ham's son, declaring that he would be a "servant of servants" unto his brothers.

David Brion Davis has written that no other biblical passage "has had such a disastrous influence through human history." Slaveholding Christians held it up time and again as justification for African servitude, the implication being that Africans were descendants of the cursed Canaan. It was certainly more acceptable than the notion of polygenesis, which denied the idea of a common human origin and, in so doing, flatly contradicted the story of creation. Davis seems to agree with the conclusion of Alexander Crummell, a respected free African American, who argued in 1862 that the belief that black slavery was a consequence of the Curse of Ham was "almost universal" in the Christian world.[28]

The obvious problem, which both Davis and Winthrop Jordan are quick to point out, is that there was absolutely nothing in the story about race or blackness being a result of Noah's curse. In fact, it was not until the mid-fifteenth century, after the first Portuguese expeditions along the West African coast, that the curse became associated with blackness in the European mind. The subsequent persistence of this idea, as Jordan explains, "was probably sustained by a feeling that blackness could scarcely be anything *but* a curse." Similarly, George Fredrickson suggests the curse, as applied to blacks, was a matter of popular mythology rather than biblical exegesis. Jordan observes that black and white were emotionally loaded colors, particularly for Elizabethan Englishmen. Black connoted filth, debasement, and shame, while white conveyed purity, virtue, and beauty. Yet, at other times, the curse was applied to Asians, the inhabitants of India, and was also used to explain European serfdom and the enslavement of Turks, Slavs, and other peoples.[29]

The Curse of Ham, therefore, had been a historically capricious doctrine. The story had no inherent pertinence to color or race. Fitzhugh, with his penchant for debunking popular ideas, was happy to point this out. Charles Sumner did as well. Upon his return to the Senate in 1860, Sumner undertook a detailed rebuttal of a speech Jefferson Davis had recently made in which the future Confederate president twice invoked Noah's curse upon Ham as evidence of slavery's divine origins. Sumner pointedly suggested that Davis's expertise was military rather than biblical. As a former secretary of war and current chairman of the Committee on Military Affairs, Davis "may perhaps set a squadron in the field," Sumner noted, "but he has evidently considered very little of the text of Scripture on which he relies. The senator assumes that it has fixed the doom of the colored race, leaving untouched the white race." Davis was apparently unaware that the Polish aristocracy had used the curse as an excuse for holding white serfs, "and that even to this day the angry Polish noble addresses his white peasant as the 'son of Ham.'"[30]

In more recent years, the existence of white slavery in Islamic North Africa had provided Northerners with a compelling analogue to black slavery. From the early sixteenth century to the late eighteenth century, there may have been as many as 1,250,000 slaves held in the North African states of Tripoli, Tunis, Morocco, and, in particular, Algiers. Although this was only a tenth the number of African slaves taken to the New World during the same period, it is not an insignificant figure. Many were fishermen and coastal villagers from Spain and Italy, but most were captured sailors, including some taken from the British navy. Very few had the family resources to purchase their freedom; many died of disease and maltreatment.

This was another example of historical slavery that Sumner took a particular interest in. He spoke on the issue numerous times, and in 1853 wrote a book entitled *White Slavery in the Barbary States*. In addition to Franklin's fictitious letter of 1790 (see introduction), Sumner recounted John Jay's reaction to complaints that the British had taken slaves from New York in violation of the Treaty of Paris. Jay, then secretary for foreign affairs under the Confederation, asked how Americans would respond if the French were to liberate American captives in Algiers, but then agree to return them to their masters upon making peace. He admitted that he was making unpopular arguments, but Jay nonetheless felt compelled to observe that the only difference between the two cases was "that the American slaves at Algiers are white people, whereas the African slaves at New York were black people." Nor could Sumner resist observing that the Barbary regencies were located near the parallel of 36°30', which made Algiers, Tunis, Tripoli, and Morocco the African equivalents of Virginia, the Carolinas, Mississippi, and Texas—or as Sumner dubbed them, "The Barbary States of America." The "common peculiarities of climate, breeding, indolence, lassitude, and selfishness," he suggested, were the cause of their mutual "insensibility to the claims of justice and humanity."[31]

If the Slave Power determined that a good and stable society required the subjugation of the poor and working class, under the terms of republican philosophy or the lessons of religion and history, the American ideals of individual liberty and popular government could not long endure. Impoverished by the enervating psychology of slavery, and politically dominated by an imperious master class that qualified or denied the principle of universal liberty, Americans of all colors faced the possibility that the United States would become merely another rotation in an endless historical cycle of might makes right. According to the Boston abolitionist Joshua P. Blanchard, slaveholders had become "an aristocracy of the most oppressive and debasing nature, in which no trace is discernable of the equal rights of men." He then warned Northerners that this aristocracy, through its political machinations, was in the process of overwhelming "every principle of revolutionary freedom" in the North as well as the South.[32]

5

The Slaveocracy

Given most Southerners' apparent embrace of an Old World social order, some Northerners feared the rise of an aristocracy in the United States. This fear was implicit in northern denunciations of the Slave Power, the slaveocracy, and the southern oligarchy, as it was in their comparisons of southern slavery with medieval serfdom and divine-right monarchy. All the arguments Southerners advanced in favor of slavery had been used at one time or another in the defense of hereditary privilege. They insisted that laborers were better off in a state of servitude, and that society benefited from the suppression of the poor and the contributions of the leisure class. Consequently, as some Northerners came to believe that Americans of any race could fall victim to proslavery arguments, they worried that slaveholders, debauched by power and luxury, would use their wealth and political influence to transform America's egalitarian experiment into a European-style hierarchy.

First, Northerners had a detailed understanding of the constitutional provisions and political arrangements that gave Southerners a disproportionally large share of political power in the national government. Second, they believed the experience of mastery fostered a tyrannical disposition among slaveholders. In short, slavery taught behaviors contrary to those necessary for a viable republic. It effectively destroyed the republican principle of "virtue." Furthermore, the degradation of the southern work ethic led to a disparity of wealth that could not sustain an egalitarian society.

Fear of the slaveocracy was one of the most common themes in the antislavery movement. In 1853, the abolitionist William Jay, president of the New York City Anti-Slavery Society, estimated that there were no more than 248,000 slaveholders in the United States. "Yet this small body of men engross the greater portion of the slave region, forming in fact a powerful feudal aristocracy, possessing nearly three millions of serfs, and governing and oppressing at pleasure the rest of the population." In addition to the South itself, many Northerners believed that the slaveholding minority dominated the national government, riding roughshod over the people's rights and shaping national policy to serve their own interests. During the debate over the Kansas-Nebraska Act in 1854, Henry Bennett of New York argued that southern slaveholders had more political influence "than any aristocracy of Europe." William Lloyd Garrison likewise believed that the evils inflicted by the Slave Power "are worse than ever were inflicted by the most kingly aristocracy, or the most despotic tyranny." And according to Moses M. Davis of Wisconsin, "the tyrannical Slave power has got possession of the people, and will crush out their liberties before many more years pass by."[1]

Nevertheless, historians have long debated the legitimacy of the "slave-power conspiracy." Writing in the early 1870s, Henry Wilson suggested that "freedom became timid, hesitating, [and] yielding" after the Missouri crisis, while "slavery became bolder, more aggressive, and more dominating." Wilson, of course, was recounting his own experiences as a Republican senator in the 1850s. After the publication of Chauncey Boucher's influential article "In Re That Aggressive Slaveocracy" in 1921, many historians dismissed the Slave Power thesis, viewing it primarily as an example of paranoia in American politics. This view dominated until the publication of Russel B. Nye's *Fettered Freedom* in 1949. Nye contended that abolitionists were genuinely convinced, particularly after the annexation of Texas and the Mexican War, that a secret agreement existed among southern slaveholders "to foist slavery upon the nation, destroy civil liberty, extend slavery into the territories (possibly to whites), reopen the slave trade, control the policies of the Federal government, and complete the formation of an aristocracy founded upon and fostered by a slave economy." Yet he also doubted that this "conspiracy" was at all organized in the sense Lincoln suggested when he condemned "Stephen, Franklin, Roger, and James" for their attempt to nationalize slavery. Also taking issue with Boucher, William Gienapp argues that historians often underestimate the significance of the Slave Power argument. In his mind, it is the "essential key" to understanding the Republican Party, in that it united Northerners' fear for "white liberties," their animosity for southern planters, and their conspiratorial mind-set. Indeed, Gienapp maintains that the free-labor argument, which Eric Foner emphasizes, was less significant prior to the Panic of 1857 than the traditional republican fear of concentrated power and conspiracies against liberty. The Republicans' "main message" of the 1856 campaign was "that the slaveholding oligarchy posed a threat of unprecedented magnitude to the survival of the Republic, its values and institutions."[2]

Similarly, Leonard Richards has demonstrated that the Slave Power was a real, if not a well-organized, phenomenon. While Boucher was correct that Southerners could be "hopelessly divided" politically, they still enjoyed tremendous advantages that allowed them to dominate the federal government from the 1780s to the 1850s. Contrary to Boucher's postulate, Richards insists that Northerners had never agreed on a common group of conspirators. They did, however, agree on the political assets behind the Slave Power's success. These advantages made the Slave Power thesis perfectly rational, in that they supported a powerful tendency, if not a unified conspiracy.[3]

❖ ❖ ❖

Among the South's most obvious advantages was the three-fifths compromise. The Constitution permitted the slave states to count three-fifths of their slave population toward the apportionment of congressional representation, thus enhancing their voice in the House of Representatives and the Electoral College. At the Constitutional Convention, Gouverneur Morris contended that slavery was "the most prominent feature in the aristocratic countenance of the proposed constitution." He predicted that the equation's application to direct taxes would be meaningless, considering that direct taxes would be avoided in favor of import duties (which proved to be the case). The only effect of the three-fifths clause would be to give Southerners disproportionate representation as a reward for an institution that was utterly incongruous with the nation's founding principle. Morris foreshadowed the frustrations of many when he argued that Southerners "will not be satisfied unless they see the way open to their gaining a majority in the public councils." A mere thirteen years later, so-called slave seats provided Thomas Jefferson's margin of victory over John Adams. Driven from power, Federalists watched with alarm as new slave states came into the Union, expanding the Jeffersonians' unfair advantage. At the same time, Jefferson's party was increasingly dominated by Southerners, driving the president's northern followers to exasperation, particularly with the economically devastating foreign policy of the Virginia leadership. Much like their Federalist opponents, they began to echo Elbridge Gerry's argument that southern "property" was no more deserving of representation than northern pigs and cattle. Richards contends that these frustrations help to explain the actions of James Tallmadge and his supporters in 1819.[4]

Although free-state congressmen outnumbered slave-state congressmen (and had since the 1790s), the three-fifths rule continued to be a thorn in the side of northern politicians in the 1850s. William Seward referred to slaveholders as "modern patriarchs" who, under the aegis of the three-fifths clause, had become "political patriarchs." Lincoln, despite his fidelity to all constitutional provisions, could not help but note that it was "manifestly unfair" that South Carolina and Maine had equal representation in Congress, even though Maine was home to more than twice as many free whites. Here was yet another reason to stop slavery's expansion. If it was truly a "sacred right of self-government" for a man to go to Kansas and "decide whether he will be the equal of me or the double of me," Lincoln predicted that the day would soon arrive that northern liberties would only be detectable through a microscope: "They will surely be too small for detection with the naked eye." William Jay also pointed out that six slave states—South Carolina, Georgia, Kentucky, Louisiana, Alabama, and Mississippi—had an "aggregate free population of 189,791 less than Pennsylvania." Yet the people of those states had six times as many senators and an additional twenty-three electoral votes.[5]

The principle of state equality in the Senate enabled Southerners to at least partially counteract the political influence of the burgeoning population of the North. Admittedly, this was not the framers' intention. Most of the delegates to the Constitutional Convention believed the "Great Compromise" would be a boon to the geographically limited states of the Northeast. Every slave state, with the exception of Maryland, wanted representation in both houses to be based on population. Virginians were particularly vocal about the sacrifice they had made to appease states like Connecticut and Rhode Island. Only later, as new slave states entered the Union with comparatively small free populations, would the Senate become a bastion for the South. It was the Senate that scuttled the Tallmadge amendments and the Wilmot Proviso. Conversely, pro-southern measures like the Indian Removal Act, the Kansas-Nebraska Act, and the Lecompton Constitution faced far less resistance in the Senate than they did in the House. Even after the South lost Senate parity with the admission of California in 1850, a fair number of northern senators felt sufficiently insulated from antislavery pressures (given their six-year terms and election by state legislatures) to vote with their southern colleagues.

Indeed, northern politicians who supported southern initiatives—the so-called doughfaces—helped to turn the South's minority status into a majority political position. Although the dominant parties of the antebellum years—the Jeffersonian Republicans and Jacksonian Democrats—were based in the South, with subservient northern wings, the three-fifths clause and Senate parity were alone insufficient to maintain southern hegemony as the northern population continued to outstrip that of the slave states. Consequently, those Northerners with southern proclivities began to play a central role.

Despite their proud opposition to all forms of legal favoritism, northern Democrats seemed to lie prostrate before a mere 350,000 southern slaveholders. What explains their support for southern measures? According to Jay, slaveholders won the support of their fellow Southerners by identifying their private interests with the public welfare (meaning white supremacy). The ubiquity of racism in the North, however, cannot explain the rise of the doughface. Many Northerners *opposed* slavery (or at least the extension of it) because of their antipathy toward blacks. Instead, the rise of the doughface appears to have been the result of political calculations. Troubled by the destructive potential of sectionalism displayed during the Missouri crisis, Martin Van Buren and his New York "Bucktails" promoted their reliability to the Virginia leadership—in contrast to Republicans like DeWitt Clinton and James Tallmadge. In addition to their desire for party harmony, northern Democrats who harbored presidential ambitions needed southern approval. Southern Democrats exercised great influence in the party's national conventions, where a required two-thirds majority for nomination allowed them to veto any candidate not to their liking (which, ironically, would derail Van Buren in 1844 and Stephen Douglas in 1860). Although southern measures like the Indian Removal Act and the gag rule were unpopular in the North, Van Buren and the Bucktails supported them, which undoubtedly helped to make the New Yorker palatable to southern Democrats in 1836. As noted in chapter one, Douglas's Kansas-Nebraska Act also seemed like a craven capitulation to southern demands. "This indifference [popular sovereignty] was all the slavepower could ask," declared the Leavenworth, Kansas, *Times.* "If a house was on fire there could be but two parties. One in favor of putting out the fire.

Another in favor of the house burning. But these popular sovereignty fellows would stand aloof and argue against interfering. The house must take care of itself subject only to the constitution and the conditions of fire and wood."[6]

Because of these factors, slaveholders were able to maintain their ascendancy in the federal government. However, this does not mean their vision for the nation's future was undemocratic. As noted earlier, many Southerners were devoted to a "natural aristocracy" of whiteness, which in their minds was the only stable basis for democracy. For Calhoun and others, their laudation of herrenvolk democracy was the natural corollary of their denouncement of universal liberty.

❖ ❖ ❖

Even paternalists like Fitzhugh and Hammond fully endorsed the principle of racial aristocracy. During the debates over the acceptance of abolitionist petitions in 1836, Hammond, then a member of the House of Representatives, examined the abolitionists' comparison of southern slaveholders with European aristocrats. "Slavery does indeed create an aristocracy," he admitted. "I accept the terms. *It is a government of the best.*" Nevertheless, he insisted that the southern aristocracy avoided the disadvantages of the European variety. Slaveholding did not foster "the pride, the exclusiveness, the selfishness, the thirst for sway, the contempt for the rights of others, which distinguish the nobility of Europe." The southern aristocracy was open to all white men, whether they were slaveholders or not. This neutralized class animosities, he explained. And in so doing it prevented the "prostitution" of the Declaration of Independence by "the ignorant, uneducated, semi-barbarous" masses who pursued their "ultimate agrarianism" in Europe and the North. Using similar terms, Congressman Thomas F. Bowie of Maryland accused northern capitalists of being an aristocracy of brute strength—"the cold, heartless, selfish, cruel, and despotic power of wealth—which brings to its feet, as a humble supplicant, the labor of the white man." In the North, the poorer classes "are ground down to the earth; and the only question among them is who can make the other *work for him,* a species of *white slavery* that I utterly abhor." The southern aristocracy, if it could be called that, was the aristocracy of nature. "It is the aristocracy of enlightened intelligence, of love, of kindness, of magnanimity, of honor, of generosity, of valor, of independence, of hospitality, and, above all, of indomitable energy. And if, in the patriotism of the North, they can hate aristocracy like this, I do not envy them the emotion of their hearts."[7]

Jefferson, on the other hand, had argued that only a prodigy could avoid the onset of a tyrannical disposition after a childhood surrounded by masters and slaves. Northerners agreed, maintaining that slavery did in fact engender a "thirst for sway" and a "contempt for the rights of others." Accustomed to wielding the lash and having their every command obeyed, slaveholders naturally developed an imperious, tyrannical, and intolerant temperament. The Ohio abolitionist John Rankin—the man William Lloyd Garrison called "my anti-slavery father"—argued that slavery "cultivates a spirit of cruelty" by causing slaveholders to "think lightly of human misery." It fostered tyranny because "it is directly opposed to the fundamental principles of republicanism maintained in that part of the Declaration of Independence, which declares 'that all men are created equal.'" Given these influences, it was not surprising that slaveholders "manifested a propensity for the unjust acquisition of power." And as a result, the slave states "do practically maintain the fundamental principles of absolute monarchy." In reaction to a *Richmond Enquirer* editorial defending the superior social character of slave society, the *New York Times* asked whether the consciousness of absolute power over others actually inspired the Christian virtue of brotherly love: "Unless all history is a lie, exactly the reverse is the effect produced." Arbitrary power inevitably begot an arbitrary temper; and an unchecked dominion over others induced "a skeptical forgetfulness of higher duties and of high obligations." The *Lawrence Free State* likewise argued that "the servility of the slave naturally increases the spirit of intolerance and tyranny in the master, which is exercised not only toward the slave but towards all others."[8]

It was an axiom among the founders that republicanism required a virtuous citizenry—one that prized widespread independence over personal aggrandizement. George Washington wrote to Lafayette that "the general government . . . can never be in danger of degenerating into a monarchy, an oligarchy, an aristocracy, or any other despotic or oppressive form, so long as there shall remain any virtue in the body of the people." As John Adams famously put it, "liberty can no more exist without virtue and independence, than the body can live and move without a soul." No matter how perfectly crafted the frame of government, liberty would not be secure if a significant portion of the population put its own status and the pursuit of wealth ahead of the public good. By this reasoning, a love of "luxury" was every bit as perilous as poverty. Consequently, having developed an imperious mind-set and a sense of entitlement, slaveholders were rendered unfit for republican government. They violated not only the language of the Revolution, but also its spirit. This apprehension can be discerned at least as far back as the debates over the Constitution in the late 1780s. According to "Cato," a prominent New York Anti-Federalist, the new national legislature would enable Southerners to spread their anti-republican tendencies across the entire nation:

> The people, who may compose this national legislature from the southern states, in which, from the mildness of the climate, the fertility of the soil, and the value of its productions, wealth is rapidly acquired, and where the same causes naturally lead to luxury, dissipation, and a passion for aristocratic distinctions; where slavery is encouraged, and liberty of course, less respected, and protected; who know not what it is to acquire property by their own toil, nor to economize with the savings of industry—will these men therefore be as tenacious of the liberties and interests of the more northern states, where freedom, independence, industry, equality, and frugality, are natural to the climate and soil, as men who are your own citizens, legislating in your own state, under your inspection, and whose manners, and fortunes, bear a more equal resemblance to your own?[9]

Given the debauching influence of luxury and arbitrary command, slaveholders often seemed as intolerant of dissent in the political arena as they were on the plantation. Northerners could point to the gag rule, the annexation of Texas, the Mexican War, the Fugitive Slave Act, and the Kansas-Nebraska Act as evidence of southern domination. And when placed on the defensive, Southerners would brook no criticism or opposition. On May 22, 1856, two days after Charles Sumner decried the Slave Power's "Crime Against Kansas," Congressman Preston Brooks of South Carolina approached the senator's desk and thrashed him repeatedly with a cane. According to the *New York Times,* the Sumner assault provided conclusive proof that the slaveocracy would stop at no extremity of violence to subdue the people of the North "and force them into a tame subservience to its own dominion." To be sure, the analogy between slaveholders' behavior on the plantation and their behavior in the halls of power seemed obvious. When did it come to pass, asked the *New York Evening Post,* that Northerners had to "speak with bated breath" in the presence of their southern masters? "Are we too slaves for life, a target for their brutal blows, when we do not comport ourselves to please them?"[10]

Northern settlers in Kansas had perhaps the most compelling reasons to ask this question. Those with proslavery proclivities frequently resorted to violence and intimidation. In one incident, a gang of "pukes" in Atchison threatened to hang the Reverend Pardee Butler when he refused to sign a resolution denouncing free-state men. After berating him for two hours before a crowd, his assailants sent him downriver on a raft with orders never to return. On another occasion, a group of Missourians seized an antislavery lawyer in Leavenworth, shaved one side of his head, tarred and feathered him, and drove him out of town on a rail. Many others were assaulted and condemned in similar fashion. Southerners, announced the *Cincinnati Gazette,* could not tolerate free speech anywhere, and would soon stifle it in Washington with the bludgeon and the bowie-knife, "as they are now trying to stifle it in Kansas by massacre, rapine and murder." Ohio congressman Samuel Galloway told the House that if he and his northern colleagues were to go to Kansas "and express the very common, and as we think very reasonable, sentiments that free labor was more profitable and vastly more pleasant than slave labor, and that the people would be richer, happier, and holier with the benefits of freedom than with the blessings of slavery" they would be liable to arrest; "and, although *perfectly free,* we might in a short time have the glorious experience of the *perfection* of our freedom within the walls of a prison—a place not usually regarded as affording the largest liberty." In fact the founders themselves, along with such American luminaries as Henry Clay, would suffer a similar fate were they to reappear and give voice to their original sentiments.[11]

In addition to the apparent link between slaveholding and the development of an imperious, intolerant demeanor, slavery also produced a psychological aversion to physical labor. Benjamin Franklin argued that the presence of slaves "diminished" whites because their children became habituated to luxury. They were "proud, disgusted with labor, and, being educated in idleness, are rendered unfit to get a living by industry." Slaveholding clearly violated the labor theory of value, which had dominated Anglo-American economic theory since John Locke's defense of private property in the *Second Treatise.* Private property, according to Locke, was sacrosanct because it derived from the labor of free individuals, and was thus a physical manifestation of personal liberty, which a legitimate form of government could not take away without consent. Yet slaveholders, like other aristocrats, were able to live a life of leisure by expropriating the fruits of other people's labor, and they could pass this unfair advantage from one generation to the next. As Lincoln explained, slavery rested on the same tyrannical spirit that says "you toil and work and earn bread, and I'll eat it." The abolitionist John Rock told the Massachusetts Antislavery Society that the slaveholder's primary concern was not race, but the dollar, "and *that* he is determined to get without working for it." Therefore, it only stood to reason "he would as soon enslave white men as black men."[12]

It was not just the slaveholders themselves who developed a psychological aversion to personal industry. Because slavery stigmatized manual labor by associating it with servility, any kind of work performed by slaves was automatically eschewed by southern whites. During the debates over Missouri statehood, James Tallmadge's close friend and congressional colleague from New York John W. Taylor decried the "baleful consequences" of slavery's expansion. Free laborers would never settle in a region "where they must take rank with negro slaves," he explained. They would "labor cheerfully while labor is honorable; make it disgraceful, they will despise it. You cannot degrade it more effectually than by establishing a system whereby it shall be performed principally by slaves. The business in which they are generally engaged, be it what it may, soon becomes debased in public estimation. It is considered low and unfit for freemen." This was true regardless of social class. Consequently, slavery made the poor whites of the South just as hopeless and degraded as the slaves themselves. The result was a stagnant, backward society inhabited by the subjugated poor and a bloated aristocracy. Egalitarianism simply could not survive such an unbalanced and inequitable distribution of wealth. The southern states, according to Theodore Parker, had already jettisoned their "republican form of government." And unless their influence was checked, the same would soon hold true for the entire nation. Henry Ward Beecher, among the most eloquent critics of slave labor, denounced the South's attempt to introduce this type of society to the plains of Kansas:

The men of the South, reared where labor was a disgrace, are without mechanic arts, without habits of industry, without organizing tendencies, without the creative force which builds up new societies. They come to curse the land with a system of husbandry which the earth detests, as well it may, for the foot of the slave burns the soil like fire. It is the agriculture of exhaustion. It is the husbandry of impoverishment. If the South inoculates the State with her leprosy, the plains of Kansas are fairer and richer today as a wilderness, than they ever will be again. For Slavery robs first the slave, and then the soil. It sucks the blood from everything it touches. And nothing can fatten upon it, except the cunning few that sit upon the middle of the web—over-swollen spiders—while the rest swing in the edges thereof, mere skeleton insects.[13]

Even after the outbreak of war in 1861, Northerners continued to argue that the South represented a reactionary force, committed to the preservation of aristocratic principles. The war was a "slaveholders' rebellion," launched by would-be oligarchs in order to halt the advance of human rights. The *Atlantic Monthly* observed in 1862 that logic naturally compelled "the Confederate oligarchs of today" to pass from a defense merely of African slavery to a defense of aristocracy in the abstract. In one of the earliest accounts of the conflict, written while it was still being waged, the historian John Abbott concluded that slavery destroyed the master's republican virtue. Nothing but slavery could so corrupt the conscience as to convince a father to sell his own daughter as a "fancy girl" to the highest bidder. Thus the ultimate question to be decided by the war was "shall there be, in the United States, an aristocratic class, maintained by the Constitution, who are to enjoy exclusive privileges, living without labor upon the proceeds of the toil of others?"[14]

As noted in chapters one and three, both Lincoln and Fitzhugh drew a parallel between American slavery and the caste system of medieval Europe. Their conclusions, however, were diametrically opposed. Fitzhugh made the comparison to establish the South as being within the mainstream of history, and to defend slavery as a means of protecting the weak from the strong. Lincoln drew the analogy in order to show that the rationales for slavery were capricious and arbitrary. It was not freedom, but slavery, and past iterations of it, that represented the principle of "might makes right." Slaveholders, just like the aristocrats and monarchs of old, insisted that the people under their control were "inferior," that they were better off enslaved, or that they had been consigned by God to a menial station. Lincoln made this comparison at Peoria in 1854, in the previously quoted speech in Chicago in 1858, in his final reply to Senator Douglas at their last joint debate at Alton, and in his recognition of Jefferson's birthday the following year. At Alton he waxed poetic in a style not unlike his second inaugural six years later. The "real issue"—which transcended the Illinois senate race or any other single campaign—was the "eternal struggle" between right and wrong. "The one is the common right of humanity," he told his listeners, "and the other the divine right of kings." Whether the latter came from a king who justified living off the fruits of his subjects' labor or from a Southerner determined to rationalize slavery, it was "the same tyrannical principle."[15]

Nor was Lincoln the only Northerner to view slavery as a manifestation of Old World absolutism. "It might be thought that in a Democracy a slaveholder could be no more safely trusted with power than a monarchist," declared the *New York Tribune*. "Neither believes in the theory of popular rights; to either the Declaration of Independence is a self-evident lie or a rhetorical flourish. Each should be carefully watched to prevent him from corrupting the minds and subverting the liberties of the people." Southerners, with their predilection for tyranny and violence, simply could not be trusted with questions of right and justice. They were "incapacitated for statesmanship." According to an Indiana editor, Northerners should be willing, if necessary, to take up arms against those who were "endeavoring to re-inaugurate the regime of the dark ages," when oppression, crime, and ignorance reigned supreme. Along these same lines, Senator Lyman Trumbull gave a speech in July 1857 (which was suspiciously similar to one Lincoln had delivered a month earlier) in which he maintained that the framers of the Declaration of Independence had not intended to declare all men equal in all respects, but had meant "to repudiate the idea of a superiority of birth," by which the divine right of kings and a hereditary aristocracy were upheld in the Old World, "and which is now sought by the self-styled Democracy to be transplanted into the new."[16]

Trumbull referred to the Declaration as the polar star that Americans should never lose sight of, lest they forget the philosophical foundation of the liberty their fathers had fought to secure. Lincoln called it a standard maxim and a stumbling block to all those who would "seek to turn a free people back into the hateful paths of despotism." But as the 1850s progressed, it became distressingly clear that the star was fading and the stumbling block eroding under the constant pressure of southern assaults and Democratic qualifications. William H. Herndon warned that the dismissal of the Declaration of Independence, and the concomitant argument that it was "right to enslave all men, black and *white*," would destroy the main pillar of American liberty and set the nation on a path toward despotism. Precisely what that "despotism" would have meant for white Americans is difficult to say, however. Most antislavery writers and politicians were inexplicit, allowing Northerners to form their own conclusions. As Gienapp points out, "Americans were so accustomed to thinking in terms of conspiracies that Republicans devoted only limited effort to proving the existence of this conspiracy and focused instead on urging the necessity of concerted action against it." Considering that Americans had long believed that economic monopolies and unchecked political power were inimical to republican government, it may have been sufficient simply to point out that slaveholders denied the universal rights of man, destroyed the dignity of labor, and dominated the national government. As Lincoln suggested in his tribute to Jefferson, such an arrangement would inevitably lead to an aristocracy, in which government existed for the good of the few and a rigid social hierarchy crushed the free laborer's dream of personal advancement.[17]

Given the arbitrary nature of proslavery rationales, and the consequent possibility they could be employed against any vulnerable group, one might assume that complacency and indifference toward slavery would be the greatest possible folly. If freedom was truly a failure, as Southerners insisted, and slavery was a blessing to those who were weak or "inferior," it only stood to reason that, as a matter of principle, it should be extended to the weak and inferior members of all races. Surrendering to southern demands in Kansas and the West would legitimize and perpetuate these rationales, and would therefore destroy the security of freedom's future. Thus Northerners could ill afford to ignore the designs of the slaveocracy. Southern arguments were not only "dangerous to you and me," Herndon insisted, but "to the whole race of men." Northerners, in their "ease and comfort and fancied security," may have believed there was no danger that these infamous arguments would ever be popular; that there was no danger they would ever be enforced. To this Herndon simply replied, "THERE IS DANGER," especially when Southerners found such malleable instruments as northern Democrats in the free states.[18]

As antislavery Northerners united under the Republican banner in 1856, it remained to be seen whether they would stem the tide and restore the principle of the Declaration. To do so, they would need to convince both Northerners and Southerners that blacks could not be excluded from the phrase "all men are created equal."

⇥ 6 ⇤

Southerners and the Principle
of Universal Liberty

Because the rationales for human servitude were not inherently racial, the acceptance of black slavery rendered the liberty of all Americans contingent on circumstance. Having come to this understanding, some Northerners insisted that the only guarantee of individual liberty was universal liberty. Only by accepting the universal equality of natural rights could Americans of all races rest secure in the belief that their own liberty would always be respected, regardless of circumstance. Thus the Declaration of Independence assumed a sacred position as the ultimate palladium of human rights. According to William H. Seward, the American Revolution had been a struggle for the principle of universal liberty, which he deemed the supreme law of man. "That supreme law is necessarily based on the equality of nations, of races, and of men. It is a simple, self-evident basis. One nation, race, or individual may not oppress or injure another, because the safety and welfare of each is essential to the common safety and welfare of all. If all are not equal and free, then who is entitled to be free, and what evidence of his superiority can he bring from nature or revelation?"[1]

When Southerners rejected or qualified the Declaration, they eroded the American people's devotion to liberty as a central principle, and in so doing, placed the nation on a path to despotism. By denying that "all men" were endowed with inalienable rights, they destroyed the self-evidence of those rights. The Declaration's meaning became a prominent theme for Northerners and Southerners alike. In numerous speeches and editorials, antislavery Northerners stressed the importance of the Declaration, decrying southern denials of universal liberty, particularly in respect to Chief Justice Taney's decision in *Dred Scott v. Sanford.*

As Northerners contemplated the future of freedom in a slaveholding country, they sometimes echoed Thomas Jefferson's fears. In his *Notes on the State of Virginia,* Jefferson expressed particular concern that the people's liberty could not be sustained if they removed "its only secure basis." In his view, this basis was "a conviction in the minds of the people that these liberties are the gift of God." And he candidly admitted that he trembled for the fate of his country when he recalled that God is just. Because blacks and whites were equally members of the human race, the vagaries of circumstance could someday ensnare whites in the black man's bondage. "Considering numbers, nature and natural means only," Jefferson explained, "a revolution of the wheel of fortune, [and] an exchange of situation is among possible events." In fact, he believed such an event could easily occur through "supernatural interference."[2]

More than seventy years later, Charles Sumner informed his southern colleagues in the Senate that "it was the inspiration of Liberty Universal that conducted us through the Red Sea of the Revolution." This principle also gave the Declaration of Independence "its mighty tone, resounding through the ages." Shortly thereafter he stood before a New York audience and endorsed Jefferson's argument that the liberty of whites depended on the liberty of blacks: "As a man, he stands before you an unquestionable member of the Human Family, and entitled to *all the rights of man.* You can claim nothing for yourself, *as a man,* which you must not accord to him. *Life, liberty and the pursuit of happiness*—which you proudly declare to be your own, inalienable, God-given rights, and to the support of which your fathers pledged their lives, fortunes and sacred honor, are his by the same immortal title that they are yours." According to Sumner, universal liberty meant that all men were justly entitled to their natural rights simply by virtue of their common humanity. Without that assumption, individual liberty would never be self-evident, and, consequently, would never be fully secure.[3]

This argument points to the critical discrepancy inherent in the American Revolution. How could a slaveholding nation effectively champion human rights? From the very beginning, the founding generation struggled to reconcile its ideals with its actions. Some found it convenient to blame the British for the introduction and preservation of slavery. It is well known that Jefferson had wanted to include a condemnation of the slave trade in

the Declaration of Independence as part of his litany of charges against
George III:

> He has waged cruel war against human nature itself, violating its most
> sacred rights of life and liberty in the persons of a distant people who
> never offended him, captivating and carrying them into slavery in another
> hemisphere, or to incur miserable death in their transportation thither. . . .
> Determined to keep open a market where men should be bought and sold,
> he has prostituted his negative for suppressing every legislative attempt
> to prohibit or to restrain this execrable commerce.

Not surprisingly, Congress excised the entire passage, in part because it
strained credulity to blame the young king for the continuation of African
slavery in the British colonies. Jefferson, however, contended that Congress
made the change "in complaisance to South Carolina and Georgia"—which
was undoubtedly true. According to Don Fehrenbacher, Southerners
may have been particularly disturbed by the moralistic tone of Jefferson's
denunciation, which could easily have extended from the slave trade to
slavery itself.[4]

Thus at the moment of America's independence, the ideal of universal
liberty bowed to the reality of slavery's existence. Jefferson expressed hope
that the Revolution would eventually abate "the spirit of the master," and
prepare the way for "a total emancipation." As Lincoln later noted, Northerners and Southerners could not have united if the former had grasped
for the immediate abolition of slavery. Nevertheless, he insisted that this
submission to necessity, by itself, did not "destroy the principle that is the
charter of our liberties."[5]

◆ ◆ ◆

The Declaration of Independence may have been the sheet anchor of
American liberty, but its legacy was more nebulous than Lincoln and
other antislavery Northerners cared to believe. In the end, the "Spirit of
Seventy-Six" was just that—a spirit. Unlike the Constitution, it was not
the supreme law of the land, nor was it any law at all. Toward the end of
his life, Jefferson explained that his purpose in writing the Declaration
had been "to place before mankind the common sense of the subject," and
to do so "in terms so plain and firm as to command their assent." But as
the decades passed, what was self-evident to some Americans became an
inconvenience and anathema to others.[6]

The incongruity of human slavery in a nation dedicated to human liberty had always been painfully obvious. At the time of the Revolution, half a million Americans were slaves, constituting more than a sixth of the nation's population. For those who viewed whites and blacks as members of the same family, the fate of one race was inextricably tied to the fate of the other. "It is astonishing," wrote a Pennsylvanian in 1777, "that men who feel the value and importance of liberty . . . should keep such numbers of the human species in a state of so absolute vassalage. Every argument which can be urged in favor of our own liberties will certainly operate with equal force in favor of that of the Negroes; nor can we with any propriety contend for the one while we withhold the other." Indeed, every argument that could be urged in favor of black slavery could operate with equal force in favor of the subjugation of whites.[7]

Prior to the 1830s, most Southerners agreed with Northerners that slavery was incompatible with the ideals of 1776. Yet as slavery ceased to be regarded as a necessary evil and became a "positive good," Southerners began to sound increasingly iconoclastic with respect to the Declaration's pronouncement that "all men are created equal." Even as early as the first decade of the nineteenth century (in the aftermath of the Haitian revolution and Gabriel's abortive insurrection) Southerners winced at the invocation of America's revolutionary principles. As William Freehling notes, "the sight of a slave listening to a Fourth of July oration chilled the bravest Southerner." And according to Robert Pierce Forbes, "as the power of American republican rhetoric to inspire oppressed peoples to revolution became progressively clearer as the century unfolded, southern Old Republicans adopted a language and outlook increasingly similar to those of the Old World despotisms they had formerly denounced and despised." A case in point was an address John C. Calhoun delivered to the Senate on the organization of Oregon in June 1848. Calhoun contemplated what a future historian might say about the dissolution of the Union. "If he should possess a philosophical turn of mind," he could trace America's destruction to "the most false and dangerous of all political errors," the proposition that "all men are born free and equal." (This was the wording of the Massachusetts Bill of Rights. Calhoun considered the wording of the Declaration of Independence to be only slightly less objectionable.) In an effort to discredit such an insidious doctrine, Calhoun, not unlike John Pettit in 1854, treated it as a literal statement rather than a philosophical expression. Men did not come into the world free or equal, he intoned.

They were born in a state of abject dependence, and slowly grew "to all the freedoms of which the condition in which they were born permits." To claim otherwise was palpably absurd. And, therefore, it was also absurd to argue that the notion of equality had any logical place in the colonists' separation from Great Britain or in the governments they subsequently established. According to Calhoun, individuals did not enjoy liberty by virtue of their humanity. Instead, liberty "must necessarily be very unequal among different people, according to their different conditions."[8]

Some Southerners, such as Calhoun, denied the principle of universal freedom entirely, while others, along with the northern advocates of popular sovereignty, qualified it in an attempt to exclude blacks. In either case, the Declaration lost its power as a palladium of individual liberty—a dangerous development, given the caprice of Jefferson's "wheel of fortune." Consequently, Northerners often lamented what they sensed as a decline in the American public's devotion to universal liberty. "Our progress in degeneracy appears to me to be pretty rapid," Lincoln wrote to his old friend Joshua Speed in 1855. "As a nation we began by declaring that 'all men are created equal.' We now practically read it 'all men are created equal, except Negroes.'" Once again comparing black slavery to the subjugation of whites, he speculated that "when the Know-Nothings get control, it will read 'all men are created equal, except Negroes and foreigners and Catholics.'"[9]

Antislavery editorials and speeches were full of jeremiads on the South's, and by extension the nation's, retrogression with respect to the Declaration's preamble and the incongruity of human slavery. On a symbolic level, Northerners deplored the fact that streets named after revolutionary heroes served as venues for auctions where men, women, and children were sold to the highest bidder. The *Methodist Quarterly Review* referred to this degeneration of the public mind as "the Great American Apostasy." Washington, Henry, Madison, and Jefferson had all lamented the prejudicial influence of slavery, noted the editor, and had hoped for its ultimate extinction. But as the decades passed, it became "the self-complacent folly of pretentious, but puny-minded men among us, to laugh at the assertion of human equality, made in the Declaration of Independence."[10]

In short, as Southerners became more and more strident in their defense of their peculiar institution, and as northern Democrats acquiesced to their demands, the incompatibility of slavery and freedom became too jarring to ignore. "How strange the spectacle," lamented the *National Era*, "that less than thirty years after the death of Jefferson, the very basis of our free institutions, which his own hand laid in the Declaration of Independence, should be rooted up and cast aside by the party which he founded in his native state." It then suggested that no one currently residing in Virginia would dare to stand up to the Slave Power and defend the principles that an earlier generation of Virginians had staked their lives and sacred honor upon. During the debates over the Wilmot Proviso, Thomas Corwin told the Senate that the men of 1776 did not believe any man was born "booted and spurred" to ride another. And in an attempt to analogize southern apostasy with European tyranny, he noted that "in those days, Virginia and Virginia's sons, Washington and Jefferson, had as little respect for that maxim, *partus sequitur ventrem,* as for that other cognate dogma, 'Kings are born to rule.'" Similarly, a local schoolmaster delivering a Fourth of July oration in Ottawa, Illinois, exclaimed to his audience that the Declaration's principle of universal freedom was consecrated by the blood of their fathers and had once been held as an axiom by all Americans. But now the people "hear it almost daily assaulted, even on the floor of Congress. We are gravely told that it is a silly abstraction, that God did not create all men free and equal; that he designed some for hewers of wood and drawers of water, some as slaves, and some as masters!" The people should thank God, he remarked, that the founders did not live to see what their children had become. While they had once declared slavery to be a national disgrace and contrary to the public good, Americans were now "required to believe and declare Slavery to be a patriarchal, heaven ordained institution, the only true basis of a free government; that the capitalists should of right own the laborer; [that] the Declaration of Independence is a lie, and the fathers of this republic were silly bigots. Such are the sentiments advocated in broad daylight in this free Republic . . . ALL THIS IN THE NINETEENTH CENTURY, and in the United States!"[11]

In response to Senator Albert G. Brown's resolution in favor of a federal slave code for the territories, Henry Wilson lamented the "complete revolution" in the political sentiments of the nation's public men. At the time of the Constitutional Convention, all Americans had cherished, "as a living faith, the creed that 'all men are created equal,'" and had voiced their hope that slavery would eventually perish. But seventy years later, those who dictated the policies of the national government shamefully sacrificed the rights of man to the economic interests of the slaveholding minority. Frederick Douglass likewise decried slavery's regressive influence. In his view, the institution had quite literally "bewitched" the people. "It has taught us to read history backwards. It has given us evil for good—darkness for light, and bitter for sweet." If the signers of the Declaration could rise from their graves, they would be "banished from the councils of the nation." Their struggle for human freedom had been supplanted by the political apostasy of unworthy successors—men who accepted or defended the view that slavery was a natural and necessary condition for at least some members of the human family.[12]

Moreover, if the defenders of slavery succeeded in overthrowing the belief that "all men are created equal," the American Revolution would be stripped of its principal legacy. No longer a struggle for the rights of man, it would stand as just another rebellion, a war undertaken by fractious colonials for the limited goal of self-government. "If slavery is right," announced the Indiana abolitionist Philip S. Cleland, "the axioms set forth in [the Declaration of Independence] are glaringly false; the American Revolution was but a successful revolution; and our fathers should be regarded as a band of rebels, engaged in unlawful resistance against the lawful authority of George III." In a more facetious manner, although no less serious, Lincoln suggested that the rejections and qualifications of the Declaration eliminated any need to celebrate the anniversary of America's independence. Why should Americans bother commemorating the Declaration when it had little or no relevance to the present day? Southerners had "become so greedy to become masters" that they called the same maxim "a self-evident lie." Consequently, "on the question of liberty as a principle, we are not what we have been." Still, "the Fourth of July has not quite dwindled away," he told a Kentucky correspondent. "It is still a great day—for burning fire-crackers!!!"[13]

To make matters worse, America's retrogression exposed the United States to ridicule and charges of hypocrisy. As immigrants from New England made their way west to Kansas, they often sang "The Freeman's Song." One verse posed a telling question:

Men, who bear the Pilgrim's name,
Men, who love your country's fame,
Can ye brook your country's shame
Chains and Slavery?

In a similar vein, William Lloyd Garrison argued that his supposed "fanaticism" amounted to nothing more than his insistence that Americans either abolish slavery or cease to "prate on the rights of man." It was simply too easy to convict them of duplicity. This hypocrisy also undermined America's influence on the world stage as a symbol of freedom, while the slaveholding ascendancy provided a comforting analogue to the enemies of reform. Lincoln pointedly warned that "the one retrograde institution in America is undermining the principles of progress, and fatally violating the noblest political system the world ever saw." As he reiterated during the war, Americans had a solemn responsibility to maintain the world's "last best hope" and ensure that a government dedicated to the principle that "all men are created equal" would not perish from the earth.[14]

Southerners, however, were naturally compelled to qualify, or otherwise reject, the Declaration if they intended to justify slavery as anything more than a temporary aberration. Senator Hammond suggested that Jefferson, while a great patriot, had been overly attached to "sentimental French philosophy," which later led to the reign of terror. The *New York Evening Post* reprinted a speech John C. Breckinridge delivered in 1856 in which the soon-to-be vice president dismissed the Declaration as a dangerous abstraction that had no bearing on the Constitution. If the Declaration had the force of constitutional law, he warned, it would compel the government to "protect every man in his right to 'life, liberty, and the pursuit of happiness,'" thus undermining the rights of the states and leading the nation "rapidly to destruction."[15]

❖ ❖ ❖

In addition to political speeches, newspaper editorials, and private letters, the increasing acceptability of slavery in the United States can be easily discerned in popular imagery. One of the most abundant sources of such imagery during the antebellum period was the multitude of banknotes that circulated throughout the nation's economy. Although we may not think of it when making a purchase, examining the contents of our own pockets can offer ample proof that there is more to money than spending power. In addition to providing a circulating medium, currency and coins are works of art. While the most obvious reason for such artistry may be the need to deter counterfeiting, it also transforms our money into a powerful patriotic device. From the lowest to the highest denominations, for thousands of years people have used money as a means of celebrating leaders, institutions, and ideas.

Faced with the exigencies of the Civil War, in 1861 the United States began to develop a nationalized monetary system, complete with a national currency. As a result of this system, our monetary iconography typically commemorates our national heritage. However, with the exception of the Continental bills issued between 1775 and 1779, prior to the Civil War paper currency was a state and local creation. By the late 1850s, there were roughly seven thousand different banknote varieties in circulation. From a strictly economic perspective, this diversity lent itself to considerable confusion as the United States developed a national market. It also provided highly fertile ground for the proliferation of counterfeits. Yet from a historian's perspective, this diversity of local notes not only allows us to compare northern and southern iconography, it allows us to examine changes in the iconographic representations of liberty and slavery from the Revolution to the Civil War.[16]

Despite the potential for local variety, Northerners and Southerners employed many of the same vignettes on their currency. One of the most common was the allegorical representation of liberty as a woman holding or wearing a liberty cap. Moreover, while every state, and many towns, chose to commemorate their own leaders and historical figures (for example, nearly every note issued in South Carolina portrayed the less-than-benign countenance of John C. Calhoun), they frequently chose likenesses of Washington, Franklin, and the other founding fathers, as well as images of shipping, generic pastoral scenes, and depictions of women that occasionally bordered on the salacious.

Southern currency differed from northern currency in one key respect: Southern notes often displayed images of slaves. Considering the enormous monetary value of the institution, it is perhaps not surprising that Southerners included illustrations of slavery on their money. Representing nearly $3 billion, the investment in slaves was more than the national investment in railroads and manufacturing combined. The use of slave vignettes also demonstrates its importance to southern society as a whole. By displaying images of happy, hardworking bondsmen, Southerners attempted to validate their belief that African bondage was a blessing to blacks and whites alike.[17]

From the early eighteenth century to the adoption of the Constitution, the colonies and states issued bills of credit adorned with allegorical and sometimes fanciful images. These were often accompanied by moralistic mottos, which, during the years of the Revolution, became fervently patriotic and anti-British. Benjamin Franklin suggested many of the designs found on the Continental notes, which explains their instructive, "Poor Richard" quality. Given the symbolic importance of monetary design, it is telling that eighteenth-century Southerners never used their currency to defend the enslavement of African Americans. Indeed, anyone unfamiliar with Britain's southern colonies might have looked at their currency and assumed that the South was home to lions, elephants, and unicorns, but they would have had no idea that it was home to even a single slave. The references to slavery that did appear were both general and decidedly negative. Maryland issued an entire series of bills in 1775 that depicted a female representation of America offering a petition to her British counterpart. At the same time, America can be seen trampling on a scroll marked "slavery," while George III stands to the left trampling on the Magna Charta and personally setting fire to an American town. On a four-dollar note issued in 1776, Georgia announced that "freedom is more precious than gold," a sentiment that future generations of Georgians actively sought to qualify. The following year, South Carolina issued a twenty-dollar note with the image of a bird escaping from its cage and the motto *Iba Patria Ubi Libertas*—"Our country, the land of freedom." The thirty-dollar note of the same series presented the motto *Misera Servitus Ominis*—"All slavery is wretched." The irony of these sentiments is palpable when one considers that more than half of South Carolina's population was enslaved. Yet while these mottos may have been hypocritical, they do suggest that eighteenth-century Southerners considered slavery to be at best a necessary evil.[18]

The first slave vignettes appeared in the 1830s and rapidly proliferated over the next twenty years. Not coincidentally, this was also the period in which Southerners launched their counterattack against the burgeoning abolitionist movement. Reflecting the new interpretation of slavery as a "positive good," one popular vignette depicts slaves cheerfully riding on a wagon loaded with cotton. Another shows an idyllic depiction of a slave mother and her child, while another portrays a field hand with a basket of cotton and a very distinct smile on his face.

Although Northerners were expressing increasing hostility to the South's peculiar institution, northern engraving firms were happy to oblige the aesthetic tastes of their southern customers. During the antebellum period, the vast majority of notes issued by both northern and southern banks were engraved by printing firms in New York and Philadelphia. (Seven of the most prominent engraving firms came together in 1858 to form the American Bank Note Company, which still produces financial and other security documents today.) This explains the considerable degree of repetition in the use of popular images. After the development of reusable, interchangeable dies (which produced notes that rival, and perhaps even exceed, the quality of today's currency), bank representatives were able to choose from existing stocks of decorative borders, portraits, and vignettes, including a wide variety of slavery-related images.

Southerners clearly used these images to demonstrate the moral and historical acceptability of African bondage. Although Jefferson's observations on human equality had fallen out of favor, they were anxious to associate slavery with the statesmen and military heroes of the Revolution. This is dramatically illustrated in a vignette used by South Carolina and the Confederate government, which includes the only slave to appear on paper money who can be personally identified: Oscar Marion. Oscar, the personal servant of General Francis Marion, appears in the famous image of the revolutionary hero inviting a British officer to partake in his dinner of sweet potatoes. This seemingly unabashed connection of slavery with the American Revolution is quite unlike the sentiment South Carolinians chose to express in the 1770s. Similarly, other southern notes depicted images of slavery next to portraits of George Washington, James Monroe, Henry Clay, and even Daniel Webster. In an act of historical revisionism, the Merchants and Planters Bank of Savannah, Georgia, went so far as to position Benjamin Franklin next to a scene of an overseer addressing a slave.[19]

Despite the association of slavery and the American Revolution, there was a clear incongruity in the use of the liberty allegory and the use of slave vignettes. For Southerners, "Lady Liberty" was potentially subversive. She was not merely a symbol of individual freedom—she was a symbol of *emancipation.* When Americans think of "Lady Liberty" today, our most prominent mental image is undoubtedly that of the Statue of Liberty. However, this is not the traditional allegory. For Americans in the eighteenth and nineteenth centuries, the female personification of liberty was most readily identified by her "liberty cap." This soft conical cap had been associated with freedom for two thousand years. When a slave was emancipated in ancient Rome, he went through a ceremony in which his owner would touch him on the shoulder with a staff and present him with the traditional headgear of the working citizen. This cap was known as the *pileus,* although most historians refer to it as the Phrygian cap, due to its prominence in the ancient country of Phrygia in Asia Minor. Because of this ceremony, the Phrygian cap was a widely recognized symbol of freedom in the Roman Empire, and throughout the Middle Ages as well.[20]

Notwithstanding her association with manumission, Southerners often failed to perceive the incompatibility of the liberty allegory with the institution of slavery. This is due in large measure to the widespread adoption of "Lady Liberty" and her Phrygian cap during the Revolution. Paul Revere was the first American to employ the symbol, using it on an obelisk he designed to commemorate the repeal of the Stamp Act in 1766. Throughout the revolutionary period, the liberty cap could be seen on currency, newspaper mastheads, and regimental flags. In an obvious reference to its emancipatory connotation, it figured prominently in the *Genius of America Encouraging the Emancipation of the Blacks,* the first abolitionist painting created by an American. The French also adopted the liberty allegory during their own revolution in the 1790s. Yet the prominence of "Liberty" and the liberty cap in the United States can be most directly attributed to their use on American coins. (Although the Senate proposed using Washington's image, the president thought it would smack of monarchy and convinced Congress to adopt an emblem representative of American freedom.) Until the early twentieth century, the majority of coins were struck with the image of "Liberty" wearing her cap or holding it aloft on a pole. Consequently, it is not at all surprising that banks chose to use similar images on their paper money (which, after all, was supposed to represent gold and silver coins). On both northern and southern banknotes, the liberty vignette was more common than any other image.

Nevertheless, Southerners may not have been totally ignorant of the incompatibility of the liberty allegory with African bondage. As secretary of war, Jefferson Davis adamantly opposed the use of the liberty cap on the statue of freedom that Thomas Crawford was designing for the new United States Capitol dome. The supervising engineer of the Capitol expansion, Montgomery Meigs, told Crawford that Davis "does not like the cap of liberty introduced into the composition; that American liberty is original, and not the liberty of the freed slave." Crawford therefore had little choice but to replace the offending cap with a helmet. Moreover, while the pervasiveness of the liberty allegory on southern banknotes would suggest that most Southerners did not share Davis's aversion to the liberty cap, there is reason to believe that they were not completely unaware of its incongruity with black slavery. Although there were thousands of banknote varieties issued in the South, in only five cases do "Liberty" and slavery appear together on the same note.[21]

Bank representatives were not explicit about their motivations for choosing particular images. However, their reasoning can often be inferred. Many vignettes—cornucopias and strongboxes overflowing with coins, canals and railroads, and Hermes, the Roman god of commerce—were intended to inspire confidence and optimism, whether such confidence was justified or not. As for the images of slaves, southern bankers may simply have been reflecting the world in which they and their customers lived, a world in which slavery had become an acceptable status for at least some human beings. Furthermore, while the classical attributes of "Lady Liberty" may be unfamiliar to Americans today (she has not appeared on circulating coins or currency since 1947), and while images of black laborers may be an uncomfortable reminder of white Southerners' devotion to the institution of slavery, their coexistence on southern paper money is a striking illustration of the complex relationship between liberty and slavery in the antebellum South.

◆ ◆ ◆

According to many antislavery Northerners, one of the chief architects of the ruinous effort to qualify the Declaration of Independence was none other than the chief justice of the United States Supreme Court, Roger B. Taney. After two decades on the high court, the chief justice was old and frail, and though a Marylander, he had not always been a vociferous proslavery apologist, having emancipated his own bondsmen. In fact, he had once defended the free speech rights of an abolitionist minister (using terms Harry Jaffa describes as Lincolnesque). However, by the 1850s he was dismayed by what he saw as antislavery aggression, warning his fellow Southerners that "the knife of the assassin is at their throats." Nor was Taney alone in this assessment. Four of his fellow justices were residents of slave states. According to Don Fehrenbacher, Justice Peter Daniel of Virginia was "a brooding proslavery fanatic," while the others were "unreserved defenders of slavery."[22]

In fairness to Taney and his colleagues, Congress had spent nearly ten years trying to give the Court the final say on slavery's status in the territories. At the height of the controversy over the Wilmot Proviso, the Senate had passed a compromise, sponsored by John M. Clayton of Delaware, granting territorial tribunals authority over "questions of personal freedom" and allowing expedited appeal to the Supreme Court. Although Clayton's bill failed in the House, its language was incorporated into the Utah and New Mexico Acts of 1850, prompting Senator Thomas Corwin of Ohio to remark that Congress had passed a lawsuit rather than a law. Nevertheless, Congress was apparently comfortable with this provision, for it was copied once again into the Kansas-Nebraska Act.

As it turned out, however, the Taney Court's opportunity to rule on this issue—one that had confounded the nation for decades—did not emanate from the Mexican Cession or from Kansas. The origins of the *Dred Scott* decision could be traced back nearly a quarter of a century and to the northern reaches of the Louisiana Purchase. In December 1833, Dr. John Emerson reported for duty at Fort Armstrong in Illinois, accompanied by his recently purchased slave, Dred Scott. Emerson expressed his displeasure with the decrepit accommodations at the fort for more than two years before he finally received a transfer to Fort Snelling in Wisconsin Territory. Shortly thereafter, he purchased another slave, Harriet, who soon became Scott's wife. The Scotts traveled with their master to assignments in Louisiana and Missouri, but also spent time hired out to other officers at Fort Snelling. When Dr. Emerson took a position in Florida in 1840, his wife returned to St. Louis along with Dred and Harriet.

After the doctor's death in 1843, Eliza Emerson became the Scotts' legal owner. Although Dred's whereabouts for the next three years are unclear, the Scotts were clearly reunited in Missouri by the spring of 1846. That April they initiated legal action against Mrs. Emerson in the state circuit court in St. Louis, claiming their freedom on the basis of their prolonged residence in Illinois and Wisconsin Territory. Thus began their labyrinthine course through the state and federal legal systems.

Unfortunately for Dred and Harriet, the increasing political rancor over slavery in the territories was beginning to bleed into the judiciary. Scott lost his case on a technicality in late 1846, but in 1850 a jury reported a verdict in his favor. Mrs. Emerson appealed the circuit court's ruling to the state supreme court, which, despite its earlier decisions upholding the freedom of those who had lived in free territory, remanded the Scotts to slavery by a two-to-one decision in 1852. Speaking for the majority, Judge John F. Ryland conceded that the court had previously freed slaves in circumstances similar to those in *Scott v. Emerson,* but candidly noted that the changing times were undermining the principle of interstate comity. In the previous ten years, individuals and states had been "possessed with a dark and fell spirit with respect to slavery, whose gratification is sought in the pursuit of measures, whose inevitable consequence must be the destruction and overthrow of our government." Under these circumstances, Ryland concluded, "it does not behoove the State of Missouri to show the least countenance to any measure which might gratify this spirit."[23]

At this point, the only recourse left to Scott was the Supreme Court of the United States. But the Court had recently refused to hear a similar case on appeal from Kentucky—*Strader v. Graham*—thus leaving Dred and Harriet with little hope for a favorable outcome. The dynamics of the Scotts' case had changed, however, when Eliza remarried and transferred control over Scott and his family to her brother, John F. A. Sanford. Consequently, Scott's attorney was able to file an entirely new suit against Sanford in federal circuit court under the diverse citizenship clause of the Constitution. The presiding judge (a slaveholder and former attorney general of Missouri) ruled against Scott in 1854, paving the way for an appeal to the Taney Court.

The Court was in no way obligated to pass judgment on the larger issues surrounding Scott's suit, namely the constitutionality of the Missouri Compromise and, by extension, the principle of congressional prohibition. That it ultimately chose to grasp the nettle struck Northerners as yet another example of the Slave Power's machinations. First, the justices decided to hold the case over for reargument in December 1856, conveniently postponing it until after the presidential election. Before Buchanan's inauguration, however, they voted to reaffirm the *Strader* precedent and uphold the previous rulings of the federal circuit court and the Missouri supreme court. If Taney and his colleagues had stuck to this course, Dred Scott would have receded into obscurity and the Court's voice would not have exacerbated the national debate over slavery's expansion and the scope of human liberty. Yet within a few days, the Court reversed itself and announced its intention to issue a comprehensive ruling. Its reasoning for doing so has long been the subject of debate. Given their majority, Southerners were particularly eager for a judicial settlement. Another interpretation is that the two non-Democrats, Benjamin Curtis of Massachusetts and John McLean of Ohio, provoked a reaction from the southern majority by announcing their intention to issue detailed dissents. Not wanting the dissenters' endorsement of black citizenship and the constitutionality of the Missouri Compromise to be the Court's only statement, Taney agreed to write a detailed defense of the southern position.

Taney first had to consider whether Scott, as a slave and a black man, was a citizen of the United States with the right to sue in federal court. Prior to the ratification of the Fourteenth Amendment in 1868, there was no constitutional definition of American citizenship. Consequently, Taney turned to the nation's seminal document, the Declaration of Independence, and sought to determine whom the signers included as citizens of the new nation. Through an examination of contemporary laws and attitudes regarding race, he concluded that Africans imported as slaves, and their descendants (whether free or slave), could not be included under the rubric "all men." According to the chief justice, Americans of the 1850s had difficulty comprehending the ubiquitous denigration of Africans in the colonial and revolutionary periods: "They had for more than a century before been regarded as beings of an inferior order, and altogether unfit to associate with the white race, either in social or political relations." In fact, they had been considered so far inferior, "that they had no rights which the white man was bound to respect."[24]

This was a universal axiom, Taney explained, which no one, North or South, had ever questioned. As evidence, he pointed to colonial and state statutes, particularly those enacted in the North, that placed legal barriers between blacks and whites. Massachusetts, for example, passed laws in 1705 and 1786 invalidating interracial marriages and prescribing harsh penalties for anyone who presided over interracial weddings. (Rhode Island followed suit in 1822.) New Hampshire passed a law in 1815 prohibiting the enrollment of blacks in the state militia, which in Taney's view was indisputable evidence that blacks were not considered citizens, who alone had the privilege and obligation to defend the state. In the end, the North had abolished slavery because of the absence of economic need and a determination that the institution was socially inconvenient. It had not been an egalitarian impulse.

To a point, Taney was undoubtedly correct. Racism had been, and continued to be, widespread in the northern states. Yet it was highly disingenuous to suggest that blacks had never exercised the rights and privileges of citizens. As Curtis and McLean pointed out in their dissents, northern blacks had possessed numerous legal rights in 1787—the right to make contracts, seek redress in court, and to hold property—and had cast their votes in five states to ratify the Constitution. Taney attempted to circumvent these inconvenient facts through the specious (and constitutionally inaccurate) argument that blacks could be citizens of individual states without being citizens of the United States.

Nor was Taney correct in his suggestion that blacks actually enjoyed greater privileges in 1857 than they had in the early days of the republic. After quoting the Declaration's preamble, the chief justice opined that the words "all men are created equal" "would seem to include the whole human family, and if they were used in a similar instrument at this day, would be so understood." Lincoln noted that two of the five states that had given free blacks the right to vote—New Jersey and North Carolina—had since restricted the franchise to whites, while New York had imposed additional restrictions on black voters. Meanwhile, even as states did away with property qualifications, no state, old or new, had extended voting rights to African Americans. Southern states had also passed laws making it much more difficult for masters to emancipate their slaves. It was therefore "grossly incorrect," Lincoln concluded, to assume that public sentiment or policy was more favorable to blacks in the 1850s than it had been in the 1770s.[25]

Nevertheless, Taney insisted that it was "too clear for dispute" that the founders had never intended to include Africans among those created equal in their rights to life, liberty, and the pursuit of happiness. To argue otherwise would be to charge the signers of the Declaration with gross hypocrisy. Like Senator Douglas, he contended that if Africans were included in the Declaration of Independence, the conduct of the founders "would have been utterly and flagrantly inconsistent with the principles they asserted; and instead of the sympathy of mankind, to which they so confidently appealed, they would have deserved and received universal rebuke and reprobation."[26]

In his dissent, Justice Curtis foreshadowed Lincoln's argument that the founders' actions could not and should not be taken as a statement of their principles: "A calm comparison of these assertions of universal abstract truths, and of their own individual opinions and acts, would not leave these men under any reproach of inconsistency." Although many of them had clearly expressed disapproval of the institution, neither Jefferson nor any of the founders could launch a frontal assault on slavery where it was already entrenched on both an economic and a social level. As Lincoln was quick to point out, this had been nothing more than a concession to necessity. They had not intended to legitimize the institution. According to Curtis, they had been ready and anxious to bring the ideal of universal liberty to fruition "whenever a necessary regard to circumstances, which no statesman can disregard without producing more evil than good, would allow." The declaration that "all men are created equal" was not a statement of reality or an edict of emancipation, but rather a national ideal—a goal to live up to. Therefore, it would be neither just nor true to assert that they had intended to say that white men alone were endowed by God with natural rights.[27]

The effects of the Court's decision were manifold. Taney and his colleagues consigned Dred Scott to slavery, although he soon secured his freedom in a bizarre twist of fate. As previously noted, Eliza Emerson had remarried in 1850. Her new husband, Calvin Chaffee, was elected to Congress from Massachusetts in 1854 as an antislavery Know-Nothing and reelected as a Republican two years later. At what point Chaffee learned that his wife owned the most famous slave in America is a matter of dispute, but with the uproar over Taney's ruling, the connection became a severe embarrassment both to the congressman and to the Republican Party. Chaffee hastened to transfer Scott to Taylor Blow of St. Louis, the son of Scott's original owner, so he could be emancipated under Missouri law. Sadly, Scott succumbed to tuberculosis the following year. Yet even though he died as a free man, it was only through the largess of his master, not by virtue of his extended residence in free territory, or his status as a human being.

On a political level, the consequences of the Court's decision were dramatic. Taney ruled that Scott's residence in free territory had not emancipated him because the exclusion of slavery north of 36°30′ had been unconstitutional, a violation of the property rights guarantee of the Fifth Amendment. This was clearly an attempt to invalidate the Republican Party's principal goal of prohibiting the expansion of slavery into the territories. Republicans, however, argued that the Court, having denied Scott's citizenship and right to sue, had no authority to pass judgment in a case that was not properly before it. As David Potter explained, the obiter dictum theory was "a psychological godsend" to Republicans in that it allowed them to defy the Court without seeming to defy the law. On the other hand, Taney's assertion that Congress lacked the constitutional authority to ban slavery in the territories, and could not delegate this authority to a territorial legislature, undermined the northern interpretation of popular sovereignty, and effectively drove a wedge in the Democratic Party.[28]

Finally, and perhaps most important, the Court gave its imprimatur to the rejection of universal liberty as a fundamental principle. The potential implications of this rejection sparked a heated debate between the pro-administration *Washington Union* and the *New York Tribune*. In response to the *Tribune's* condemnation of the Court's judgment, the *Union's* editor demanded to know how the decision posed any conceivable threat to the rights or liberties of northern whites. The *Tribune* then explained that the decision constituted an outright denial of "the rights of human nature"—the ideal for which the founders had risked their lives and sacred honor. Unlike their descendants, Southerners of 1774 had understood that an assault on the rights of others destroyed the inviolability of their own rights. Americans, North and South, had therefore gone to war for the universal principle expressed in the Declaration. Of course it was true, the *Tribune* admitted, that Dred Scott was black and the descendants of Europeans were white. It insisted, however, that the rights of man "know no distinction founded on this difference of origin and color." Thus Americans could not afford to predicate their rights on the "fickle breath" of popular or judicial majorities. Their security could only rest "on the firm basis of eternal justice," and "whatever assails or defies that basis renders all rights unstable, our own included." In its sneering rejoinder, the *Union* congratulated the *Tribune* for "its full appreciation of its own color," and criticized its "fanatical" theories and "general homilies upon humanity." It also repeated Taney's reasoning that the inclusion of slaves in the Declaration of Independence "is directly in the teeth of all our history." Indeed, if slaves were included, why did Scott not claim his freedom by virtue of "the rights of human nature" instead of the comparatively limited principle of the Missouri Compromise?[29]

Although, in the *Union*'s view, "the Tribune utterly fails to meet the case we put to it," other Northerners offered similar arguments. The editor of the *Pittsburgh Gazette* viewed the Court's decision as an affront to American principles that would "awaken the friends of freedom to renewed efforts." The *Chicago Tribune* likewise warned its readers that the Court was "part of a grand conspiracy against freedom." Its decision "sweeps away all the legislation of the fathers against the extension of slavery," and provided cover for the Slave Power's "efforts at despotism." Thurlow Weed's *Albany Evening Journal* announced that "the three hundred and forty-seven thousand five hundred and twenty-five Slave holders in the Republic" had succeeded in converting the Supreme Court "into a propagandist of human slavery." Weed then appealed to "all who love republican institutions and who hate aristocracy" to prepare for the struggle "which threatens your liberty and will test your manhood." In Milwaukee, Sherman Booth's *Free Democrat* labeled the decision "the most important public document that has been published in this country since the founding of the government." It was a "counterrevolution" that "subverted the public liberties of the nation" by declaring freedom unconstitutional.[30]

According to the editor of the *New Englander*, the consequences of the chief justice's ruling could easily redound to the detriment of white Americans. By qualifying the Declaration, the Court "absolutely destroys the fundamental principles upon which our democracy is built." If men were not entitled to liberty by virtue of their status as human beings, the rationales for oppression could be applied to anyone, white or black: "The Amendment which Judge Taney would make in the Declaration, that 'all men are created equal,' destroys the *self-evidence* of the truth. It is not self-evident, nay, it is not true, that white men, as creatures of God, are different from the rest of the race as creatures of God. The whole self-evidence is founded upon the common nature of man, and the moment the proposition is limited, so as to be applied to one only of the branches of the human family, it becomes an idle vaunt of the superior race, founded on no universal necessity, but on a mere consideration of external circumstances." Indeed, without universal liberty, the vicissitudes of circumstance would place the weak entirely at the mercy of the strong. If the Slave Power could reinterpret "all men are created equal" to mean "all men, but negroes, are created equal," and if, as Taney suggested, "the citizens of each state" could be converted to "a portion of the citizens of each state," there was nothing in the Constitution that could stand firm. "It can be made to mean anything a dominant party chooses to have it."[31]

7

Republicans, Northern Democrats, and the Principle of Universal Liberty

Shortly before the inauguration of James Buchanan, Joshua R. Giddings captured Northerners' attention when he challenged his Democratic colleagues in the House to uphold the principles of the Declaration of Independence: "I ask any member of the Democratic party, North or South, whether that party is ready to stand by those principles? I pause for an answer. I hear no reply. Sir, such is the response I always get to my well-defined interrogatories." Southerners unequivocally rejected universal liberty, he observed, while northern Democrats sat in silence. In fact, the latter were in a most uncomfortable position. If they were to renounce the Declaration, they would be cast off by their constituents; if they sustained it, they would be repudiated by the South. "Thus they vibrate between heaven and hell." Giddings then took note of Senator John Pettit's characterization of the Declaration as "a self-evident lie," and contended that the entire Democratic Party now sanctioned that libel, whether tacitly or explicitly.[1]

While Southerners, under the banner of slavery's beneficence, threatened American liberty by rejecting or qualifying the Declaration of Independence, northern Democrats did the same under the banner of popular sovereignty. The latter could hardly define slavery as anything less than legitimate, given their adoption of Douglas's "care not" philosophy with respect to the institution's future. Consequently, as Giddings suggested, antislavery Northerners believed that Southerners and northern Democrats both stood guilty of maligning and distorting the founding fathers' legacy. And they offered the same arguments in response to northern Democrats' denials and qualifications of the Declaration as they did to

Southerners' denials and qualifications. In fact Republicans and northern Democrats both went to great lengths to align themselves with the revolutionary generation. It is important, therefore, to evaluate the purposes and historical accuracy of their respective arguments—with respect not only to their territorial policies, but also the differences that underlay their mutual opposition to secession.

As a national policy, popular sovereignty implied national approval of the institution of slavery whenever and wherever a local majority wanted it. Lincoln therefore contended that Pettit only said "what consistency and candor" required all of Douglas's supporters to say. Indeed, Pettit was not the only Northerner guilty of egregious apostasy. Antislavery Northerners also denounced the influential Massachusetts senator Rufus Choate. Troubled by the sectional character of the Republican Party, Choate had declared for Buchanan in 1856 and, in a letter to the Whig Central Committee of Maine, had criticized Republicans for quoting "the glittering and sounding generalities of natural right which make up the Declaration of Independence." Many New Englanders expressed dismay that such a sentiment had come from one of their own. "Glittering generalities!" cried Ralph Waldo Emerson. "Blazing ubiquities, rather!" Charles Francis Adams, the grandson of John Adams, likewise criticized Choate for undermining the ideals of the Revolution and subverting the people's liberty with his "poison to freedom."[2]

Although northern Democrats may have had no love for the institution of slavery, their acceptance of its expansion and perpetuation logically compelled them to join the southern apologists who discarded the principle of universal liberty or qualified it to exclude blacks. In so doing, they sustained the host of arbitrary proslavery rationales, thereby destroying the assumption of human freedom and, therefore, the self-evidence of individual liberty. Shortly after Pettit's infamous speech, the *New York Evangelist* chastised the senator for his inability to distinguish mankind's equality of *rights* from men's inevitable inequality of *condition.* "The truth is, the doctrine of equality in original rights is founded upon a *limited,* and not on universal similarity among men. All are MEN; all rest upon the generic and central trunk of a common humanity, a common nature as intellectual and moral beings, a common origin and relation as the creatures of God. It is not necessary to be a Senator in order to be a man; neither is it necessary to have a white skin, or an expanded intellect." This universality of natural rights was necessary, explained the editor, given the transience of circumstance and the subjective lens through which human conditions could be viewed. Strength, intelligence, wealth, and beauty were all fragile foundations for the enjoyment of personal freedom. "Essential humanity as the basis and criterion of rights, is compatible with a great variety in the condition of beings." Without this foundation, "the whole doctrine of rights is a mere fiction. . . . Even the Senator from Indiana might justly be a freeman one moment, and a bondsman the next, but for that equality of right which he spurns, and whose assertion in the Declaration of Independence he calls a 'self-evident lie.'" Similarly, Frederick Douglass denounced Pettit's conceited arguments on the physical, moral, and intellectual differences among human beings. If Pettit could be said to have proven anything, it was merely that "all men are not equally stupid." No antislavery man had ever interpreted the Declaration in the ridiculous manner that the senator took it upon himself to refute. "The writer of this is a Negro, but he has no desire whatever to be thought equal with Mr. Pettit, except in the right to life, liberty, and the pursuit of happiness—and this is precisely the equality contended for in the Declaration of Independence, which this unmannerly and coarse blasphemer pronounces a SELF-EVIDENT LIE."[3]

❖ ❖ ❖

Republicans and northern Democrats each accused the other of misrepresenting the intentions of the founding fathers who signed the Declaration of Independence. According to Douglas, the Declaration was not a grand statement of universal freedom. It merely proclaimed that Americans, having been denied their inalienable rights as British subjects, were justified in their repudiation of the British crown. Less than two months after the passage of the Kansas-Nebraska Act in 1854, Douglas attended a Fourth of July celebration at Philadelphia's Independence Square. After listening to a recital of the Declaration, the Little Giant spoke for over an hour, defending his measure as another triumph in the American people's original and continuing struggle for self-government. Nothing that occurred in the following years shook him from this conviction. As he told Senator Seward in response to the New Yorker's defense of the Topeka Constitution in 1856, he would not sacrifice "the political and constitutional rights of twenty millions of white people for the benefit of three millions of negroes." Following his reelection to the Senate in 1859, Douglas expounded on the conformity of popular sovereignty in the territories with the American colonies' struggle for self-government in a lengthy exposition he wrote for *Harper's Magazine.* With the assistance of the historian George Bancroft, he presented the resolutions of colonial assemblies and the First Continental Congress to prove that "the Declaration of Independence was founded and the battles of the Revolution were fought" for Americans' exclusive right to pass legislation involving "all local and internal concerns, slavery included." It was not the rights of man for which they fought, but rather "the inalienable right of local self-government." Consequently, the Republicans' broad misinterpretation of the constitutional provision giving Congress the right to make "all needful rules and regulations for the territories" was analogous to the tyranny of the British Parliament as expressed in the Declaratory Act. Harry Jaffa argues, correctly, I believe, that it was "merely rhetorical deception" for Douglas to equate the prohibition of slavery in the territories with the right "to bind them 'in all cases whatsoever.'"[4]

Whether Douglas's logic convinced many readers is open to debate. Robert Johannsen doubts that it did, noting that the Little Giant's reasoning was turgid, tedious, and contrived, and by attempting to frame it as a historical precedent, may actually have hurt popular sovereignty's appeal as a practical solution. Nevertheless, other northern Democrats offered similar historical arguments. The Democratic Party of Pennsylvania resolved that popular sovereignty extended to the territories "the rule of 'equal and exact justice to all men,' of all sections of the confederacy, which was designed by the framers of our government, and which was defined as one of its essential principles by the immortal Jefferson." The Republican insistence that their policy agreed with that of Jefferson was "an old fraud," announced the Democratic Club of Syracuse, New York. Treating the territories as "infants" rather than self-governing communities was in opposition to the "doctrine of Jefferson and Jackson."[5]

Douglas included slavery within the rightful prerogatives of white majorities because, like Chief Justice Taney, he deemed Africans "inferior," and therefore not included under the rubric of "all men." The authors of the Declaration had referred only to "men of European birth and European descent." This, he maintained, was amply proven by their actions. He repeatedly asked whether Jefferson could possibly have meant to declare that his own African bondsmen, "which he held and treated as property, were created his equals by divine law." If he had, would he not stand guilty of violating God's law every day of his life by holding them as slaves? Jefferson had in fact been the owner of more than 175 slaves when he wrote the Declaration, and he made little effort to emancipate them over the course of his life or upon his death. For Douglas, the answer was clear: Jefferson had not intended to include blacks among those men who were "created equal" and therefore entitled to self-government. He noted that neither Jefferson nor any other slaveholding delegate emancipated his bondsmen during the Revolution. Furthermore, when the Declaration was signed, slavery was legal in every colony, which meant that every delegate represented a slave-holding constituency. "Are you willing to have it said," Douglas demanded, "that every man who signed the Declaration of Independence declared the negro his equal, and then was hypocrite enough to continue to hold him as a slave, in violation of what he believed to be the divine law?" This was precisely what Republicans were doing, he insisted—charging the signers of the Declaration with abject hypocrisy.[6]

While Douglas viewed the Declaration as an endorsement of self-government for those of European descent, Republicans viewed it as a palladium of individual liberty, regardless of race. At their first national convention, held at Philadelphia in 1856, the new party resolved that "the maintenance of the principles promulgated in the Declaration of Independence and embodied in the Federal Constitution are essential to the preservation of our Republican institutions." Therefore, "with our Republican fathers we hold it to be a self-evident truth that all men are endowed with the inalienable right to life, liberty, and the pursuit of happiness." It had been "the primary object" of the national government (as evidenced by the Fifth Amendment) to secure these rights to all persons "within its exclusive jurisdiction"—which included the District of Columbia and the territories. Only by this means (restricting slavery to the states where it already existed) could Americans define slavery as a temporary aberration and thus maintain freedom as a national ideal. At a Republican meeting in Brooklyn, James A. Briggs (a supporter of Salmon Chase who, in an effort to weaken the presidential prospects of William Seward, invited Lincoln to speak at Cooper Union) announced that he was a Republican "because he believed that all men were created free and equal . . . that no man had a right to hold another man in bondage . . . that freedom was the natural condition of every man, of every woman, and every child on God's earth." Congressman James Humphrey of New York likewise observed that the Republican platform rested on the Declaration of Independence. He then predicted that America was about to face "the conflict of the century," which would decide whether the United States was to be a slave nation or a free nation. Humphrey's colleague in the House Anson Burlingame struck at Douglas's conception of the Declaration as a guarantee of self-government for political communities but not a promise of universal human liberty: "We hold that this government was not formed to protect the rights of States alone, but the great rights of man."[7]

With respect to the argument that the founders could not have included a race they held as slaves, Lincoln, as noted in chapter one, argued that Douglas's logic amounted to "nothing at all." The Declaration of Independence was not a reflection of reality or an edict of emancipation. Acquiescing in the existence of slavery where it was already entrenched had been a matter of unavoidable necessity. However, the Declaration *was* an expression of the ideal of universal liberty, and should therefore serve as a maxim and guide for the nation's future.

As for Calhoun's and Pettit's argument that Jefferson's proclamation of "equality" contradicted the obvious reality that some men were superior to others, it is true, as Pauline Maier has suggested, that Jefferson's language was not as clear as it could have been. The phrase "all men are created equal" was not directly linked to the enumeration of inalienable rights— "life, liberty, and the pursuit of happiness." Yet despite those who would dismiss it as a ridiculous proclamation that all men were equal in condition, the Declaration's defense of "equality" applied only to these natural rights. As Charles Sumner explained, these rights applied to all men (at least in principle), transcending the vagaries of condition and circumstance, and thus ensuring the self-evidence of each individual's liberty: "The Declaration of Independence was a Declaration of Rights, and the language employed, though general in its character, must obviously be restrained within the design and sphere of a Declaration of Rights, involving no such absurdity as was attributed to it yesterday by the Senator from Indiana [John Pettit]." By this reasoning, the acceptance of slavery's expansion and indefinite continuation, either through the indifference of popular sovereignty or an explicit defense of the institution, was contrary to the principles espoused by the founding fathers and inimical to the liberty of the American people.[8]

Antislavery Northerners adamantly denied that their movement was dangerous or novel. They saw themselves as the political heirs of the founding fathers. Given his assumption that blacks were inferior (and therefore not included in the Declaration), Douglas insisted throughout the joint debates that popular sovereignty conformed to the nation's founding principles. Again and again, he linked it to "the great principle" of self-government and, in response to Lincoln's assertion in the "House

Divided" speech that the Union could not endure permanently half slave and half free, argued that the founding fathers had in fact made the nation divided into free and slave states. As he told the audience at Galesburg, there was "but one path of peace in this republic, and that is to administer this government as our fathers made it, divided into free and slave States, allowing each State to decide for itself whether it wants slavery or not."[9] To Lincoln's mind, Douglas's interpretation of America's founding ideals was an outrage. It was the Republican Party that sought to maintain the original policy of the founders. The founders themselves had placed slavery in the course of ultimate extinction—a policy that had remained in place until 1854. As evidence of their inclusion of blacks in the Declaration, and their views on the future of slavery (which did not endorse Douglas's version of popular sovereignty), Lincoln repeatedly pointed to the prohibition of the African slave trade and the Northwest Ordinance.

> I insist that our fathers did not make this nation half slave and half free, or part slave and part free, I insist that they found the institution of slavery existing here. They did not make it so, but they left it so because they knew of no way to get rid of it at that time. When Judge Douglas undertakes to say that, as a matter of choice, the fathers of the government made this nation part slave and part free, he assumes what is historically a falsehood. More than that: when the fathers of the government cut off the source of slavery by the abolition of the slave-trade, and adopted a system of restricting it from the new Territories where it had not existed, I maintain that they placed it where they understood, and all sensible men understood, it was in the course of ultimate extinction; and when Judge Douglas asks me why it cannot continue as our fathers made it, I ask him why he and his friends could not let it remain as our fathers made it?[10]

Like Washington, Jefferson, and Adams, Republicans viewed themselves as combatants in the eternal struggle between freedom and tyranny. Southerners may have echoed the revolutionary generation's hostility to distant and arbitrary government, but unlike the founders, they feared centralized government as a threat to slavery rather than liberty. Henry Wilson offered a litany of quotations to prove that the framers of the American government considered slavery to be incompatible with the legacy of the Revolution: Washington "wished as much as any man living to see slavery abolished by legislative authority." Franklin regarded slavery as "an atrocious debasement of human nature." Madison, the father of the Constitution, pronounced slavery "a dreadful calamity," and he "thought it wrong to admit in the Constitution the idea that there could be property in man." Gouverneur Morris, who edited the final document, denounced slavery as "a nefarious institution." Luther Martin believed that "God was Lord of all, viewing with equal eye the poor African slave and his American master"; and he would "authorize the General Government to make such regulations as should be most advantageous for the gradual abolition of slavery and the emancipation of the slaves which were already in the States." George Mason declared that slavery produced "the most pernicious effects on manners"; that "every master of slaves is born a petty tyrant"; and that "it brought the curse of Heaven on a country."[11]

Notwithstanding their differences on immediatism, both abolitionists and Republicans embraced the argument that antislavery constituted a renewal of the founders' policy. As early as 1845, Salmon Chase had insisted that the new Liberty Party was actually "the Liberty party of 1776 revived." Indeed, it was the same party that had struggled throughout history against "the party of false conservatism and slavery." Fifteen years later, James Doolittle proudly exclaimed that the Republican Party "stands today upon precisely the principles of the old Republican party of Thomas Jefferson." Similarly, the *New York Tribune* pointedly noted that "the doctrines of Jefferson" had found their natural home in the Republican Party. And according to the abolitionist Henry Highland Garnett, the endorsement of equal rights in the Declaration of Independence "would lead the framers of it, were they now living, to fight in our cause."[12]

Not surprisingly, Republicans and northern Democrats were somewhat selective in their use of the founders' legacy. Douglas pointed to the Ordinance of 1784, which he deemed the "Jeffersonian Plan" for the territories, as a philosophical prototype for the Kansas-Nebraska Act (in that the ordinance granted settlers full control over their own internal policies). Yet he quickly brushed aside Jefferson's proposal that all new territories, North and South, should be closed to slavery after 1800, a proposal that, much to Jefferson's regret, had fallen one vote short of passage. (Jaffa argues that Jefferson's passionate desire to arrest slavery's expansion in 1784 illustrates the chasm that separated Douglas's thoughts from the founders'.) Republicans, on the other hand, invoked the Northwest Ordinance, which had prohibited slavery in all the territory the national government controlled in 1787 (a point Douglas conspicuously ignored in his *Harper's* article). In addition to Douglas's frequent reminder that the founders had made no effort to eliminate slavery, or even to emancipate their own slaves, when they signed the Declaration of Independence, other Democrats were quick to note that it was Jefferson who had acquired Louisiana, and had signed the measure allowing slavery in the new territory. Furthermore, it was the same Thomas Jefferson who had lamented the creation of an artificial dividing line between free and slave territory—the very line that the Kansas-Nebraska Act had abolished. It therefore stood to reason, according to northern Democrats, that Jefferson's language in the Declaration contained "a full and complete endorsement" of popular sovereignty.[13]

❖ ❖ ❖

Douglas may have been on firmer historical ground than Lincoln realized or cared to admit. Although it was clearly misleading to claim that the founders made the nation half slave and half free, confirming Lincoln's argument that they knowingly included blacks in the Declaration of Independence is a challenge. As Philip Detweiler pointed out fifty years ago, and as Pauline Maier has noted more recently, the founders spent surprisingly little time debating what the Declaration's preamble actually meant. "Attention centered upon the conclusion—the announcement of independence." In one of the first histories of the Revolution, David Ramsay wrote in 1789 that the Declaration was essentially "the act of the united colonies for separating themselves from the government of Great-Britain"—a point of view that, according to Detweiler, prevailed in most of the histories and textbooks produced in Jefferson's lifetime. Consequently, the modern historian who would assert that the phrase "all men" was understood by the delegates to the Continental Congress to include African slaves "has a fragile foundation on which to build."[14]

In fact, the Declaration as a whole received relatively little attention in the fifteen years after its promulgation. Because Jefferson was known to be an excellent writer—and a miserable debater—Congress gave him the task of composing a document that many saw as little more than an ornamental formality. Although it was significant enough to shift Independence Day from July 2 (when Congress approved Richard Henry Lee's resolution dissolving the colonies' political ties with Britain) to July 4, it would seem that the Declaration itself was quickly forgotten after it had served its purpose. Early Fourth of July orations rarely invoked it. Its wording was not incorporated into any state constitution prior to that of Wisconsin in 1848. The delegates to the Constitutional Convention largely ignored it, as did the authors of *The Federalist Papers.* Nor did the Antifederalists appeal to the Declaration in their protests against the Constitution. The Declaration soon gained new life, however, with the development of party politics in the 1790s. Prior to this time, it was not widely known that Jefferson was the principal author. Most Americans thought of it as the work of the entire Congress (not unfairly, considering the revisions to Jefferson's original draft). But as Jefferson became the leader of the Republican opposition, the Declaration became an indelible part of his legacy, in the eyes of his supporters and his critics. The former lauded Jefferson's words as the seminal expression of the nation's political philosophy. In terms amenable to Lincoln's interpretation, Republican newspapers suggested that the Declaration should be celebrated not only "as affecting the separation of one country from the jurisdiction of another; but as being the result of a rational discussion and definition of the rights of man, and the end of civil government." Federalists, on the other hand, denounced Jefferson as a revolutionary pro-French demagogue and a howling atheist. And they dismissed the Declaration as a fanatical anti-British screed. As Simon P. Newman has demonstrated, Federalists often celebrated Washington's birthday in lieu of the Fourth of July. Others attempted to downplay Jefferson's importance. When John Marshall re-counted the drafting of the Declaration in his *Life of George Washington,* he consigned Jefferson (then the sitting president) to a footnote. Furthermore, given the obvious influence of John Locke's *Second Treatise* on Jefferson's ideas and phrasing, some Federalists hinted that the Sage of Monticello was little more than a plagiarist and suggested that it was Locke who truly deserved credit for the Declaration of Independence.[15]

But once Republicans gained the political ascendancy with Jefferson's accession to the White House in 1801, they were in a position to write the Declaration's legacy on their own terms. In her influential *History of the Rise, Progress, and Termination of the American Revolution,* Mercy Otis Warren lavished praise on this "celebrated paper," which had "done so much honor . . . to the genius and heart of the gentleman who drew it." She believed the Declaration should be "read by the rising youth of the American states, as a palladium of which they should never lose sight." Its principles were "grounded on the natural equality of man, their right of adopting their own modes of government, the dignity of the people, and that sovereignty which cannot be ceded either to representatives or to kings." Perhaps not surprisingly, Jefferson was well pleased with this "truthful account," and promptly ordered copies for himself and his entire cabinet.[16]

This was the legacy of the Declaration that gained widespread acceptance after the Treaty of Ghent. According to Maier, it was the second
generation of Americans who, finding themselves somehow lacking in
comparison to their fathers, lifted the Declaration up to the status of
"American scripture." As part of this effort, Congress commissioned the
artist John Trumbull to paint a grand (and ultimately ahistorical) tableau
of the signing ceremony, which was later exhibited in several eastern cities
before its final installation in the Capitol rotunda. Publishers also catered
to the public's interest with biographies of the signers, of whom only four
were still alive in 1820: William Floyd, Charles Carroll, John Adams, and
Thomas Jefferson. In its appraisal of one such work, the *North American
Review* heaped encomiums on both the book and its subject: "The declaration of Independence—a national monument, not more lasting than
brass, but as durable in its effects and associations, as the republic itself
and the name of freedom—still deserves every illustration, which documents, tradition, or the arts can afford."[17]

The Declaration also assumed a special place because, in the end, it was
the only national document that proclaimed the inalienable rights of man,
making it a much-sought-after ally to those battling injustice. It was this
legacy that Lincoln and the new Republican Party appealed to in the 1850s.

◆ ◆ ◆

Lincoln was correct when he observed that some Southerners had denied
the truth of the Declaration "for a period of years" prior to Pettit's "shame-
ful" pronouncement that it was "a self-evident lie." But he was wrong to
accuse Douglas and Taney of being the first to assail it "in the sneaking way
of pretending to believe it and then asserting it did not include the Negro."
Indeed, Douglas missed an opportunity to severely embarrass his opponent
after Lincoln announced that it would be "a matter of great astonishment
to me" if it could be shown that a single American had ever attempted to
exclude blacks from the Declaration prior to the Kansas-Nebraska Act.[18]

In fact, the congressional debates of 1819–1820 included arguments quite
similar to those made by Democrats and Republicans more than three
decades later. Just as Lincoln pointed to Kansas-Nebraska as a dangerous
turning point, James Tallmadge and his northern allies had characterized
Missouri's admission to the Union as a watershed moment in American
history, one that would determine the character of the nation. Having decried the existence of slavery since the Revolution, Americans in general,
and Southerners in particular, now faced an opportunity to put their words

into action. Prohibiting slavery's expansion would demonstrate that the American people still subscribed to the proposition that all men are created equal, while according to Tallmadge, allowing Missouri's admission as a slave state would imply "the moral right of slavery." (Lincoln employed nearly the same phrase in 1854.) "How gladly would the legitimates of Europe chuckle," the New Yorker declared, "to find an American Congress in debate on such a question!"

> You boast of the freedom of your Constitution and your laws; you have claimed, in the Declaration of Independence, "That all men are created equal . . .'"; and yet you have slaves in your country. The enemies of your Government . . . point to your inconsistencies, and blazon your supposed defects. If you allow slavery to pass into Territories where you have the lawful power to exclude it, you will justly take upon yourself all the charges of inconsistency; but, confine it to the original slaveholding States, where you found it at the formation of your Government, and you stand acquitted of all imputation.

Tallmadge's fellow New Yorker, and soon-to-be House speaker, John W. Taylor likewise proclaimed that "if we reject the [Tallmadge] amendment and suffer this evil, now easily eradicated, to strike its roots so deep in the soil that it can never be removed, shall we not furnish some apology for doubting our sincerity when we deplore its existence?" Similarly, New Hampshire's Arthur Livermore considered the prohibition of slavery in Missouri to be an opportunity "if not to diminish, at least to prevent, the growth of a sin which sits heavy on the souls of every one of us. By embracing this opportunity, we may retrieve the national character, and, in some degree, our own."[19]

In response to this reasoning, some Southerners began to dismiss the Declaration's impact on American life. Senator William Pinkney of Maryland presaged Senator Pettit's interpretation when he observed that "the self-evident truths announced in the Declaration of Independence are not truths at all, if taken literally." John Randolph expressed the same sentiment as he looked back upon the Missouri controversy in 1826. Invoking the Declaration was dangerous business, he argued. Taken to its logical extreme, it meant "all men are born free and equal." This he could not abide, "for the best of all reasons, because it is not true." In his mind, the Declaration was merely a "fanfaronade of abstractions."[20]

Unbeknownst to Lincoln, Southerners had also attempted to exclude blacks from the term "all men." Don Fehrenbacher goes so far as to argue that, after 1820, the vast majority of Americans subscribed to the southern interpretation that the Declaration of Independence did not proclaim universal human rights, "but rather applied to whites alone." In the course of the debates over Missouri's admission, Senator James Barbour of Virginia, exasperated by northern invocations of the Declaration, demanded: "What has that to do with this question? Who were the parties—the slaves? . . . Did it enter into any human mind that it had the least reference to this species of population?" Other Southerners presaged Douglas's argument that the Declaration was a guarantee of self-government for whites only, with black slavery as a legitimate subject of majority rule. Congressman Louis McLane of Delaware announced his concurrence with the Declaration's principles, but denied that Africans were included: "The Revolution found them in a state of servitude, the acknowledgment of our actual independence left them so, and the Constitution of the United States perpetuated their condition." He maintained that the principle of "equality" should be extended to the white citizens of Missouri, thus granting them the right to choose their own institutions as they saw fit. In the same vein, Congressman John Tyler of Virginia, later the tenth president of the United States, expressed his love for the principle of equality "as an abstract truth," but did not believe it could be applied *in extenso.* Therefore, since Congress could not raise the black man to the same level as the white (constitutionally or otherwise), it should at least guarantee the political equality of white Americans. "Extend an equality to the people of Missouri," he implored. "Place them upon a footing with the people of New York, Connecticut, and of the other states." This "equality" did not pertain to life, liberty, and the pursuit of happiness, but rather to the people's right "to alter, to amend, [or] to abolish their constitutions." A future vice president, Senator Richard M. Johnson of Kentucky, agreed. The Declaration was "the foundation of all civil rights, and the palladium of our liberties," he averred, yet like Tyler, he interpreted these rights and liberties as the foundation of self-government for whites alone. To him the Declaration's overriding principle was that "all communities stand upon an equality." This was precisely Douglas's position after 1854.[21]

❖ ❖ ❖

Yet while the Republican interpretation of the Declaration may not have been dominant for as long as Lincoln suggested, and while Douglas's analysis did in fact antecede the Kansas-Nebraska Act, it was not disingenuous to contend that Douglas's measure constituted a dangerous turning point. The principle of popular sovereignty, as applied to black slavery, was an ipso facto qualification of the principle of universal liberty. And Douglas presented Kansas-Nebraska as the new *national policy* for addressing slavery's expansion.

Accordingly, Lincoln and other Republicans pilloried Douglas as a traitor to Jeffersonian principles. "I understand you are preparing to celebrate the 'Fourth,'" Lincoln told a Springfield audience in 1857. "What for? The doings of that day had no reference to the present."

> But I suppose you will celebrate, and will even go as far as to read the Declaration. Suppose, after you read it once in the old-fashioned way, you read it once more with Judge Douglas's version. It will then run thus: "We hold these truths to be self-evident, that all British subjects who were on this continent eighty-one years ago, were created equal to all British subjects born and then residing in Great Britain."
>
> And now I appeal to all—to Democrats as well as others—are you really willing that the Declaration shall thus be frittered away?—thus left no more, at most than an interesting memorial of the dead past?—thus shorn of its vitality and practical value, and left without the germ or even the suggestion of the individual rights of man in it?

Less than a month after Douglas's nomination for president by the northern wing of his party, a Wisconsin editor likewise presented this "new Declaration of Independence" as a limited and ultimately capricious guarantee of individual freedom. "We hold these truths to be self-evident: that the European race on this continent, and their descendants, and emigrants who shall come here, are created equal. . . . We hold this truth to be equally self-evident: that negroes, the Chinese, the Indians, the Japanese, and all other inferior races, should have every right, every privilege, every immunity, consistent with the safety and welfare of the State; and each State and Territory must decide for itself as to the nature and extent of those rights, privileges and immunities."[22]

In a rousing speech later that summer, Senator Carl Schurz contrasted the Jeffersonian view of the Declaration as a great manifesto of human liberty with Douglas's less-inspired interpretation. In the latter, the Declaration was nothing more than a "diplomatic dodge" intended to secure foreign support by inveigling "noble-hearted fools" with disingenuous protestations of Americans' devotion to human freedom. Schurz therefore argued that it was Douglas, not the Republicans, who had maligned the founders as "a batch of artful pettifoggers," "accomplished humbuggers," and slaveholding hypocrites who had said one thing and meant another. "There is your great American Revolution," he exclaimed, "no longer the great champion of universal principles, but a mean Yankee trick." He then suggested that if the authors of the Declaration could rise from their graves they would surely have some choice words for the Little Giant. Jefferson, "his lips curled with the smile of contempt," would be heard to say, "Sir, you may abuse us as much as you please, but have the goodness to spare us with your vindications of our character and motives." In the end, Schurz assured his audience that the progressive ideas of the Declaration would prevail. Because only those with a dull or disordered mind could fail to understand its principles, it was in vain "for demagogism to raise its short arms against the truth of history."[23]

◆ ◆ ◆

The belief that individual liberty depended on universal liberty persisted through the 1860 presidential campaign and its aftermath. A particularly dramatic incident took place in May at the Republican National Convention in Chicago. Although Don Fehrenbacher and Eric Foner have disputed the view that the new party platform was substantively less radical than the 1856 version (the declaration that slavery could not constitutionally exist in any territory remained in place), the delegates did attempt to soften their condemnation of slavery in order to appeal to moderate Northerners, particularly in Pennsylvania, Indiana, and Illinois. They dropped the reference to slavery and polygamy as "twin relics of barbarism," denounced John Brown's raid on Harpers Ferry as "the gravest of crimes," and affirmed "the right of each state to order and control its own domestic institutions." The platform committee also eliminated the party's 1856 endorsement of the Declaration of Independence. Incensed by what he perceived as a craven surrender of principles, Giddings blamed Horace Greeley for this "low insidious effort" to muffle the party's invocation of the rights of man. He promptly introduced an amendment stating "that the maintenance of the principle promulgated in the Declaration of Independence . . . is essential to the preservation of our republican institutions." The amendment was rejected, whereupon Giddings moved to exit the hall in a show of opposition. "It seemed to me," said George William Curtis, "that the spirits of all the martyrs to freedom were marching out of the convention behind the venerable form of that indignant and outraged old man." Curtis then rose to renew Giddings's motion, which provoked an enthusiastic response from the convention. According to a witness who recounted the scene in the *Boston Herald* twenty years later, Curtis "spoke as with a tongue of fire in [the Declaration's] support, daring the representatives of the party of freedom, meeting on the borders of the free prairies in a hall dedicated to the advancement of liberty, to reject the doctrine of the Declaration of Independence affirming the equality and defining the rights of man." His speech "fell like a spark upon tinder," and the convention adopted the amendment with deafening shouts of approval.[24]

Following Lincoln's election, Northerners were quick to note the absurdity of southern secession as a "revolution" in the defense of human bondage. Yet many Southerners did in fact couch their arguments in the language of 1776. "The tea has been thrown overboard," proclaimed the *Charleston Mercury.* "The revolution of 1860 has been initiated." The *New Orleans Picayune* observed that the Confederacy was "acting over again the history of the American Revolution of 1776." In his inaugural address, Jefferson Davis announced that the South had "merely asserted the right which the Declaration of Independence of July 4, 1776 defined to be 'inalienable.'" Indeed, according to South Carolina's "Declaration of the Causes of Secession," the colonies had struggled for the "right of self-government," as expressed in the proclamation that the colonies "are, and of right ought to be, free and independent states." Not coincidently, the new declaration concluded with the announcement that South Carolina was "a separate and independent State." However, while Southerners embraced the right of self-government and the right to abolish government "when it becomes destructive of the ends for which it was established," they carefully avoided any mention of what those "ends" were. They excised that part of the Declaration that defined government as the means of securing the people's rights to life, liberty, and the pursuit of happiness.[25]

Northerners responded to these arguments with adamant denials that the indefinite preservation of slavery was a cause analogous to that of the American Revolution. Leaders from across the antislavery spectrum conceded that the right of revolution was undeniable when minority rights were consistently violated. But this was surely not the case for the South. In fact the principal aim of the new Confederacy directly violated the purpose of legitimate government—the preservation of life, liberty, and property. (Once again, Northerners and Southerners disagreed as to whether slavery was a form of property or a denial of liberty.) To highlight this point, Northerners compared the goals of the founding fathers to the secessionists' aims. "Mr. Jefferson's Declaration of Independence was made in the interest of natural rights against Established Institutions," observed the *New York Tribune,* while "Mr. Jeff. Davis's caricature thereof is made in the interest of an unjust, outgrown, decaying Institution against the apprehended encroachments of Natural Human Rights." Despite his self-proclaimed paralysis, even President Buchanan noted that Southerners had no justification for revolution, which could only be invoked against intolerable oppression. "We appear to be on the eve of the oddest revolution history has yet seen," announced the *National Anti-Slavery Standard.* It was a revolution "for the greater security of injustice, and the firmer establishment of tyranny." And while it had been disingenuously launched as a defense of popular liberty, it was a strictly reactionary movement, "such as has more than once set up again a throne that had been toppled down, and brought back a discarded monarch." Thus the new Confederacy would be "one of the most horrible despotisms that ever blackened the earth, for the white man as well as the black."[26]

But while Republicans and northern Democrats both denounced secession, their motivations reflected their divergent views on the nature of America's experiment in popular government. Douglas continued to condemn Republicans for their racial fanaticism and political inflexibility, yet he would ultimately sustain them in their opposition to disunion. Allen Guelzo has recently observed that Douglas and his supporters "knew no law but the *vox populi*"—a law that secession put at risk. When a political party comes to power through a fair democratic process, the minority, no matter how disaffected, is obliged to acquiesce. If it does not, popular government becomes an untenable proposition. As Locke had explained in the *Second Treatise,* "if the consent of the majority shall not in reason be received as the act of the whole, and conclude every individual, nothing but the consent of every individual can make any thing to be the act of the whole. But such a consent is next impossible ever to be had." Consequently, when individuals refused to submit to the determination of the majority, government would "signify nothing," and men would then return to the state of nature. Lincoln made precisely the same argument when he noted in his first inaugural address that secessionists necessarily flew to anarchy or despotism. In short, secession would prove to the world that the American experiment in popular government had been a failure, and that democracy simply did not work.[27]

Yet Republicans, unlike northern Democrats, defended the American union as the exemplar of majority rule *circumscribed by the universal rights of man.* Despite Douglas's constant appeals to self-government, popular sovereignty violated that principle by tolerating the indefinite continuation of human slavery. "When the white man governs himself, that is self-government," Lincoln explained, "but when he governs himself and also governs another man, that is more than self-government—that is despotism." Lincoln's election as president, on the other hand, was a legitimate example of majority rule. The prohibition of slavery in the territories was not a violation of southern rights, but rather an affirmation of human rights. As Lincoln would later observe in the Gettysburg Address, the founding fathers had not only created a government of the people, by the people, and for the people, but one "dedicated to the proposition that all men are created equal."[28]

The fate of the Declaration of Independence was clearly on Lincoln's mind as he made his way by train from Springfield to Washington in February 1861. After an exhausting journey, and a seemingly endless succession of expectant crowds, the president-elect found renewed inspiration as he traveled through the scenes of America's revolution. Speaking at the New Jersey state assembly in Trenton, he recounted his boyhood fascination with the "struggles for the liberties of the country" and, in particular, Washington's victory against the Hessians in the winter of 1776. "I recollect thinking then, boy even though I was, that there must have been something more than common that those men struggled for." That something was not national independence alone, he maintained, but rather an "original idea" that "held out a great promise" to all mankind. He then expressed the hope that he could serve as a "humble instrument" in the current struggle to maintain that principle and perpetuate the liberties of the American people.[29]

On February 22, Washington's birthday, Lincoln woke up in Philadelphia's Continental House and prepared for his first visit to Independence Hall. The troubled state of the country had been dramatically confirmed the night before, when Frederick Seward, the son of the incoming secretary of state, had arrived with a letter from his father and General Scott. The letter corroborated the private detective Alan Pinkerton's discovery that southern sympathizers in Baltimore had hatched a well-organized plot to kill the president-elect as he traveled by carriage through the city. Despite the heightened alarm, Lincoln refused to forgo his scheduled engagements. Standing before city officials in the hallowed hall where the Continental Congress had declared America's independence, he expressed his "deep emotion" and determination to maintain the foundation of American liberty. He noted that "all the political sentiments I entertain have been drawn, so far as I have been able to draw them, from the sentiments which originated in and were given to the world from this hall. I have never had a feeling, politically, that did not spring from the sentiments embodied in the Declaration of Independence." As he had done at Trenton, Lincoln then pondered the dangers faced by the Congress and the Continental Army and asked what "great principle or idea" had held the country together for so long. "It was not the mere matter of separation of the colonies from the motherland," as Douglas had argued, "but that sentiment in the Declaration of Independence which gave liberty not alone to the people of this country, but hope to all the world, for all future time." It was a promise "that in due time the weights would be lifted from the shoulders of all men, and that all should have an equal chance. This is the sentiment embodied in the Declaration of Independence."[30]

"Now, my friends," he asked in conclusion, "can this country be saved on that basis? If it can, I will consider myself one of the happiest men in the world if I can help to save it. If it cannot be saved upon that principle, it will be truly awful. But if this country cannot be saved without giving up that principle. . . ." He paused. "I was about to say I would rather be assassinated on this spot than surrender it."[31]

In the century and a half since Lincoln stood in Independence Hall, Americans have struggled to comprehend the reasons why the United States careened into fratricidal conflict. As I have attempted to demonstrate, some Northerners viewed slavery as a threat to the philosophical structure of free society. This threat was inextricably linked to their economic opposition to slavery and to their fear of the Slave Power. Any American, of any race or ethnic background, could fall victim to the argument that they were "inferior," that they would be better off in a state of subjugation, that society would be better off if they were enslaved, or that history and religion justified their enslavement. In short, all the arguments used to justify the exclusion of blacks from the rights of man destroyed the self-evidence of those rights. Having rejected the Declaration's principle that all men are naturally free, Americans could no longer invoke their own humanity as an inviolable defense against tyranny.

As the new president delivered his inaugural address, Douglas sat in the background, holding Lincoln's hat and expressing approval as Lincoln condemned secession as a fatal violation of the democratic process. One can only speculate about what Douglas may have thought as the president gave his views on the conflict's origins. Lincoln argued that the national crisis emanated from the inability to reconcile the South's belief that slavery was right and ought to be extended with the North's belief that slavery was wrong and ought to be restricted. One of the key motivations behind the Republican Party's effort to halt slavery's expansion had been the desire of antislavery Northerners to signify national disapproval of the institution. Indeed, the moral and philosophical implications of the Republican platform were not lost on Southerners. According to the *Richmond Enquirer*, accepting the confinement of slavery to the states where it already existed would be "pregnant with the admission that slavery is wrong, and but for the constitution should be abolished." It would be tantamount to an admission that human beings should not be reduced to bondage, regardless of their perceived "inferiority," their "fitness for liberty," the alleged threat they posed to society, or the historical examples of servitude. Unlike Southerners and northern Democrats, antislavery Northerners understood that these rationales were too arbitrary to be confined to men and women of African descent. The preservation of American freedom would therefore depend on the American people's belief that the liberty of all men was a self-evident truth.[32]

Notes

INTRODUCTION

1. Walter Isaacson, *Benjamin Franklin: An American Life* (New York: Simon & Schuster, 2003), 466–67.

2. Gordon S. Wood, *The Americanization of Benjamin Franklin* (New York: Penguin Books, 2004), 228–29; David Waldstreicher, *Runaway America: Benjamin Franklin, Slavery, and the American Revolution* (New York: Macmillan, 2004), 237–38.

3. "Sidi Mehemet Ibrahim on the Slave Trade," *Philadelphia Federal Gazette,* Mar. 23, 1790.

4. Abraham Lincoln, *The Collected Works of Abraham Lincoln,* vol. 2, Roy P. Basler, ed. (New Brunswick, N.J.: Rutgers Univ. Press, 1953), 222–23.

5. Michael F. Holt, *The Political Crisis of the 1850s* (New York: John Wiley and Sons, 1978); William E. Gienapp, *Origins of the Republican Party, 1852–56* (New York: Oxford Univ. Press, 1987); Avery O. Craven, *The Coming of the Civil War* (New York: Charles Scribner's Sons, 1942); James G. Randall, "The Blundering Generation," *Mississippi Valley Historical Review* 27 (June 1940); John Ashworth, *Slavery, Capitalism, and Politics in the Antebellum Republic,* vol. 2: *The Coming of the Civil War: 1850–1861* (Cambridge, Eng.: Cambridge Univ. Press, 2007), 335.

6. Leon F. Litwack, *North of Slavery: The Negro in the Free States, 1790–1860* (Chicago: Univ. of Chicago Press, 1961); Eugene H. Berwanger, *The Frontier against Slavery: Western Anti-Negro Prejudice and the Slavery Extension Controversy* (Urbana: Univ. of Illinois Press, 1967).

7. Eric Foner, *Free Soil, Free Labor, Free Men: The Ideology of the Republican Party before the Civil War* (New York: Oxford Univ. Press, 1970); James L. Huston, *Calculating the Value of the Union: Slavery, Property Rights, and the Economic Origins of the Civil War* (Chapel Hill: Univ. of North Carolina Press, 2003); David M. Potter, *The Impending Crisis, 1848–1861* (New York: Harper & Row, 1976).

8. Nicole Etcheson, *Bleeding Kansas: Contested Liberty in the Civil War Era* (Lawrence: Univ. Press of Kansas, 2004); Bill Cecil-Fronsman, "Advocate the

Freedom of White Men, as Well as that of Negroes: The *Kansas Free State* and Antislavery Westerners in Territorial Kansas,” *Kansas History: A Journal of the Central Plains* 20 (Summer 1997), 102–15; Leonard L. Richards, *The Slave Power: The Free North and Southern Domination, 1780–1860* (Baton Rouge: Louisiana State Univ. Press, 2000).

9. Michael A. Morrison, *Slavery and the American West: The Eclipse of Manifest Destiny and the Coming of the Civil War* (Chapel Hill: Univ. of North Carolina Press, 1997); Garry Wills, *Lincoln at Gettysburg: The Words That Remade America* (New York: Simon and Schuster, 1992); Major L. Wilson, *Space, Time, and Freedom: The Quest for Nationality and the Irrepressible Conflict, 1815–1861* (Westport, Conn.: Greenwood, 1974); Douglas L. Wilson, *Lincoln before Washington: New Perspectives on the Illinois Years* (Urbana: Univ. of Illinois Press, 1998), 172.

10. Harry V. Jaffa, *Crisis of the House Divided: An Interpretation of the Issues in the Lincoln-Douglas Debates* (Garden City, N.Y.: Doubleday, 1959), 349; David Zarefsky, *Lincoln, Douglas, and Slavery: In the Crucible of Public Debate* (Chicago: Univ. of Chicago Press, 1990), 177; Stephen B. Oates, *With Malice Toward None: A Life of Abraham Lincoln* (New York: Harper & Row, 1977), 159; Allen C. Guelzo, *Abraham Lincoln: Redeemer President* (Grand Rapids, Mich.: William B. Eerdmans Publishing Co., 1999), 193–97.

11. Winthrop D. Jordan, *White Over Black: American Attitudes Toward the Negro, 1550–1812* (Chapel Hill: Univ. of North Carolina Press, 1968).

12. Russel B. Nye, “The Slave Power Conspiracy, 1830–1860,” *Science and Society* 10, no. 3 (Summer 1946): 262–74; Thomas D. Morris, *Southern Slavery and the Law, 1619–1860* (Chapel Hill: Univ. of North Carolina Press, 1996); Lawrence R. Tenzer, *The Forgotten Cause of the Civil War: A New Look at the Slavery Issue* (Manahawkin, N.J.: Scholars’ Publishing House, 1997); William I. Bowditch, *White Slavery in the United States* (New York: American Anti-Slavery Society, 1855), 4–7; *Lawrence* (Kans.) *Herald of Freedom*, Nov. 10, 1855.

13. Carol Wilson and Calvin D. Wilson, “White Slavery: An American Paradox,” *Slavery and Abolition* 19, no. 1 (1998), 1–23; Harriet Beecher Stowe, *The Key to Uncle Tom’s Cabin: Presenting the Original Facts and Documents upon which the Story is Founded, Together with Corroborative Statements Verifying the Truth of the Work* (Boston: John P. Jewett and Co., 1853).

14. *Portage City* (Wisc.) *Record*, Oct. 20, 1858, reprinted June 6, 1860; *Salem* (Ohio) *Anti-Slavery Bugle*, June 2, 1855; James M. Ashley, *Success of the Calhoun Revolution: The Constitution Changed and Slavery Nationalized by the Usurpations of the Supreme Court* (Washington, D.C.: Buell and Blanchard, 1860), 24.

15. Francis G. Couvares et al., *Interpretations of American History: Patterns and Perspectives*, vol. 1: *Through Reconstruction* (New York: The Free Press, 2000), 304; Kenneth M. Stampp, *The Peculiar Institution: Slavery in the Antebellum South* (New York: Alfred A. Knopf, 1972).

16. James Brewer Stewart, *Holy Warriors: The Abolitionists and American Slavery* (New York: Hill and Wang, 1976), 77–78; “The Missouri Question,” *Panoplist and Missionary Herald*, Feb. 1820; Parker quoted in the *Liberator*, June 11, 1858.

17. Trumbull quoted in James A. Rawley, *Bleeding Kansas and the Coming of the Civil War* (New York: J. B. Lippincott Co., 1969), 151.

18. *Marysville* (Ohio) *Tribune,* Sept. 17, 1856; *Coshocton* (Ohio) *Progressive Age,* Aug. 19, 1857; *Portage City* (Wisc.) *Record,* June 17, 1857.

19. *Springfield Journal* quoted in the *Decatur* (Ill.) *State Chronicle,* June 12, 1856.

20. *New York Times,* May 25, 1854.

1. THE MYTH OF THE FREE-STATE DEMOCRAT

1. Charles Robinson to Thomas Wentworth Higginson, Aug. 27, 1855, Thomas W. Higginson Collection, Kansas State Historical Society.

2. *Lecompton* (Kans.) *Union,* Dec. 11, 1856; Drew R. McCoy, *The Elusive Republic: Political Economy in Jeffersonian America* (Chapel Hill: Univ. of North Carolina Press, 1980).

3. Philip S. Foner, *History of the Labor Movement in the United States,* vol. 1: *From Colonial Times to the Founding of the American Federation of Labor* (New York: International Publishers, 1947), 260–61.

4. James A. Rawley, *Race and Politics: Bleeding Kansas and the Coming of the Civil War* (New York: J. B. Lippincott Co., 1969), 26–57.

5. *Congressional Globe,* 32d Cong., 2 Sess., 560.

6. David M. Potter, *The Impending Crisis, 1848–1861* (New York: Harper & Row, 1976), 145–61; Rawley, *Race and Politics,* 26–57.

7. H. M. Flint, *Life of Stephen A. Douglas, His Most Important Speeches and Reports* (New York: Derby & Jackson, 1860), 78; Abraham Lincoln, *The Life and Writings of Abraham Lincoln,* Philip Van Doren Stern, ed. (New York: The Modern Library, 1999), 352.

8. Rawley, *Race and Politics,* 54–55.

9. The most current estimate of the number of people killed in Kansas for political reasons is fifty-six. Dale Watts notes that the 157 violent deaths that occurred in Kansas's territorial period, while hardly insignificant, compare favorably to the 583 who died violently in California in 1855 alone. Dale E. Watts, "How Bloody Was Bleeding Kansas? Political Killings in Kansas Territory, 1854–1861," *Kansas History: A Journal of the Central Plains* 18 (1995), 116–29.

10. Nicole Etcheson, *Bleeding Kansas: Contested Liberty in the Civil War Era* (Lawrence: Univ. Press of Kansas, 2004), 63–64, 91–93.

11. Sara Robinson, *Kansas: Its Interior and Exterior Life* (Boston: Crosby and Nichols, 1857), 69; *Report of the Special Committee Appointed to Investigate the Troubles in Kansas* (Washington, D.C.: Cornelius Wendell, Printer, 1856), 652–57.

12. Lincoln, *Life and Writings,* 348–73.

13. Ibid., 506.

14. Ibid., 374.

15. Ibid., 412–13.

16. Ibid., 375.

17. *Congressional Globe,* 33rd Cong., 1st sess., appendix, 212–21.

18. Lincoln, *Life and Writings,* 375; Samuel W. Parker, *Kansas and Nebraska: The Deed and Its Results* (Washington, D.C.: Congressional Globe Office, 1854), 7.

19. Robert W. Johannsen, *Stephen A. Douglas* (Chicago: Univ. of Illinois Press, 1973), 570.

20. Lincoln, *Life and Writings*, 424.

21. Ibid., 423.

22. Johannsen, *Stephen A. Douglas*, 642–43; David Herbert Donald, *Lincoln* (London: Random House, 1995), 220.

23. Lincoln, *Life and Writings*, 464.

24. Ibid., 504.

25. Ibid., 417.

26. Rawley, *Race and Politics*, 206.

27. Kenneth Stampp, *America in 1857: A Nation on the Brink* (New York: Oxford Univ. Press, 1992), 175.

28. In fairness to Buchanan, Kenneth Stampp argues that the president probably had no idea the Lecompton convention would defy his wishes until late October, when the "swindle" became known. However, his decision to accept it, when he could easily have rejected it, was "one of the most tragic miscalculations any president has ever made." Stampp, *America in 1857*, 281–82; Donald, *Lincoln*, 204.

29. James L. Huston, *Stephen A. Douglas and the Dilemmas of Democratic Equality* (Lanham, Md.: Rowman & Littlefield, 2007), 74; Potter, *Impending Crisis*, 68. Many Northerners disagreed with the "natural limits" argument. The charter of the Massachusetts Emigrant Aid Society observed that Kansas's soil was "well adapted to the staples of Virginia and Kentucky," and especially to hemp production, which flourished along the Missouri River. "Report of the Committee of the Massachusetts Emigrant Aid Society, 1854," Spencer Research Library, Kansas Collection, Univ. of Kansas.

30. *Congressional Globe*, 35th Cong., 1st sess., 4–5; *Fort Scott Democrat*, July 15, 1858.

31. *New York Times*, Apr. 21, 1858; Charles Robinson to Thomas Ewing, Apr. 13, 1858, Historical Constitutions, Kansas State Historical Society, Topeka; Philip Shriver Klein, *President James Buchanan: A Biography* (University Park: Pennsylvania State Univ. Press, 1962), 286–312.

32. Huston, *Stephen A. Douglas*, 77. Rawley also notes Douglas's "insensitivity to antislavery sentiment as a moral force, and his miscalculation of it as a political force." Rawley, *Race and Politics*, 37; *Political Debates Between Hon. Abraham Lincoln and Hon. Stephen A. Douglas in the Celebrated Campaign of 1858 in Illinois* (Columbus, Ohio: Follett, Foster and Co., 1860), 34–35; Johannsen, *Stephen A. Douglas*, 618, 672.

33. Stephen B. Oates, *With Malice Toward None: A Life of Abraham Lincoln* (New York: Harper & Row, 1977), 139.

34. *Journal of the Illinois State Historical Society* 16, no. 2 (1926): 526.

35. Lincoln, *Life and Writings*, 496–97. In 1854 Lincoln had expressed some hope that climate would prevent slavery's expansion into Kansas, but he then noted that five slave states—Missouri, Delaware, Maryland, Kentucky, and Virginia, as well as Washington, D.C.—were north of the Missouri Compromise line. He also saw no reason why slavery would not spill across the western border of Missouri, where the institution was thoroughly entrenched.

36. Ibid., 483.

37. Ibid., 540, 449–50.

2. INFERIORITY

1. Kimberly C. Shankman, *Compromise and the Constitution: The Political Thought of Henry Clay* (New York: Lexington Books, 1999).

2. Abraham Lincoln, *The Complete Works of Abraham Lincoln*, John Nicolay and John Hay, eds. (New York: The Lamb Publishing Co., 1905), 200–201; Abraham Lincoln, *The Life and Writings of Abraham Lincoln*, Philip Van Doren Stern, ed. (New York: The Modern Library, 1999), 451, 455.

3. Russel B. Nye, *Fettered Freedom: Civil Liberties and the Slavery Controversy* (Urbana: Univ. of Illinois Press, 1972), 307; Charles Elliott, *The Sinfulness of American Slavery* (Cincinnati, Ohio: L. Swormstedt and J. H. Power, 1850), 244–45; *New York Times,* June 5, 1860; *National Era,* Mar. 4, 1858.

4. H. M. Flint, *Life of Stephen A. Douglas, His Most Important Speeches and Reports* (New York: Derby & Jackson, 1860), 27–29.

5. Winthrop D. Jordan, "Enslavement of Negroes in America to 1700," in *Colonial America: Essays in Politics and Social Development* (New York: McGraw-Hill, 1993), 261.

6. Gene M. Brack, *Mexico Views Manifest Destiny, 1821–1846: An Essay on the Origins of the Mexican War* (Albuquerque: Univ. of New Mexico Press, 1975), 120.

7. Dale T. Knobel, *Paddy and the Republic: Ethnicity and Nationality in Antebellum America* (Middletown, Conn.: Wesleyan Univ. Press, 1986). Knobel presents Irish stereotypes in much the same way Winthrop Jordan presents black stereotypes—as a "social mirror" through which members of a dominant group could define themselves by contrast. *Salem* (Ohio) *Anti-Slavery Bugle,* Sept. 20, 1856.

8. Eric Foner, *Free Soil, Free Labor, Free Men: The Ideology of the Republican Party before the Civil War* (New York: Oxford Univ. Press, 1970), 231.

9. *Coshocton* (Ohio) *Progressive Age,* Aug. 19, 1857; *Fond Du Lac* (Wisc.) *Daily Herald,* Aug. 20, 1856. These are just a few of the many examples of Republican solicitude for foreign-born voters. Given the large German population, particularly in the Northwest, Republicans could ill afford to antagonize them. (As Eric Foner and William Gienapp observe, German Protestants aroused far less animosity than Irish Catholics.) It is also true that Republicans could not alienate antislavery Know-Nothings. However, I would agree with Foner and Tyler Anbinder's argument that the Know-Nothings' antislavery bona fides were at least as important to northern voters as the party's nativist appeal, and that Republicans were thus able to attract most northern Know-Nothings while making very few concessions to nativist sentiment. Foner, *Free Soil, Free Labor, Free Men,* 258–59; Tyler Anbinder, *Nativism and Slavery: The Northern Know Nothings and the Politics of the 1850s* (New York: Oxford Univ. Press, 1992).

10. *Washington Union* and *National Era,* quoted in the *Columbus Republican Journal,* Feb. 23, 1859; *Monroe* (Wisc.) *Sentinel,* July 18, 1860.

11. James M. Ashley, *Success of the Calhoun Revolution: The Constitution Changed and Slavery Nationalized by the Usurpations of the Supreme Court* (Washington, D.C.: Buell and Blanchard, 1860); Benjamin Stanton, *Negro Equality—The Right of One Man to Hold Property in Another—The Democratic Party a Disunion Party—The Success of the Republican Party the Only Salvation for*

the Country. Speech of Hon. Benjamin Stanton (Washington, D.C.: Buell and Blanchard, 1860), 2.

12. Foner, *Free Soil, Free Labor, Free Men,* 266; C. Vann Woodward, *The Strange Career of Jim Crow* (New York: Oxford Univ. Press, 1955); Leon F. Litwack, *North of Slavery: The Negro in the Free States, 1790–1860* (Chicago: Univ. of Chicago Press, 1961); James A. Rawley, *Race and Politics: Bleeding Kansas and the Coming of the Civil War* (New York: J. B. Lippincott Co., 1969), 66.

13. *Congressional Globe,* 32d Cong., 2d sess., 238–39; Lincoln, *Life and Writings,* 456.

14. "If the strong of the earth are to enslave the weak here," Lovejoy added, "it would justify angels in enslaving men, because they are superior; and archangels in turn would be justified in subjugating those who are inferior in intellect and position, and ultimately it would transform Jehovah into an infinite Juggernaut, rolling the huge wheels of his Omnipotence." Quoted in the *Liberator,* Apr. 26, 1860; *Janesville* (Wisc.) *Daily Gazette,* Apr. 19, 1860; *Elyria* (Ohio) *Independent Democrat,* Apr. 11, 1860; *Racine* (Wisc.) *Daily Journal,* Apr. 18, 1860, and *Berkshire County* (Mass.) *Eagle,* Apr. 12, 1860; James Ford Rhodes, *History of the United States from the Compromise of 1850* (New York: Macmillan, 1913), 436–38.

15. *Canton* (Ohio) *Repository,* Feb. 18, 1857; *Alton* (Ill.) *Weekly Courier,* Aug. 30, 1855.

16. Daniel Webster, *The Papers of Daniel Webster,* Charles M. Wiltse and Harold D. Moser, eds., 14 vols. (Hanover, N.H.: Univ. Press of New England, 1974), 236.

17. *Lawrence* (Kans.) *Herald of Freedom,* Nov. 22, 1856; *Columbus Republican Journal,* Feb. 23, 1859.

18. Russel B. Nye, *Fettered Freedom: Civil Liberties and the Slavery Controversy* (Urbana: Univ. of Illinois Press, 1972), 251; *Marshall* (Mich.) *Statesman,* Oct. 22, 1856; William H. Seward, *The Works of William H. Seward,* George Baker, ed. (Boston: Houghton Mifflin, 1884), 289.

19. *The American Jubilee,* Mar. 1855.

20. William Chambers, *American Slavery and Colour* (London: W. & R. Chambers, 1857), 1–2.

21. *Smethport* (Pa.) *M'Kean Miner,* Sept. 22, 1860.

22. William Henry Fry, *Republican Campaign Text-Book for the Year 1860,* quoted in the *New York Times,* Aug. 15, 1860.

23. George Fitzhugh, *Sociology for the South, or the Failure of Free Society* (Richmond, Va.: A. Morris, 1854), 95; Christopher A. Luse, "Slavery's Champions Stood at Odds: Polygenesis and the Defense of Slavery," *Civil War History* 4, no. 53 (2007): 379–412.

24. *Milwaukee Free Democrat,* quoted in *Portage City* (Wisc.) *Record,* June 17, 1857.

25. Fry, *Republican Campaign Text-Book;* James L. Huston, *Calculating the Value of the Union: Slavery, Property Rights, and the Economic Origins of the Civil War* (Chapel Hill: Univ. of North Carolina Press, 2003).

26. *Milwaukee Free Democrat,* quoted in *Portage City* (Wisc.) *Record,* June 17, 1857.

27. "Considerations for Working Men," *Portage City* (Wisc.) *Record,* Oct. 20, 1858, reprinted June 6, 1860.

3. THE GOOD OF THE SLAVE

1. Thomas R. Bayne to Zoe Adams, Sept. 11, 1895, Kansas State Historical Society.

2. Thomas R. Dew, *Review of the Debate in the Virginia Legislature of 1831 and 1832* (New York: Negro Universities Press, 1968), 288; Kevin C. Julius, *The Abolitionist Decade, 1829–1838: A Year-by-Year History of Early Events in the Antislavery Movement* (New York: McFarland, 2004), 92–93; William J. Cooper Jr. and Thomas E. Terrill, *The American South: A History* (Lanham, Md.: Rowman and Littlefield, 2008), 259–60.

3. Stephen B. Oates, *The Fires of Jubilee: Nat Turner's Fierce Rebellion* (New York: Harper & Row, 1975).

4. Hammond quoted in William W. Freehling, *Prelude to Civil War: The Nullification Controversy in South Carolina, 1816–1836* (New York: Harper & Row, 1965), 299.

5. William Goodell, *Slavery and Anti-Slavery: A History of the Great Struggle in Both Hemispheres* (New York: William Goodell, 1853).

6. *Richmond Enquirer,* Dec. 15, 1855.

7. William E. Gienapp, *Origins of the Republican Party, 1852–56* (New York: Oxford Univ. Press, 1987), 265–66; "Philadelphia National Convention, Circular of the National Committee, Appointed at Pittsburg, February 22, 1856," reprinted in the *New York Times,* Apr. 12, 1856.

8. "Modern 'Democracy,' the Ally of Slavery, Speech of Hon. M. W. Tappan, of New Hampshire, in the House of Representatives, July 29, 1856," *Republican Campaign Documents of 1856: A Collection of the Most Important Speeches and Documents Issued by the Republican Association of Washington, During the Presidential Campaign of 1856* (Washington, D.C.: Lewis Clephane, 1857), 14; "Politics of the Country, Speech of Hon. I. Washburn, Jr., of Maine, In the House of Representatives, June 21, 1856," *Republican Campaign Documents of 1856,* 8; "The Democratic Party as It Was and as It Is!, Speech of Hon. Timothy C. Day, of Ohio, in the House of Representatives, Apr. 23, 1856," *Republican Campaign Documents of 1856,* 7; *Speech of Hon. John M. Read, on the Power of Congress Over the Territories; and in Favor of Free Kansas, Free White Labor, and of Fremont and Dayton, at the Eighth Ward Mass Meeting, Held in the Assembly Buildings, on Tuesday Evening, September 30, 1856* (Philadelphia: s.n., 1856), 15; *Decatur* (Ill.) *State Chronicle,* Aug. 14, 1856.

9. Carl R. Osthaus, *Partisans of the Southern Press: Editorial Spokesmen of the Nineteenth Century* (Lexington: Univ. Press of Kentucky, 1994), 12; Abraham Lincoln, *The Life and Writings of Abraham Lincoln,* Philip Van Doren Stern, ed. (New York: The Modern Library, 1999), 404–5, 413.

10. *Richland County* (Wisc.) *Observer,* Oct. 21, 1856; *Canton* (Ohio) *Repository,* Sept. 24, 1856; *Whitewater* (Wisc.) *Register,* Mar. 20, 1858.

11. *Charleston Standard,* quoted in *Marysville* (Ohio) *Tribune,* Sept. 17, 1856; *Muscogee Herald,* quoted in *Alton* (Ill.) *Weekly Courier,* Sept. 29, 1856; *Southside Democrat,* quoted in *Elyria* (Ohio) *Independent Democrat,* Oct. 22, 1856; Solo-

mon W. Downs quoted in *Canton* (Ohio) *Repository*, Sept. 24, 1856; *Richmond Enquirer*, quoted in *Alton* (Ill.) *Weekly Courier*, Sept. 29, 1856; *Manitowoc* (Wisc.) *Tribune*, Oct. 2, 1856.

12. Harvey Wish, *George Fitzhugh: Propagandist of the Old South* (Baton Rouge: Louisiana State Univ. Press, 1943).

13. Fitzhugh later included the entire text of *Slavery Justified* as an appendix to *Sociology for the South*.

14. George Fitzhugh, *Sociology for the South, or the Failure of Free Society* (New York: Burt Franklin, 1854), 241; George Fitzhugh, *Cannibals All! or Slaves without Masters*, C. Vann Woodward, ed. (Cambridge: Harvard Univ. Press, 1960), 18.

15. Fitzhugh, *Cannibals All!*, 21.

16. Fitzhugh, *Sociology*, 34, 51, 229; Patrick Allitt, *The Conservatives: Ideas and Personalities throughout American History* (New Haven, Conn.: Yale Univ. Press, 2009), 42.

17. Merrill D. Peterson, *The Jefferson Image in the American Mind* (New York: Oxford Univ. Press, 1960), 169–70.

18. Fitzhugh, *Sociology*, 246; *Cannibals All!*, 18.

19. Fitzhugh, *Cannibals All!*, 18.

20. William H. Herndon, *The Hidden Lincoln: From the Letters and Papers of William H. Herndon*, Emanuel Hertz, ed. (New York: The Viking Press, 1938), 96; *Springfield Daily Illinois State Journal*, Apr. 10, 1856; *Republican Campaign Documents of 1856*, 2; Although Fitzhugh rarely ventured away from home, in the spring of 1855 he accepted an invitation to debate Wendell Phillips in New Haven, Connecticut. While there, he also visited his distant kinsman Gerrit Smith. As always, the Virginian was attentive and amiable, but saw nothing that significantly changed his opinion of free society.

21. On rare occasions, Fitzhugh's editorials were signed "G. F." or "F." However, the majority were anonymous; Wish, *George Fitzhugh*, 78, 144.

22. Eugene D. Genovese, *The World the Slaveholders Made: Two Essays in Interpretation* (Middletown, Conn.: Wesleyan Univ. Press, 1969), 129; Albert J. Beveridge, *Abraham Lincoln, 1809–1858* (New York: Houghton Mifflin, 1928), 31; Robert J. Loewenberg, "John Locke and the Antebellum Defense of Slavery," *Political Theory* 13 (May 1985): 281; Robert Johannsen, *Lincoln the South and Slavery: The Political Dimension* (Baton Rouge: Louisiana State Univ. Press, 1991), 79.

23. *Congressional Globe*, 36th Cong., 1st sess., Jan. 3, 1860; Lawrence R. Tenzer, *The Forgotten Cause of the Civil War: A New Look at the Slavery Issue* (Manahawkin, N.J.: Scholars' Publishing House, 1997), 216–17; Genovese, *World the Slaveholders Made*, 135; Wish, *George Fitzhugh*, 126.

24. Allan Nevins, *Ordeal of the Union*, 2 vols. (New York: Charles Scribner's Sons, 1947), 1, 515; Eric McKitrick, *Slavery Defended: The View of the Old South* (Englewood Cliffs, N.J.: Prentice Hall, 1963), 58–67.

25. Wish, *George Fitzhugh*, 171; John Ashworth, *Slavery, Capitalism, and Politics in the Antebellum Republic*, vol. 1: *Commerce and Compromise, 1820–1850* (New York: Cambridge Univ. Press, 1995), 235, 237.

26. *Richmond Enquirer*, May 5, 1856.

27. Fitzhugh, *Cannibals All!*, 201, 220.

28. Hogeboom also arranged for the publication of the correspondence in a forty-page pamphlet, *George Fitzhugh and A. Hogeboom, A Controversy on Slavery, Between George Fitzhugh, Esq., of Virginia, Author of "Sociology for the South," etc., and A. Hogeboom, Esq., of New York* (Oneida, N.Y.: Oneida Sachem Office, 1857).

29. *Richmond Enquirer*, Sept. 19, 1856.

30. Wish, *George Fitzhugh*, 151.

31. Pickens quoted in James M. Ashley, *Success of the Calhoun Revolution: The Constitution Changed and Slavery Nationalized by the Usurpations of the Supreme Court* (Washington, D.C.: Buell and Blanchard, 1860), 23.

32. George Washington Van Vleck, *The Panic of 1857: An Analytical Study* (New York: Columbia Univ. Press, 1943), 88.

33. James L. Huston, *The Panic of 1857 and the Coming of the Civil War* (Baton Rouge: Louisiana State Univ. Press, 1987), 125–27.

34. Drew Gilpin Faust, *James Henry Hammond and the Old South: A Design for Mastery* (Baton Rouge: Louisiana State Univ. Press, 1982), 246.

35. Huston, *Panic of 1857*, 127; *Atchison* (Kans.) *Freedom's Champion*, Apr. 3, 1858; *Congressional Globe*, 35th Cong., 1st sess., May 24, 1858, appendix, 399.

36. Charles Sumner, *The Works of Charles Sumner*, vol. 5 (Boston: Lee and Shepard, 1872), 11; Wish, *George Fitzhugh*, 285.

37. *Cedar Falls* (Iowa) *Gazette*, Nov. 2, 1860.

4. THE GOOD OF SOCIETY

1. Eugene D. Genovese, *The World the Slaveholders Made: Two Essays in Interpretation* (Middletown, Conn.: Wesleyan Univ. Press, 1969), 129.

2. Kenneth M. Stampp, *The Peculiar Institution: Slavery in the Ante-Bellum South* (New York: Alfred A. Knopf, 1956), 29–31.

3. Steven A. Channing, *Crisis of Fear: Secession in South Carolina* (New York: Simon and Schuster, 1970).

4. George M. Fredrickson, *The Black Image in the White Mind: The Debate on Afro-American Character and Destiny, 1817–1914* (New York: Harper & Row, 1971); James Oakes, *The Ruling Race: A History of American Slaveholders* (New York: Alfred A. Knopf, 1982), 139–40. Oakes also maintains that slaveholders put a premium on upward mobility in much the same way Northerners did: "Except for its defense of bondage, the slaveholders' ideology was strikingly similar to the Republican ideology of the 1850s."

5. Brown quoted in Michael A. Morrison, *Slavery and the American West: The Eclipse of Manifest Destiny and the Coming of the Civil War* (Chapel Hill: Univ. of North Carolina Press, 1997), 175.

6. John C. Calhoun, *The Works of John C. Calhoun*, Richard K. Cralle, ed., 6 vols. (New York: D. Appleton, 1854–1857).

7. *Richmond Enquirer*, July 8, 1856; Bill Cecil-Fronsman, "Advocate the Freedom of White Men, as Well as that of Negroes: The *Kansas Free State* and

Antislavery Westerners in Territorial Kansas," *Kansas History: A Journal of the Central Plains* 20, no. 2 (Summer 1997): 102–15; *Atchison* (Kans.) *Squatter Sovereign,* Feb. 20, 1855.

8. William L. Barney, *The Secessionist Impulse: Alabama and Mississippi in 1860* (Princeton, N.J.: Princeton Univ. Press, 1974), 187; J. Mills Thornton III, *Politics and Power in a Slave Society: Alabama, 1800–1860* (Baton Rouge: Louisiana State Univ. Press, 1978).

9. Stephens quoted in Frank Moore, ed., *The Rebellion Record: A Diary of American Events,* 11 vols. (New York: G. P. Putnam, 1861–1865), 44–49.

10. U.S. Department of the Interior, *Eighth Census,* vol. 1: *Population of the United States in 1860* (Washington, D.C.: Government Printing Office, 1864).

11. Thomas Jefferson, *Notes on the State of Virginia* (New York: Harper & Row, 1964), 157.

12. Robert Middlekauff, *The Glorious Cause: The American Revolution, 1763–1789* (New York: Oxford Univ. Press, 1982), 644–45.

13. Edmund S. Morgan, *American Slavery, American Freedom: The Ordeal of Colonial Virginia* (New York: W. W. Norton, 1975), 382–83.

14. Ibid., 324–25.

15. George Fitzhugh, *Cannibals All! or Slaves without Masters,* C. Vann Woodward, ed. (Cambridge, Mass.: Harvard Univ. Press, 1960), 135.

16. Paul M. Angle, ed., *Created Equal? The Complete Lincoln-Douglas Debates of 1858* (Chicago: Univ. of Chicago Press, 1958), 17.

17. McDuffie quoted in Charles Elliott, *Sinfulness of American Slavery* (Cincinnati, Ohio: L. Swormstedt & J. H. Power, 1850), 83–84; *Marysville* (Ohio) *Tribune,* Sept. 1, 1858.

18. *Cedar Falls* (Iowa) *Gazette,* Nov. 2, 1860; Hammond quoted in *Whitewater* (Wisc.) *Register,* Mar. 20, 1858.

19. Don Jordan and Michael Walsh, *White Cargo: The Forgotten History of Britain's White Slaves in America* (New York: New York Univ. Press, 2008), 12–16.

20. James L. Huston, *Stephen A. Douglas and the Dilemmas of Democratic Equality* (Lanham, Md.: Rowman & Littlefield, 2007), 88.

21. "Philadelphia National Convention, Circular of the National Committee, Appointed at Pittsburg, February 22, 1856," reprinted in the *New York Times,* Apr. 12, 1856.

22. *Portland Weekly Oregonian,* Aug. 25, 1860.

23. Iveson L. Brookes, *A Defense of the South Against the Reproaches and Encroachments of the North: In Which Slavery Is Shown to Be an Institution of God Intended to Form the Basis of the Best Social State and the Only Safeguard to the Permanence of a Republican Government* (Hamburg, S.C.: Republican Printing Office, 1850).

24. Thomas R. Dew, *Review of the Debate in the Virginia Legislature of 1831 and 1832* (New York: Negro Universities Press, 1968), 288; William Gilmore Simms, *Southern and Western Magazine and Review* (Charleston, S.C.: Burges & James, 1845), 6.

25. Hunter quoted in David Donald, *Charles Sumner and the Coming of the Civil War* (New York: Alfred A. Knopf, 1960), 349.

26. George Fitzhugh, "Origin of Civilization—What Is Property?—Which Is the Best Slave Race?" *De Bow's Review* 25 (Dec. 1858): 662–63.

27. *Congressional Globe*, 36th Cong., 1st sess., Feb. 29, 1860; *Washington* (D.C.) *National Era*, Apr. 6, 1854; ibid., Mar. 15, 1860.

28. David Brion Davis, *Inhuman Bondage: The Rise and Fall of Slavery in the New World* (New York: Oxford Univ. Press, 2006), 64.

29. Winthrop D. Jordan, *White Over Black: American Attitudes Toward the Negro, 1550–1812* (Chapel Hill: Univ. of North Carolina Press, 1968), 19; George Fredrickson, *Racism: A Short History* (Princeton, N.J.: Princeton Univ. Press, 2002), 45.

30. Sumner quoted in the *New York Times*, June 5, 1860.

31. Charles Sumner, *White Slavery in the Barbary States* (Boston: John P. Jewett and Co., 1853), 12–13.

32. J. P. Blanchard, *Principles of the Revolution: Showing the Perversion of Them and the Consequent Failure of Their Accomplishment* (Boston: Damrell and Moore, 1855), 10.

5. THE SLAVEOCRACY

1. William Jay, *Miscellaneous Writings on Slavery* (Boston: Damrell & Moore, 1853), 497; *Congressional Globe*, 33d Cong., 1st sess., May 17, 1854; William Lloyd Garrison, *The Letters of William Lloyd Garrison: From Disunionism to the Brink of War, 1850–1860*, Louis Ruchames, ed. (Cambridge, Mass.: Harvard Univ. Press, 1976), 130; Moses M. Davis to John F. Potter, Oct. 25, 1857, Potter Papers.

2. Henry Wilson, *History of the Rise and Fall of the Slave Power in America* (Boston: James R. Osgood and Co., 1875), 165; Russel B. Nye, *Fettered Freedom: Civil Liberties and the Slavery Controversy* (Urbana: Univ. of Illinois Press, 1972), 223–49; William E. Gienapp, *Origins of the Republican Party, 1852–56* (New York: Oxford Univ. Press, 1987), 365.

3. Leonard L. Richards, *The Slave Power: The Free North and Southern Domination, 1780–1860* (Baton Rouge: Louisiana State Univ. Press, 2000).

4. Don E. Fehrenbacher, *The Slaveholding Republic: An Account of the United States Government's Relation to Slavery,* completed and edited by Ward M. McAfee (New York: Oxford Univ. Press, 2001), 31; James L. Huston, *Calculating the Value of the Union: Slavery, Property Rights, and the Economic Origins of the Civil War* (Chapel Hill: Univ. of North Carolina Press, 2003), 20; Richards, *Slave Power,* 35–36.

5. William H. Seward, *The Works of William H. Seward,* George E. Baker, ed. (Boston: Houghton, Mifflin, 1887), 456; Abraham Lincoln, *The Life and Writings of Abraham Lincoln,* Philip Van Doren Stern, ed. (New York: The Modern Library, 1999), 366–67; Jay, *Miscellaneous Writings,* 421.

6. *Leavenworth* (Kans.) *Times*, Dec. 6, 1859.

7. James Henry Hammond, *Remarks of Mr. Hammond of South Carolina on the Question of Receiving Petitions for the Abolition of Slavery in the District of Columbia* (Washington, D.C.: Duff Green, 1836), 15–16; Marion Mills Miller, ed.,

Great Debates in American History: From the Debates in the British Parliament on the Colonial Stamp Act (1764–1765) to the Debates in Congress at the Close of the Taft Administration (1912–1913), vol. 4. (New York: Current Literature Publishing Company, 1913), 331.

8. John Rankin, *Letters on American Slavery, Addressed to Mr. Thomas Rankin* (Boston: Isaac Knapp, 1838), 68–71; *New York Times,* July 20, 1855; *Lawrence* (Kans.) *Free State,* Apr. 7, 1855.

9. Washington Irving, *The Life of George Washington* (New York: G. P. Putnam's Sons, 1876), 565; John Adams, *Novanglus and Massachusettensis: Political Essays, Published in the Years 1774 and 1775* (Bedford, Mass.: Applewood Books, 2009), 25; *New York Journal,* Oct. 25, 1787.

10. *New York Times,* May 24, 1856; *New York Evening Post,* May 23, 1856.

11. *Cincinnati Gazette,* May 24, 1856; Miller, *Great Debates in American History,* 327.

12. Benjamin Franklin, *The Works of Benjamin Franklin* (London: B. F. Stevens, 1882), 316; Lincoln, *Life and Writings,* 530.

13. Miller, *Great Debates in American History,* 49; Eric Foner, *Free Soil, Free Labor, Free Men: The Ideology of the Republican Party before the Civil War* (New York: Oxford Univ. Press, 1970), 40–72; James L. Huston, "The American Revolutionaries, the Political Economy of Aristocracy, and the American Concept of the Distribution of Wealth, 1765–1900," *American Historical Review* 98 (Oct. 1993), 1079–1105; Henry Ward Beecher, *Defense of Kansas* (Washington, D.C.: Buell and Blanchard, 1856).

14. *Atlantic Monthly,* vol. 9 (Boston: Ticknor and Fields, 1862), 31; John S. C. Abbott, *The History of the Civil War in America* (New York: Henry Bill, 1863), 24.

15. Lincoln, *Life and Writings,* 423.

16. *New York Tribune,* Apr. 7, 1856; *Fort Wayne Daily Times,* May 31, 1856; *Alton* (Ill.) *Weekly Courier,* July 7, 1857.

17. Lincoln, *Life and Writings,* 423; *Springfield* (Ill.) *State Chronicle,* Apr. 10, 1856; Gienapp, *Origins of the Republican Party,* 365.

18. *Springfield* (Ill.) *State Chronicle,* Apr. 10, 1856.

6. SOUTHERNERS AND THE PRINCIPLE OF UNIVERSAL LIBERTY

1. *Speech of William H. Seward, at the Dedication of Capital University, Columbus, Ohio, September 14, 1853* (Auburn, N.Y.: Knapp and Peck, Printers, 1853), 8.

2. Thomas Jefferson, *Notes on the State of Virginia* (Richmond: J. W. Randolph, 1853), 174–75.

3. Charles Sumner, *Recent Speeches and Addresses* (Boston: Ticknor and Fields, 1856), 366, 488.

4. *Journals of the Continental Congress, 1774–1789,* vol. 5 (Washington, D.C.: Government Printing Office, 1906), 498; Don E. Fehrenbacher, *The Slaveholding Republic: An Account of the United States Government's Relation to Slavery,* completed and edited by Ward M. McAfee (New York: Oxford Univ. Press, 2001), 17.

5. Jefferson, *Notes on the State of Virginia,* 175; Abraham Lincoln, *The Life and Writings of Abraham Lincoln,* Philip Van Doren Stern, ed. (New York: The Modern Library, 1999), 450.

6. Gordon S. Wood, *Revolutionary Characters: What Made the Founders Different* (New York: Penguin Group, 2006), 101.

7. Fred Shelly, ed., "Ebenezer Hazard's Travels through Maryland in 1777," *Maryland Historical Magazine* 44 (1951): 50.

8. William W. Freehling, *Prelude to Civil War: The Nullification Controversy in South Carolina, 1816–1836* (New York: Oxford Univ. Press, 1965), 52; Robert Pierce Forbes, *The Missouri Compromise and Its Aftermath: Slavery and the Meaning of America* (Chapel Hill: Univ. of North Carolina Press, 2007), 145; John C. Calhoun, *The Works of John C. Calhoun,* vol. 4 (New York: D. Appleton and Co., 1888), 507–8.

9. Lincoln, *Life and Writings,* 395.

10. *Methodist Quarterly Review,* Apr. 1857.

11. *Washington* (D.C.) *National Era,* Jan. 24, 1856; Marion Mills Miller, ed., *Great Debates in American History: From the Debates in the British Parliament on the Colonial Stamp Act (1764–1765) to the Debates in Congress at the Close of the Taft Administration (1912–1913),* vol. 4 (New York: Current Literature Publishing Company, 1913), 152; *Ottawa* (Ill.) *Free Trader,* July 7, 1860.

12. Henry Wilson, *Territorial Slave Code, Speech of Hon. Henry Wilson of Massachusetts* (Washington, D.C.: Scammel & Co., 1860), 2; Frederick Douglass, *The Frederick Douglass Papers: 1855–63,* John W. Blassingame, ed. (New Haven, Conn.: Yale Univ. Press, 1979), 224.

13. Daniel John McInerney, *The Fortunate Heirs of Freedom: Abolition and Republican Thought* (Lincoln: Univ. of Nebraska Press, 1994), 34; Lincoln, *Life and Writings,* 390.

14. Nicole Etcheson, *Bleeding Kansas: Contested Liberty in the Civil War Era* (Lawrence: Univ. Press of Kansas, 2004), 35–36; Lincoln, *Life and Writings,* 375.

15. *The Pro-Slavery Argument; As Maintained by the Most Distinguished Writers of the Southern States, Containing the Several Essays, on the Subject, of Chancellor Harper, Governor Hammond, Dr. Simms, and Professor Dew* (Charleston, S.C.: Walker, Richards, and Co., 1852), 251; *New York Evening Post,* quoted in the *Wellsborough* (Pa.) *Agitator,* Oct. 30, 1856.

16. Bray Hammond, *Sovereignty and an Empty Purse: Banks and Politics in the Civil War* (Princeton, N.J.: Princeton Univ. Press, 1970), 23; Stephen Mihm, *A Nation of Counterfeiters: Capitalists, Con Men, and the Making of the United States* (Cambridge, Mass.: Harvard Univ. Press, 2007).

17. James L. Huston, *Calculating the Value of the Union: Slavery, Property Rights, and the Economic Origins of the Civil War* (Chapel Hill: Univ. of North Carolina Press, 2003).

18. Eric P. Newman, *Early Paper Money of America* (Iola, Wisc.: Krause Publications, 1990), 119–22, 419.

19. Darragh Johnson, "Researcher's Work Restores Forgotten Man's Story," *Washington Post,* Feb. 15, 2007, p. DZ01.

20. Yvonne Korshak, "The Liberty Cap as a Revolutionary Symbol in America and France," *Smithsonian Studies in American Art* 1, no. 2 (Autumn 1987): 52–69.

21. Robert L. Gale, *Thomas Crawford: American Sculptor* (Pittsburgh, Pa.: Univ. of Pittsburgh Press, 1964), 124.

22. Don E. Fehrenbacher, *The Dred Scott Case: Its Significance in American Law and Politics* (New York: Oxford Univ. Press, 1978).

23. Earl M. Maltz, *Dred Scott and the Politics of Slavery* (Lawrence: Univ. Press of Kansas, 2007), 69.

24. *A Report of the Decision of the Supreme Court of the United States, and the Opinions of the Judges thereof, in the Case of Dred Scott versus John F. A. Sanford* (New York: D. Appleton and Co., 1857), 407.

25. Ibid., 410; Lincoln, *Life and Writings*, 421. The disenfranchisement of blacks was more extensive than Lincoln suggested. Delaware restricted the franchise to whites in 1792, as did Kentucky in 1799, Maryland in 1801, New Jersey in 1807, Connecticut in 1814, Rhode Island in 1822, Tennessee in 1834, North Carolina in 1835, and Pennsylvania in 1838. By the eve of the Civil War, blacks could only vote in Massachusetts, New Hampshire, Vermont, Maine, and (if they owned sufficient property) New York.

26. *Dred Scott v. Sanford*, 410.

27. Ibid., 574–75.

28. David M. Potter, *The Impending Crisis, 1848–1861* (New York: Harper & Row, 1976), 284.

29. *New York Tribune*, Mar. 25, 1857; *Washington Union*, Mar. 28, 1857.

30. Lorman A. Ratner and Dwight L. Teeter, *Fanatics and Fire-Eaters: Newspapers and the Coming of the Civil War* (Chicago: Univ. of Illinois Press, 2003), 54; *Albany Evening Journal*, Mar. 9, 1857.

31. *New Englander*, Aug. 1857.

7. REPUBLICANS, NORTHERN DEMOCRATS, AND THE PRINCIPLE OF UNIVERSAL LIBERTY

1. *New York Tribune*, Feb. 1, 1857.

2. Abraham Lincoln, *The Life and Writings of Abraham Lincoln*, Philip Van Doren Stern, ed. (New York: The Modern Library, 1999), 375; Daniel Walker Howe, *The Political Culture of the American Whigs* (Chicago: Univ. of Chicago Press, 1984), 367; Charles Francis Adams, *An Oration, Delivered Before the Municipal Authorities of the City of Fall River, July 4, 1860* (Boston: Almy & Milne, Daily News Steam Printing House, 1860), 15.

3. *New York Evangelist*, Mar. 2, 1854; *Frederick Douglass Papers*, Mar. 3, 1854.

4. Marion Mills Miller, ed., *Great Debates in American History: Slavery from 1790 to 1857* (New York: Current Literature Publishing Company, 1913), 332; Stephen A. Douglas, "The Dividing Line Between Federal and Local Authority: Popular Sovereignty in the Territories," *Harper's Magazine* XIX (1859): 521–26; Harry V. Jaffa, *A New Birth of Freedom: Abraham Lincoln and the Coming of the Civil War* (Lanham, Md.: Rowman & Littlefield, 2000), 481.

5. Robert W. Johannsen, *Stephen A. Douglas* (Chicago: Univ. of Illinois Press, 1973), 709–10; *Proceedings of the Pennsylvania Democratic State Convention:*

Held at Harrisburg, March 4th, 1856 (Philadelphia, Pa.: Wm. Rice, Pennsylvanian Office, Printer, 1856), 21.

6. Stephen A. Douglas, *Speeches of Senator S. A. Douglas, on the Occasion of His Public Receptions by the Citizens of New Orleans, Philadelphia, and Baltimore* (Washington, D.C.: Lemuel Towers, 1859), 5; *Political Debates Between Hon. Abraham Lincoln and Hon. Stephen A. Douglas, in the Celebrated Campaign of 1858, in Illinois; Including the Preceding Speeches of Each at Chicago, Springfield, etc.; Also the Two Great Speeches of Mr. Lincoln in Ohio, in 1859* (Columbus, Ohio: Follett, Foster and Co., 1860), 176.

7. *All the Republican National Conventions from Philadelphia, June 17, 1856: Proceedings, Platforms, and Candidates,* Henry Harrison Smith, ed. (Washington, D.C.: Robert Beall, 1896), 12; *Brooklyn Daily Eagle,* Jan. 31, 1854; Dec. 29, 1858; Oct. 13, 1860.

8. Pauline Maier, *American Scripture: Making the Declaration of Independence* (New York: Alfred A. Knopf, 1997); Miller, *Great Debates in American History,* 296.

9. John G. Nicolay and John Hay, eds., *The Complete Works of Abraham Lincoln,* vol. 4 (New York: Francis D. Tandy Co., 1894), 263.

10. Ibid., 374–75.

11. Henry Wilson, *Territorial Slave Code: Speech of Hon. Henry Wilson of Massachusetts.* (Washington, D.C.: Scammel & Co., 1860), 4.

12. Robert B. Warden, *An Account of the Private Life and Public Services of Salmon Portland Chase* (Cincinnati, Ohio: Wilstach, Baldwin and Co., 1874), 21; Daniel John McInerney, *The Fortunate Heirs of Freedom: Abolition and Republican Thought* (Lincoln: Univ. of Nebraska Press, 1994), 54.

13. *Brooklyn Daily Eagle,* May 10, 1856.

14. Philip F. Detweiler, "The Changing Reputation of the Declaration of Independence: The First Fifty Years," *William and Mary Quarterly* 19, no. 4 (Oct. 1962): 557–74.

15. (Philadelphia) *Dunlap's American Daily Advertiser,* July 7, 1792; John Marshall, *The Life of George Washington,* vol. 2 (Philadelphia, Pa.: C. P. Wayne, 1807), 377.

16. Mercy Otis Warren, *History of the Rise, Progress, and Termination of the American Revolution* (Boston: Manning and Loring, 1805).

17. *North American Review* XVI (1823): 195.

18. Lincoln, *Life and Writings,* 513–14.

19. *Annals of Congress,* 15th Cong., 2d sess., 1211 (Feb. 16, 1819); Robert Pierce Forbes, *The Missouri Compromise and Its Aftermath: Slavery and the Meaning of America* (Chapel Hill: Univ. of North Carolina Press, 2007), 37–45.

20. *Annals of Congress,* 16th Cong., 1st sess., 405; *Register of Debates,* 19th Cong., 1st sess., 125–27 (Mar. 2, 1826).

21. *Annals of Congress,* 16th Cong., 1st sess., 325–26 (Feb. 1, 1820), 1154–55 (Feb. 7, 1820), 1383–84 (Feb. 17, 1820), 350 (Feb. 1, 1820).

22. Lincoln, *Life and Writings,* 424–25; *Monroe* (Wisc.) *Sentinel,* July 18, 1860.

23. *Mauston* (Wisc.) *Star,* Sept. 5, 1860.

24. Eric Foner, *Free Soil, Free Labor, Free Men: The Ideology of the Republican Party before the Civil War* (New York: Oxford Univ. Press, 1970), 132; Carl Schurz,

Report of the George William Curtis Memorial Committee (New York: The Chronicle Press, 1905), 12–13.

25. *Charleston Mercury,* Nov. 8, 1860; Frank Moore, ed., *The Rebellion Record,* vol. 1 (New York: D. Van Nostrand, 1861), 254; Jefferson Davis, *The Rise and Fall of the Confederate Government* (New York: D. Appleton and Co., 1881), 232.

26. *New York Tribune,* May 21, 1862; *New York National Anti-Slavery Standard,* Dec. 1, 1860.

27. Allen C. Guelzo, *Abraham Lincoln as a Man of Ideas* (Carbondale: Southern Illinois Univ. Press, 2009), 83–84; John Locke, *Two Treatises of Government* [1690], Peter Laslett, ed. (Cambridge, Eng.: Cambridge Univ. Press, 1988), 332–33.

28. Lincoln, *Life and Writings,* 362.

29. Harold Holzer, *Lincoln President-Elect: Abraham Lincoln and the Great Secession Winter, 1860–1861* (New York: Simon and Schuster, 2008), 372–73.

30. Lincoln, *Life and Writings,* 644–45.

31. Ibid.

32. *Richmond Enquirer,* June 16, 1856.

Bibliography

PRIMARY SOURCES

NEWSPAPERS
Albany Evening Journal
Alton (Ill.) *Weekly Courier*
Atchison (Kans.) *Freedom's Champion*
Atchison (Kans.) *Squatter Sovereign*
Berkshire County (Mass.) *Eagle*
Boston Liberator
Brooklyn Daily Eagle
Canton (Ohio) *Repository*
Cedar Falls (Iowa) *Gazette*
Charleston Mercury
Cincinnati Gazette
Columbus Republican Journal
Coshocton (Ohio) *Progressive Age*
Decatur (Ill.) *State Chronicle*
Elyria (Ohio) *Independent Democrat*
Fond Du Lac (Wisc.) *Daily Herald*
Fort Wayne Daily Times
Janesville (Wisc.) *Daily Gazette*
Lawrence (Kans.) *Free State*
Lawrence (Kans.) *Herald of Freedom*
Leavenworth (Kans.) *Times*
Lecompton (Kans.) *Union*
Manitowoc (Wisc.) *Tribune*
Marshall (Mich.) *Statesman*
Mauston (Wisc.) *Star*
Milwaukee Free Democrat
Monroe (Wisc.) *Sentinel*

New York Evangelist
New York Evening Post
New York Journal
New York National Anti-Slavery Standard
New York Times
New York Tribune
Ottawa (Ill.) *Free Trader*
Philadelphia Federal Gazette
Portage City (Wisc.) *Record*
Portland Weekly Oregonian
Racine (Wisc.) *Daily Journal*
Richland County (Wisc.) *Observer*
Richmond Enquirer
Rochester (N.Y.) *Frederick Douglass' Paper*
Salem (Ohio) *Anti-Slavery Bugle*
Smethport (Pa.) *M'Kean Miner*
Springfield Daily Illinois State Journal
Washington (D.C.) *National Era*
Washington (D.C.) *Union*
Wellsborough (Pa.) *Agitator*
Whitewater (Wisc.) *Register*

PERIODICALS
Atlantic Monthly
De Bow's Review
Dunlap's American Daily Advertiser
Harper's Monthly Magazine
Methodist Quarterly Review
New Englander
North American Review

GOVERNMENT PUBLICATIONS
Annals of Congress
Congressional Globe
Journals of the Continental Congress, 1774–1789. 5 vols. Washington, D.C.: Government Printing Office, 1906.
Report of the Decision of the Supreme Court of the United States, and the Opinions of the Judges thereof, in the Case of Dred Scott versus John F. A. Sanford. New York: D. Appleton and Co., 1857.
Report of the Special Committee Appointed to Investigate the Troubles in Kansas. Washington, D.C.: Cornelius Wendell, Printer, 1856.
U.S. Department of the Interior. *Eighth Census,* Vol. 1: *Population of the United States in 1860.* Washington, D.C.: Government Printing Office, 1864.

MANUSCRIPT COLLECTIONS

Civil War Collection. Missouri Historical Society, St. Louis.

Governor's Office Files. Administration of Charles A. Robinson. Kansas State Historical Society, Topeka.

Kansas Civil War Collection. Kansas State Historical Society, Topeka.

Potter, John F. Papers. State Historical Society of Wisconsin, Madison.

Robinson, Charles, and Sara T. D. Papers. Kansas State Historical Society, Topeka.

PUBLISHED WORKS

Abbott, John S. C. *The History of the Civil War in America*. 2 vols. Springfield, Mass.: Gurdon Bill, 1863–66.

Adams, Charles Francis. *An Oration, Delivered Before the Municipal Authorities of the City of Fall River, July 4, 1860*. Fall River, Mass.: Almy & Milne, Daily News Steam Printing House, 1860.

Appeal of the Independent Democrats in Congress to the People of the United States: Shall Slavery Be Permitted in Nebraska? Washington, D.C.: n.p., 1854.

Ashley, James M. *Success of the Calhoun Revolution: The Constitution Changed and Slavery Nationalized by the Usurpations of the Supreme Court*. Washington, D.C.: Buell and Blanchard, 1860.

Beecher, Henry Ward. *Defense of Kansas*. Washington, D.C.: Buell and Blanchard, 1856.

Blanchard, J. P. *Principles of the Revolution: Showing the Perversion of Them and the Consequent Failure of Their Accomplishment*. Boston: Damrell and Moore, 1855.

Bowditch, William I. *White Slavery in the United States*. New York: American Anti-Slavery Society, 1855.

Chambers, William. *American Slavery and Colour*. London: W. & R. Chambers, 1857.

Davis, Jefferson. *The Rise and Fall of the Confederate Government*. New York: D. Appleton and Co., 1881.

Dew, Thomas R. *Review of the Debate in the Virginia Legislature of 1831 and 1832*. Reprint, New York: Negro Universities Press, 1968.

Douglas, Stephen A. *Speeches of Senator S. A. Douglas, on the Occasion of His Public Receptions by the Citizens of New Orleans, Philadelphia, and Baltimore*. Washington, D.C.: Lemuel Towers, 1859.

Elliott, Charles. *Sinfulness of American Slavery*. Cincinnati: L. Swormstedt & J. H. Power, 1850.

Fitzhugh, George. *Cannibals All! or Slaves without Masters*. Edited by C. Vann Woodward. Cambridge, Mass.: Harvard University Press, 1960.

———. *Sociology for the South, or the Failure of Free Society*. Richmond, Va.: A. Morris, 1854.

Fitzhugh, George, and A. Hogeboom. *A Controversy on Slavery, Between George Fitzhugh, Esq., of Virginia, Author of "Sociology for the South," etc., and A. Hogeboom, Esq., of New York*. Oneida, N.Y.: Oneida Sachem Office, 1857.

Flint, H. M. *Life of Stephen A. Douglas, His Most Important Speeches and Reports*. New York: Derby & Jackson, 1860.

Fry, William Henry. *Republican Campaign Text-Book for the Year 1860*. New York: A. H. Burdick, 1860.

Goodell, William. *Slavery and Anti-Slavery: A History of the Great Struggle in Both Hemispheres.* New York: William Goodell, 1853.

Hammond, James Henry. *Remarks of Mr. Hammond of South Carolina on the Question of Receiving Petitions for the Abolition of Slavery in the District of Columbia.* Washington, D.C.: Duff Green, 1836.

Jay, William. *Miscellaneous Writings on Slavery.* Boston: Damrell & Moore, 1853.

Jefferson, Thomas. *Notes on the State of Virginia.* Richmond, Va.: J. W. Randolph, 1853.

Marshall, John. *The Life of George Washington.* 2 vols. Philadelphia: C. P. Wayne, 1807.

Political Debates Between Hon. Abraham Lincoln and Hon. Stephen A. Douglas in the Celebrated Campaign of 1858 in Illinois. Columbus, Ohio: Follett, Foster and Co., 1860.

Proceedings of the Pennsylvania Democratic State Convention: Held at Harrisburg, March 4th, 1856. Philadelphia: Wm. Rice, Pennsylvanian Office, Printer, 1856.

The Pro-Slavery Argument; As Maintained by the Most Distinguished Writers of the Southern States, Containing the Several Essays, on the Subject, of Chancellor Harper, Governor Hammond, Dr. Simms, and Professor Dew. Charleston, S.C.: Walker, Richards, and Co., 1852.

Rankin, John. *Letters on American Slavery, Addressed to Mr. Thomas Rankin.* Boston: Isaac Knapp, 1838.

Republican Campaign Documents of 1856: A Collection of the Most Important Speeches and Documents Issued by the Republican Association of Washington, During the Presidential Campaign of 1856. Washington, D.C.: Lewis Clephane, 1857.

Robinson, Sara. *Kansas: Its Interior and Exterior Life.* Boston: Crosby and Nichols, 1857.

Schurz, Carl. *Report of the George William Curtis Memorial Committee.* New York: The Chronicle Press, 1905.

Seward, William H. *Speech of William H. Seward, at the Dedication of Capital University, Columbus, Ohio, September 14, 1853.* Auburn, N.Y.: Knapp and Peck Printers, 1853.

Stanton, Benjamin. *Negro Equality—The Right of One Man to Hold Property in Another—The Democratic Party a Disunion Party—The Success of the Republican Party the Only Salvation for the Country. Speech of Hon. Benjamin Stanton.* Washington, D.C.: Buell and Blanchard, 1860.

Stowe, Harriet Beecher. *The Key to Uncle Tom's Cabin: Presenting the Original Facts and Documents upon which the Story is Founded, Together with Corroborative Statements Verifying the Truth of the Work.* Boston: John P. Jewett and Co., 1853.

Sumner, Charles. *White Slavery in the Barbary States.* Boston: John P. Jewett and Co., 1853.

Warren, Mercy Otis. *History of the Rise, Progress, and Termination of the American Revolution.* Boston: Manning and Loring, 1805.

Wilson, Henry. *Territorial Slave Code, Speech of Hon. Henry Wilson of Massachusetts.* Washington, D.C.: Scammel & Co., 1860.

EDITED COLLECTIONS

Adams, John. *Novanglus and Massachusettensis: Political Essays, Published in the Years 1774 and 1775.* Bedford, Mass.: Applewood Books, 2009.

Angle, Paul M., ed. *Created Equal? The Complete Lincoln-Douglas Debates of 1858.* Chicago: University of Chicago Press, 1958.

Calhoun, John C. *The Works of John C. Calhoun.* Edited by Richard K. Cralle. 6 vols. New York: D. Appleton, 1854–1857.

Douglass, Frederick. *The Frederick Douglass Papers: 1855–63.* Edited by John W. Blassingame. New Haven, Conn.: Yale University Press, 1979.

Garrison, William Lloyd. *The Letters of William Lloyd Garrison: From Disunionism to the Brink of War, 1850–1860.* Edited by Louis Ruchames. 6 vols. Cambridge, Mass.: Harvard University Press, 1976.

Herndon, William H. *The Hidden Lincoln: From the Letters and Papers of William H. Herndon.* Edited by Emanuel Hertz. New York: The Viking Press, 1938.

Lincoln, Abraham. *The Collected Works of Abraham Lincoln.* Edited by Roy P. Basler. 9 vols. New Brunswick, N.J.: Rutgers University Press, 1953–55.

Locke, John. *Two Treatises of Government* [1690]. Edited by Peter Laslett. Cambridge, Eng.: Cambridge University Press, 1988.

Miller, Marion Mills, ed. *Great Debates in American History: From the Debates in the British Parliament on the Colonial Stamp Act (1764–1765) to the Debates in Congress at the Close of the Taft Administration (1912–1913).* 4 vols. New York: Current Literature Publishing Company, 1913.

Moore, Frank, ed. *The Rebellion Record: A Diary of American Events.* 11 vols. New York: G. P. Putnam, 1861–1865.

Seward, William H. *The Works of William H. Seward.* Edited by George Baker. Boston: Houghton Mifflin, 1884.

Sumner, Charles. *Recent Speeches and Addresses.* Boston: Ticknor and Fields, 1856.

———. *The Works of Charles Sumner.* 11 vols. Boston: Lee and Shepard, 1870–75.

Webster, Daniel. *The Papers of Daniel Webster.* Edited by Charles M. Wiltse and Harold D. Moser. 14 vols. Hanover, N.H.: University Press of New England, 1974.

SECONDARY SOURCES

Allitt, Patrick. *The Conservatives: Ideas and Personalities throughout American History.* New Haven, Conn.: Yale University Press, 2009.

Barney, William L. *The Secessionist Impulse: Alabama and Mississippi in 1860.* Princeton, N.J.: Princeton University Press, 1974.

Beveridge, Albert J. *Abraham Lincoln, 1809–1858.* New York: Houghton Mifflin, 1928.

Boritt, Gabor S., ed. *Why the Civil War Came.* New York: Oxford University Press, 1996.

Brack, Gene M. *Mexico Views Manifest Destiny, 1821–1846: An Essay on the Origins of the Mexican War.* Albuquerque: University of New Mexico Press, 1975.

Cecil-Fronsman, Bill. "Advocate the Freedom of White Men, as Well as that of Negroes: The *Kansas Free State* and Antislavery Westerners in Territorial Kansas." *Kansas History: A Journal of the Central Plains* 20 (Summer 1997): 102–15.

Channing, Steven A. *Crisis of Fear: Secession in South Carolina.* New York: Simon & Schuster, 1970.

Cooper, William J., Jr., and Thomas E. Terrill. *The American South: A History.* Lanham, Md.: Rowman & Littlefield, 2008.

Craven, Avery O. *The Coming of the Civil War.* New York: Charles Scribner's Sons, 1942.

Davis, David Brion. *Inhuman Bondage: The Rise and Fall of Slavery in the New World.* New York: Oxford University Press, 2006.

Detweiler, Philip. "The Changing Reputation of the Declaration of Independence: The First Fifty Years." *William and Mary Quarterly* 19, no. 4 (Oct. 1962): 557–74.

Donald, David. *Charles Sumner and the Coming of the Civil War.* New York: Alfred A. Knopf, 1960.

———. *Lincoln.* London: Random House, 1995.

Dumond, Dwight Lowell. *A History of the United States.* New York: H. Holt and Co., 1942.

Ellis, Joseph J. *American Sphinx: The Character of Thomas Jefferson.* New York: Vintage Books, 1998.

Etcheson, Nicole. *Bleeding Kansas: Contested Liberty in the Civil War Era.* Lawrence: University Press of Kansas, 2004.

Faust, Drew Gilpin. *James Henry Hammond and the Old South: A Design for Mastery.* Baton Rouge: Louisiana State University Press, 1982.

Fehrenbacher, Don E. *The Dred Scott Case: Its Significance in American Law and Politics.* New York: Oxford University Press, 1978.

———. *Prelude to Greatness: Lincoln in the 1850's.* Stanford: Stanford University Press, 1962.

Foner, Eric. *Free Soil, Free Labor, Free Men: The Ideology of the Republican Party before the Civil War.* New York: Oxford University Press, 1970.

Foner, Philip S. *History of the Labor Movement in the United States,* Vol. 1: *From Colonial Times to the Founding of the American Federation of Labor.* New York: International Publishers, 1947.

Fredrickson, George M. *The Black Image in the White Mind: The Debate on Afro-American Character and Destiny, 1817–1914.* Middletown, Conn.: Wesleyan University Press, 1987.

———. *Racism: A Short History.* Princeton, N.J.: Princeton University Press, 2002.

Freehling, William W. *Prelude to Civil War: The Nullification Controversy in South Carolina, 1816–1836.* New York: Harper & Row, 1965.

Gale, Robert L. *Thomas Crawford: American Sculptor.* Pittsburgh, Pa.: University of Pittsburgh Press, 1964.

Genovese, Eugene D. *The World the Slaveholders Made: Two Essays in Interpretation.* Middletown, Conn.: Wesleyan University Press, 1969.

Geyl, Pieter. "The American Civil War and the Problem of Inevitability." *New England Quarterly* 24 (1951): 147–68.

Gienapp, William E. *Origins of the Republican Party, 1852–56.* New York: Oxford University Press, 1987.

———. "The Republican Party and the Slave Power," in *New Perspectives on Race and Slavery in America: Essays in Honor of Kenneth M. Stampp,* edited by Robert H. Abzug and Stephen E. Maizlish, 51–58. Lexington: University of Kentucky Press, 1986.

Guelzo, Allen C. *Abraham Lincoln as a Man of Ideas.* Carbondale: Southern Illinois University Press, 2009.

———. *Abraham Lincoln: Redeemer President.* Grand Rapids, Mich.: William B. Eerdmans Publishing Co., 1999.

Hammond, Bray. *Sovereignty and an Empty Purse: Banks and Politics in the Civil War.* Princeton, N.J.: Princeton University Press, 1970.

Haxby, James A. *United States Obsolete Banknotes, 1782–1866.* 4 vols. Iola, Wisc.: Krause Publications, 1988.

Holt, Michael F. *The Political Crisis of the 1850s.* New York: John Wiley & Sons, 1978.

Holzer, Harold. *Lincoln: President-Elect; Abraham Lincoln and the Great Secession Winter, 1860–1861.* New York: Simon & Schuster, 2008.

Howe, Daniel Walker. *The Political Culture of the American Whigs.* Chicago: University of Chicago Press, 1984.

Huston, James L. *Calculating the Value of the Union: Slavery, Property Rights, and the Economic Origins of the Civil War.* Chapel Hill: The University of North Carolina Press, 2003.

———. *The Panic of 1857 and the Coming of the Civil War.* Baton Rouge: Louisiana State University Press, 1987.

———. *Stephen A. Douglas and the Dilemmas of Democratic Equality.* Lanham, Md.: Rowman & Littlefield, 2007.

Irving, Washington. *The Life of George Washington.* New York: G. P. Putnam's Sons, 1876.

Isaacson, Walter. *Benjamin Franklin: An American Life.* New York: Simon & Schuster, 2003.

Jaffa, Harry V. *Crisis of the House Divided: An Interpretation of the Issues in the Lincoln-Douglas Debates.* Garden City, N.Y.: Doubleday, 1959.

———. *A New Birth of Freedom: Abraham Lincoln and the Coming of the Civil War.* Lanham, Md.: Rowman & Littlefield, 2000.

Johannsen, Robert W. *Lincoln, the South, and Slavery: The Political Dimension.* Baton Rouge: Louisiana State University Press, 1991.

———. *Stephen A. Douglas.* Chicago: University of Illinois Press, 1973.

Jordan, Don, and Michael Walsh. *White Cargo: The Forgotten History of Britain's White Slaves in America.* New York: New York University Press, 2008.

Jordan, Winthrop D. *White Over Black: American Attitudes Toward the Negro, 1550–1812.* Chapel Hill: The University of North Carolina Press, 1968.

Julius, Kevin C. *The Abolitionist Decade, 1829–1838: A Year-by-Year History of Early Events in the Antislavery Movement.* New York: McFarland, 2004.

Klein, Philip Shriver. *President James Buchanan: A Biography.* University Park: Pennsylvania State University Press, 1962.

Knobel, Dale T. *Paddy and the Republic: Ethnicity and Nationality in Antebellum America.* Middletown, Conn.: Wesleyan University Press, 1986.

Korshak, Yvonne. "The Liberty Cap as a Revolutionary Symbol in America and France." *Smithsonian Studies in American Art* 1, no. 2 (Autumn 1987): 52–69.

Litwack, Leon F. *North of Slavery: The Negro in the Free States, 1790–1860.* Chicago: University of Chicago Press, 1961.

Loewenberg, Robert J. "John Locke and the Antebellum Defense of Slavery." *Political Theory* 13 (May 1985): 266–91.

Luse, Christopher A. "Slavery's Champions Stood at Odds: Polygenesis and the Defense of Slavery." *Civil War History* 4, no. 53 (2007): 379–412.

Maier, Pauline. *American Scripture: Making the Declaration of Independence.* New York: Alfred A. Knopf, 1997.

Maltz, Earl M. *Dred Scott and the Politics of Slavery.* Lawrence: University Press of Kansas, 2007.

McCoy, Drew R. *The Elusive Republic: Political Economy in Jeffersonian America.* Chapel Hill: The University of North Carolina Press, 1980.

McKitrick, Eric. *Slavery Defended: The View of the Old South.* Englewood Cliffs, N.J.: Prentice Hall, 1963.

Middlekauff, Robert. *The Glorious Cause: The American Revolution, 1763–1789.* New York: Oxford University Press, 1982.

Mihm, Stephen. *A Nation of Counterfeiters: Capitalists, Con Men, and the Making of the United States.* Cambridge, Mass.: Harvard University Press, 2007.

Moore, Glover. *The Missouri Controversy, 1819–1821.* Lexington: University of Kentucky Press, 1953.

Morgan, Edmund S. *American Slavery, American Freedom: The Ordeal of Colonial Virginia.* New York: W. W. Norton, 1975.

Morris, Thomas D. *Southern Slavery and the Law, 1619–1860.* Chapel Hill: The University of North Carolina Press, 1996.

Morrison, Michael A. *Slavery and the American West: The Eclipse of Manifest Destiny and the Coming of the Civil War.* Chapel Hill: University of North Carolina Press, 1997.

Nevins, Allan. *Ordeal of the Union.* 2 vols. New York: Charles Scribner's Sons, 1947.

Newman, Eric P. *Early Paper Money of America.* Iola, Wisc.: Krause Publications, 1990.

Nye, Russel B. *Fettered Freedom: Civil Liberties and the Slavery Controversy.* Urbana: University of Illinois Press, 1972.

Oakes, James. *The Ruling Race: A History of American Slaveholders.* New York: Alfred A. Knopf, 1982.

Oates, Stephen B. *The Fires of Jubilee: Nat Turner's Fierce Rebellion.* New York: Harper & Row, 1975.

———. *With Malice Toward None: A Life of Abraham Lincoln.* New York: Harper & Row, 1977.

Osthaus, Carl L. *Partisans of the Southern Press: Editorial Spokesmen of the Nineteenth Century.* Lexington: The University Press of Kentucky, 1994.

Peterson, Merrill D. *The Jefferson Image in the American Mind.* New York: Oxford University Press, 1960.

Potter, David M. *The Impending Crisis, 1848–1861.* New York: Harper & Row, 1976.

Ramsdell, Charles W. "The Natural Limits of Slavery Expansion." *Mississippi Valley Historical Review* 16 (September 1929): 151–71.

Randall, James G. "A Blundering Generation." *Mississippi Valley Historical Review* 27 (June 1940): 3–28.

Ratner, Lorman A., and Dwight L. Teeter. *Fanatics and Fire-Eaters: Newspapers and the Coming of the Civil War.* Chicago: University of Illinois Press, 2003.

Rawley, James A. *Bleeding Kansas and the Coming of the Civil War.* New York: J. B. Lippincott Co., 1969.

Reid, Ronald Forrest. *The American Revolution and the Rhetoric of History.* Los Angeles: The University of California Press, 1978.

Rhodes, James Ford. *History of the United States from the Compromise of 1850.* New York: Macmillan, 1913.

Richards, Leonard L. *The Slave Power: The Free North and Southern Domination, 1780–1860.* Baton Rouge: Louisiana State University Press, 2000.

Shankman, Kimberly C. *Compromise and the Constitution: The Political Thought of Henry Clay.* New York: Lexington Books, 1999.

Silbey, Joel H. *Storm Over Texas: The Annexation Controversy and the Road to Civil War.* New York: Oxford University Press, 2005.

Stampp, Kenneth M. *America in 1857: A Nation on the Brink.* New York: Oxford University Press, 1992.

———. *The Peculiar Institution: Slavery in the Antebellum South.* New York: Alfred A. Knopf, 1972.

Tenzer, Lawrence R. *The Forgotten Cause of the Civil War: A New Look at the Slavery Issue.* Manahawkin, N.J.: Scholars' Publishing House, 1997.

Thornton, J. Mills, III. *Politics and Power in a Slave Society: Alabama, 1800–1860.* Baton Rouge: Louisiana State University Press, 1978.

Van Vleck, George W. *The Panic of 1857: An Analytical Study.* New York: Columbia University Press, 1943.

Waldstreicher, David. *Runaway America: Benjamin Franklin, Slavery, and the American Revolution.* New York: Macmillan, 2004.

Warden, Robert B. *An Account of the Private Life and Public Services of Salmon Portland Chase.* Cincinnati, Ohio: Wilstach, Baldwin and Co., 1874.

Wieck, Carl F. *Lincoln's Quest for Equality: The Road to Gettysburg.* DeKalb, Ill.: Northern Illinois University Press, 2002.

Wilson, Carol, and Calvin D. Wilson. "White Slavery: An American Paradox." *Slavery and Abolition* 19, no. 1 (1998): 1–23.

Wish, Harvey. *George Fitzhugh: Propagandist of the Old South.* Baton Rouge: Louisiana State University Press, 1943.

Wood, Gordon S. *The Americanization of Benjamin Franklin.* New York: Penguin Books, 2004.

Woodward, C. Vann. *The Strange Career of Jim Crow.* New York: Oxford University Press, 1955.

Zarefsky, David. *Lincoln, Douglas, and Slavery: In the Crucible of Public Debate.* Chicago: The University of Chicago Press, 1990.

Index

Abbott, John, 97
Abolitionists, 5–6; danger of inferiority rationale, 37–38; and the legacy of the founders, 127; and light-skinned slaves, 9–10; prejudice of, 42; Republicans distinguished from, 10–11, 26; Southern reaction to, 51–52, 82, 109
Adams, Charles Francis, 121
Adams, John, 89, 93, 121, 126, 130
Ashley, James M., 10, 41
Ashworth, John, 5, 63–64
Atchison, David Rice, 18

Bancroft, George, 122
Banks, Nathaniel P., 29
Barbour, James, 132
Barksdale, William, 43
Bayne, Thomas R., 50
Beecher, Henry Ward, 96–97
Bell, John, 20
Bennett, Henry, 88
Benton, Thomas Hart, 18, 25
Berwanger, Eugene, 5
Birney, James G., 11
Blair, Francis P., 53
Bliss, Philemon, 68
Boucher, Chauncey, 88–89
Bowie, Thomas F., 92
Brack, Gene, 39

Breckinridge, John C., 31, 82, 107
Brooks, Preston, 79, 94
Brown, Albert Gallatin, 81, 105
Brown, John, 71, 134
Brown, Joseph E., 72
Buchanan, James, 12, 40–41, 56, 67–68, 120, 136; on the Lecompton Constitution, 28–31
Burlingame, Anson, 124
Butler, Andrew, 67
Butler, Pierce, 1

Calhoun, John C., 39, 47; opposition to universal liberty, 103–4, 125; and white equality, 72–73, 92
Cass, Lewis, 19, 25
Catholics, 40, 44
Cecil-Fronsman, William, 6
Chaffee, Calvin, 117
Chambers, William, 46
Chase, Salmon P., 10, 124, 127
Chestnut, James, 62
Chinese: characterized as "inferior," 41
Choate, Rufus, 121
Clay, Henry, 36, 95, 110
Clayton, John M., 112
Cleland, Philip S., 106
Compromise of 1850, 18–19
Corwin, Thomas, 105, 112

Craven, Avery, 5
Crawford, Thomas, 111
Curtis, Benjamin, 114–16
Curtis, George William, 134–35

Davis, David Brion, 84
Davis, Jefferson, 47, 68, 74; appeal to the Declaration of Independence, 135; and Curse of Ham, 85; opposition to "liberty cap," 111; and peonage, 80–81
Davis, Moses M., 88
Day, Timothy C., 54
Detweiler, Philip, 128
Dew, Thomas R., 50–52, 82
Dixon, Archibald, 18, 43
Doolittle, James, 61–62, 127
Douglas, Stephen A., 3, 6, 12–13, 22–23, 27, 33, 36–37, 44, 66, 69, 82, 91, 97, 116, 120–21, 130, 138; appeal to the revolutionary heritage of popular sovereignty, 122–28, 132–34; on "inferior races," 25–26, 38, 77; and introduction of Kansas-Nebraska, 17–21; on the "natural limits of slavery," 29–31; opposition to Lecompton Constitution, 28, 32; opposition to secession, 136, 139; and peonage, 80–81
Douglass, Frederick, 26, 105–6; on equality, 122
Downs, Solomon W., 56
Dred Scott decision, 14, 25, 32, 34, 49, 101; blacks excluded from citizenship and Declaration of Independence, 114–16; origins of, 113–14; as a threat to American liberty, 117–19

Edgerton, Sidney, 83
Elliot, Charles, 37
Emerson, Eliza, 113, 117
Emerson, John, 113
Emerson, Ralph Waldo, 121
Etcheson, Nicole, 6

Filmer, Robert, 59
Fitzhugh, George: author of "complexion" editorials, 60–61; background of, 57; on Curse of Ham, 85; historians' views on, 61–62; on inferiority,

47–48; on land as a "safety valve," 65–66; on superiority of slave labor, 58–60, 63–64, 68–69, 74, 79, 97; on voting rights, 77
Foner, Eric, 6, 42, 89, 134
Forbes, Robert Pierce, 103
Franklin, Benjamin, 1–3, 51, 86, 95, 108, 110, 126–27
Fredrickson, George M., 71–72, 85
Freehling, William, 103
Freeman, Marcus, 50
Fry, William Henry, 47–48
Fugitive slave law, 9, 94

Gag rule, 5, 91, 94
Garrison, William Lloyd, 9–11, 51, 60, 88, 93, 106
Geary, John W., 28
Genovese, Eugene, 61–62, 70
Germans: Republican appeal to, 12–13, 25, 34, 40
Giddings, Joshua R., 120, 134–35
Gienapp, William, 5, 7, 53; on the Slave Power and fear of conspiracy, 88–89, 99
Goodell, William, 45
Grant, Ulysses S., 42
Grayson, William J., 62–63
Greeley, Horace, 29, 32, 134
Guelzo, Allen, 8, 136

Hammond, James Henry, 47–49, 52, 62, 107; and racial aristocracy, 92; on superiority of slave labor, 67–68, 79
Herndon, William H., 55, 60, 98–99
Herrenvolk democracy, 64, 71–74
Holt, Michael, F., 7
Houston, Sam, 20
Hunter, Robert M. T., 62, 68, 81, 83
Huston, James L., 6, 31, 80

Indian Removal Act, 90–91
Irish: Republican appeal to, 12–13, 25, 45, 84; characterized as "inferior," 39–41

Jackson, James, 1–3, 51
Jaffa, Harry V., 7–8, 112, 123, 127

Japanese: characterized as "inferior," 41
Jay, John, 86
Jay, William, 87–88, 90–91
Jefferson, Thomas, 16, 25, 34, 41, 50, 55, 59, 70, 89, 105, 107, 110, 116; on civic virtue, 75; Democrats' appeal to, 123–24, 127–28, 134; and the history of the Declaration of Independence, 128–30; opposition to slave trade, 101–2; on slavery's psychological impact, 93; on slavery's threat to American liberty, 101, 104
Johannsen, Robert, 61, 123
Johnson, Andrew, 38, 81
Johnson, Herschel V., 69, 79
Johnson, Richard M., 132
Jordan, Winthrop, 8, 84–85

Kansas-Nebraska Act, 6, 8, 13, 43, 61, 88, 90–91, 94, 112, 122, 127–28, 130, 133; Buchanan on, 30; introduction and passage of, 17–20; Lincoln's reaction to, 21–25, 27–28, 32–35
Knobel, Dale, 39–40
Know-Nothing Party, 11, 44, 104, 117

Lane, James, 31
Lane, Joseph, 81–82
Lecompton Constitution, 28–32, 90
Liberty Party, 127
Lincoln, Abraham, 4, 60, 66, 69, 88, 124, 128, 131; historiography, 7–8, 61; defense of Declaration of Independence, 13, 15, 22–27, 32–35, 98–99, 104, 106–7, 121, 132–33, 137–38; on the founding fathers, 102, 116, 125–26, 129–30, 137; inauguration of, 139; on "inferiority," 36–37, 43; opposition to Kansas-Nebraska Act, 19, 21–22, 27–28, 32–35; and prejudice of northern whites, 12, 26–27; on subjectivity of proslavery arguments, 3, 34–35, 55, 83–84, 96–98; on three-fifths clause, 90
Litwack, Leon, 5, 42
Locke, John, 59, 70; influence on Jefferson, 129; on majority rule, 136; on property rights, 75–76, 95
Lovejoy, Elijah, 37

Lovejoy, Owen, 10; on "inferiority," 37–38, 43–44

Madison, James, 104, 127
Mason, George, 127
Mason, James, 62, 68
McDuffie, George, 52, 78
McLane, Louis, 132
Missouri Compromise, 18–19, 29, 114, 118
Money: slavery vignettes on southern banknotes, 107–12
Morgan, Edmund, 10, 76–77
Morris, Gouverneur, 76, 89, 127
Morris, Thomas D., 8
Morrison, Michael, 7

New Mexico Territory, 17, 81
Northwest Ordinance, 126–27
Nye, Russel B., 8, 37, 45, 88

Oakes, James, 72
Ordinance of 1784, 127
Osthaus, Carl, 55

Panic of 1857, 66, 89
Parker, Samuel, 25
Parker, Theodore, 11, 42, 96
Peonage, 80–82
Pettit, John, 23–26, 36–37, 42–43, 103, 120–22, 125, 130
Pickens, Francis, 66
Pierce, Franklin, 20, 28
Polk, James K., 30
Potter, David, 6, 30, 117
Pryor, Roger, 43

Race: white slaves, 8–10, 46, 52, 70
Randall, James G., 5
Randolph, John, 131
Rankin, John, 93
Read, John M., 54
Reeder, Andrew, 28
Republicanism, ideology of, 7, 75–78, 93–94
Richards, Leonard, 6, 89–90
Richardson, William A., 17
Robinson, Charles, 16, 21, 31

Robinson, Sara, 21
Rock, John, 96

Schurz, Carl, 133–34
Scott, Winfield, 137
Seward, Frederick, 137
Seward, William H., 29, 66–67, 90, 122, 124; and slavery as a threat to Northern laborers, 45, 68; and universal liberty, 100
Shannon, Wilson, 28
Slave Power, 12, 27, 45, 49, 61, 79, 8, 105, 138; and aristocracy, 92–99; historiography of, 6–7, 87–89; political advantages of, 89–92, 114, 119
Smith, William Loughton, 1
Stampp, Kenneth, 10
Stanton, Benjamin, 41, 78
Stephens, Alexander H., 20, 31, 74
Stewart, James Brewer, 11
Stowe, Harriet Beecher, 9, 11, 42, 53
Sumner, Charles, 10, 68; assaulted by Preston Brooks, 94; on the Curse of Ham, 85; on "inferiority," 38, 41; on slavery in North Africa, 85–86; on universal liberty, 101, 125

Tallmadge, James, 90–91, 96, 130–31
Taney, Roger B., 25, 49, 101, 112–19, 123, 130
Tappan, Mason W., 54
Taylor, John W., 96, 131

Tenzer, Lawrence R., 8, 62
Toombs, Robert, 81
Trumbull, John, 130
Trumbull, Lyman, 12, 32, 98
Turner, Nat, 51, 71, 82
Tyler, John, 132

Uncle Tom's Cabin, 9, 63

Van Buren, Martin, 91
Van Evrie, John, 40, 56, 64, 74

Wade, Benjamin, 29
Walker, Robert J., 28, 30
Warren, Mercy Otis, 129
Washburn, Israel, 54, 60
Washington, George, 1, 93, 104–5, 108, 110–11, 126, 129, 137
Webster, Daniel, 30, 44, 110
Weed, Thurlow, 118
Wickliffe, Robert, 40–41, 56
Williams, Eric, 10
Wills, Garry, 7
Wilson, Calvin, 8–9
Wilson, Carol, 8–9
Wilson, Douglas, 7
Wilson, Henry, 29, 42–43, 81, 88, 105, 126
Wilson, Major, 7
Wise, Henry, 31, 73

Zarefsky, David, 8